Fat Blame

CultureAmerica

Erika Doss

Philip J. Deloria

Series Editors

Karal Ann Marling

Editor Emerita

Fat Blame

**How the War on Obesity
Victimizes Women and Children**

April Michelle Herndon

 University Press of Kansas

Published by the
University Press of
Kansas (Lawrence,
Kansas 66045), which
was organized by
the Kansas Board
of Regents and is
operated and funded
by Emporia State
University, Fort Hays
State University,
Kansas State
University, Pittsburg
State University, the
University of Kansas,
and Wichita State
University

© 2014 by the University Press of Kansas
All rights reserved

Library of Congress Cataloging-in-Publication Data is available.
Library of Congress Control Number: 2014936965
ISBN 978-0-7006-1965-8 (cloth)

British Library Cataloguing-in-Publication Data is available.

Printed in the United States of America

10 9 8 7 6 5 4 3 2 1

The paper used in this publication is recycled and contains 30
percent postconsumer waste. It is acid free and meets the minimum
requirements of the American National Standard for Permanence of
Paper for Printed Library Materials Z39.48-1992.

Contents

Preface

There were many times I thought seriously about not writing this book. In fact, at some points, I was nearly certain I wasn't going to write it. When I've posed questions about "the obesity epidemic" or suggested to a colleague that perhaps we ought to think more carefully about obesity, I've been charged with many things. I've been told I was glorifying fatness. I've been accused of not caring about people's health. Once or twice, I was even accused of being racist for not understanding or caring about issues such as "diabesity" among minorities because I was questioning the Let's Move! campaign.[1] In truth, I decided to continue writing the book because those experiences taught me that there is a serious need for more dialogue—even though the conversations may prove difficult.

As a field, Fat Studies has done a tremendous amount of work to open new conversations about fatness and provide compelling means of revisiting ongoing debates. As a Fat Studies scholar, I have drawn deeply from the discipline and from scholars who have helped forge the field of Fat Studies and critical conversations about obesity. The work of Paul Campos, Sondra Solovay, Abigail Saguy, Michael Gard and Jan Wright, and many other forerunners has proven invaluable. I also drew a great deal on my own background as an American Studies scholar who has taught everything from English to Women's and Gender Studies to Science and Technology Studies and who once served as the director of programming for the Intersex Society of North America. Those experiences and the training and preparation they required have helped to make this book an interdisciplinary examination of contemporary America's obsession with fatness and how women and children are being victimized by those discussions and policies. In its focus and methodology, this book adds to the continuing conversation about childhood obesity while pushing readers to think about how the panic over childhood obesity actually threatens the well-being of both children and their mothers.

When I realized I didn't have all the answers, I thought long and hard about what it meant to own that and to write a book that examines the issue of obesity without necessarily reducing the matter to simple metrics like the numbers on the bathroom scale. The lure of the scale and of the language of the obesity epidemic is that they make everything seem so simple; one number tells people all they need to know about an individual, about his or her family, and about the health not only of that individual but also of the entire nation. I knew I'd be asking readers to give up a great deal to come along with me on a different kind of journey, a journey where I ask them to think seriously about how the war on obesity has become a war against women and children. But I'm asking.

Acknowledgments

Somehow, I thought writing the acknowledgments would be the fun part, but I'm paralyzed with fear that I will forget someone. Given that, let me begin by saying thank you to anyone who has ever helped me—in any way—with this project. There have been far too many of you to name.

There are, however, some individuals who deserve special thanks. My work in Fat Studies would have never been possible without my graduate school mentors. I had the good fortune to run into three colleagues, in particular, who encouraged me to continue my work—even when others suggested I was crazy for asking people to look at fatness as anything other than pathological. Jon Robison, Cressida Heyes, and Alice Dreger all played key roles in my development as a Fat Studies scholar—each in very different but important ways.

Over the years, I've maintained a close relationship with my dissertation director, Alice Dreger. As this project sat on the back burner while I was teaching a four/four load (often with four preps!), Alice continued to urge me to write whenever I could. She sent me news articles and links to blogs, and I have no doubt that part of why she did it was to encourage me to keep working. I'm indebted to her for all the conversations about my work in Fat Studies that we've had over the years. She has been my mentor, my confidant, and the person who lovingly kicked me when I needed it, and I'm proud to know her as a colleague and friend.

I also have to acknowledge the friends I made along my trek through academia who have supported my work. I only spent one year at Gustavus Adolphus College, but I made lasting friendships there with a group of incredibly smart women. My thanks to Alisa Rosenthal, Jill Locke, Peg O'Connor, and Lisa Heldke for making opportunities for me to come back to campus to talk about my work and for always being there when I needed a sounding board for my ideas.

Here at Winona State University (WSU), I've made equally supportive friends. Dan Lintin, Kara Lindaman, Ruth Forsythe, Jane Carducci, and Cindy Killion were my human shields while I waded through tenure and promotion and this project. I also have to thank all of my colleagues in the English Department. When I tell people how well our department functions, they often think I'm lying. I'm not. Our English Department is somehow filled with the most normal and functional academics I've ever met, and I can never fully express my gratitude for their having taken an interdisciplinary scholar like me in as one of their own. I know many of them taught extra sections of freshman composition so I could have my sabbatical and finally finish this project, but they never complained. They are truly good eggs.

I'm also grateful to WSU for the funding I received to help with the project. Dean Ralph Townsend and the Winona State University Foundation both provided funding for rights and permissions, and I'm grateful for their financial assistance. Also, Susan Byom, in our Interlibrary Loan Department, saved me more than once with her skills and connections, as did other librarians at WSU, such as Allison Quam.

Like most scholars, I've benefited greatly from colleagues, too numerous to name, who attended conferences to see me give my papers and offer me encouragement and advice. The scholarly community at conferences such as that held by the National Women's Studies Association has been so helpful for my thinking and my psyche as I worked on this project. The online activist community has also been supportive and helpful. I'm especially thankful to Marilyn Wann and Ragen Chastain for their work on their own activist projects and for loaning me their many connections to the fat-positive community, including the individuals and families from the I STAND campaign who allowed me to use their photos for my work.

I'm deeply grateful to the editors and staff at the University Press of Kansas for taking on this project when it was in its budding stages and seeing me through to the end. Even when I was ready to give up, they still wanted the book and encouraged me to keep going. My work here is all the better for their efforts.

On a more personal note, I owe thanks to my mom and dad. I know they don't always understand what exactly it is that I do, but they tell me to do what makes me happy. My mom, in particular, has waited a very long time to see this book in print.

Above all, I want to thank S. Through the gnashing of teeth as I labored on this volume and the intense moments of doubt followed by joyous dancing when a chapter was finished, S. never wavered. Even when I didn't believe in myself, S. believed in me and in this project. There's no way I could have completed this book without that support.

Fat Blame

The Mother of All Wars

The reason why the "obesity epidemic" has come about could not be less important. The future will be decided along moral and ideological— that is, political—grounds.
—Michael Gard and Jan Wright, *The Obesity Epidemic*[1]

COLLATERAL DAMAGE

In September 2000,[2] Anamarie Regino, a three-year-old Mexican American girl living in New Mexico, was taken away from her parents because she was obese and experiencing health problems believed to be directly related to her obesity. At the time, many thought removing Anamarie from her home was an extreme measure. Since then, however, courts in Iowa, New Mexico, New York, Pennsylvania,[3] and Ohio[4] have also removed children from their homes, and doing so is quickly becoming seen as a logical means of making children thin and getting the attention of all parents. When such cases are reported, media outlets often cite statistics about the rise in childhood obesity, and they almost always mention the children's weights in the headlines of their articles. But what's rarely discussed are the psychological consequences of removing a child from a home or whether any weight loss achieved in the process is actually maintained in a meaningful way. In other words, the long-term psychosocial and physiological consequences and data are often neglected in favor of reporting on pounds and assuring the public that something is being done.

We know from the Regino case, which is one of the few cases where both the child and the parents later spoke openly to the media about their experiences, that the psychological toll of Anamarie's removal from her home and family has been long lived. At the age of fourteen, Anamarie reflected on the 2011 call made by physician David Ludwig and lawyer Lindsey Murtagh for obese children to be removed from homes; in a televised interview, she said,

"It's not right, what [Dr. Ludwig] is doing, because to get better you need to be with your family, instead of being surrounded by doctors."[5] In the same news interview, Anamarie's mother stated that the damage done to her child by her removal could not be undone with money or therapy and that the two months Anamarie was away from home were "hell."[6] At the time of the interview on ABC's *Good Morning America,* it was clear to anyone watching that Anamarie was still a very fat teenager in spite of the hell that she and her family had endured. Even more tragic is that both of her parents have now passed, and one can only imagine that the two-month separation from her family, imposed by court order, stings all the more after their early deaths. Given Anamarie's outcry against removing children from their homes based on her own experience, some people might ask how something like this could have happened and how such practices could continue even now. The truth is it happened because her parents, especially her mother, were constructed as negligent, working-class immigrants who either didn't understand how to properly care for their child or simply didn't care enough to do so, making the Regino case one of the earliest bellweathers signaling the ways in which the war on obesity would soon become a war against women and children, especially those also marginalized by other categorizations, such as race and class.

Perhaps most disturbing is that so many people in the American culture have come to see these types of interventions as logical, commonsense approaches to dealing with childhood obesity, as evidenced by the plethora of Facebook memes and online comments on news stories about obese children that boldly state childhood obesity is, in fact, child abuse.

As I will show throughout this book, concerns about fatness are regularly coconstructed alongside other cultural concerns, with fatness providing a kind of shorthand for talking about many different worries regarding the demise of American culture. What is unfortunately forgotten, however, is that the shorthand often eclipses the underlying problems and the fact that there are real people being affected by these conversations and interventions. The Regino case isn't, of course, only about obesity; it is also about all the other social categories and issues with which obesity has become associated and for which weight can become a stand-in, such as race, gender, class, and immigrant status—or even just parenting styles that may be different. Although interventions in what are deemed public health crises are most often presented as necessary and benign, they are not, as scholars such as John Evans and Brian Davies have pointed out, value neutral.[7] The war on obesity is as much about tensions surrounding gender, race, and class as it is about obesity, and the Reginos are just one of the millions of families harmed by the ways the panic over obesity has been mapped onto the bodies of women and children as the first sites of intervention in what is arguably positioned as the epidemic of our time.

In the same way that taking Anamarie Regino out of her home might seem like a commonsense approach, so, too, have the existence of the obesity epidemic and the need to intervene become rational concepts to most Americans. Yet, many well-respected scholars from a variety of fields have questioned the very existence of an obesity epidemic,[8] and even mainstream venues such as the *New York Times* now regularly publish pieces where the logic that overweight or obese equals unhealthy is challenged, especially the health consequences of fatness among people who are physically active.[9] This is not to say that there may not be some health effects of being fat; rather, it is to question how much those health effects matter in a person's overall life or whether the health effects of being fat are any more significant to one's life span than, for instance, being male. Keep in mind, though, that this is when looking at weight *itself,* not conditions that may or may not be tied to weight, such as diabetes or heart disease. Since obesity doesn't cause those conditions (the medical community regularly acknowledges that there are correlations but not causations), the effects of obesity on health warrant separate study. When Americans ask, "Is being fat bad for you?" the best and most fair answer that can be reached from all the existing data is, "Maybe."

Although largely out of sight for mainstream Americans, hot debates continue in the scientific community regarding the data on overweight's health effects—and not always just because of scientific disagreements. There are decidedly political and social aspects to how some scientists want to present data to the general public. Recently, the journal *Nature* rebuked the chair of Harvard's School of Public Health's Nutrition Department, Walter Willett, for his assertion that a landmark study suggesting the effects of overweight on health are fairly benign was junk science. Willett came out hard against a meta-analysis that included nearly 3 million people and ninety-seven studies that showed being overweight was not, in fact, a death sentence. The meta-analysis, conducted by Katherine Flegal, an epidemiologist at the National Center for Health Statistics, is widely accepted as a touchstone among a growing field of studies that posit some measure of fatness, in and of itself, is not necessarily unhealthy. Willett, who is a very visible figure in debates about obesity, was asked about Flegal's study during an interview on National Public Radio (NPR) and responded by saying, "[It] is really a pile of rubbish, and no one should waste their time reading it."[10] Many scientists and researchers came immediately to Flegal's defense, and according to Trevor Butterworth's piece in *Forbes,* Willett admitted his biggest concern was that such a study was "dangerous," for he feared that it would lead people to think it was okay to be overweight and that it might be co-opted by soft drink companies and other special interest groups.[11] In other words, although he said the study was rubbish, his overriding concern apparently wasn't getting closer to the truth about the effects of overweight on health but rather ensuring that the findings wouldn't be used in ways he deemed inappropriate.

Willett's worry about such a study being co-opted by soft drink companies seems in keeping with current discussions about what causes obesity and how to best address it as a growing problem. Although everything from endocrine disruptors to so-called thrifty genes to viruses has been posited as the cause for obesity, many of the most popular mainstream arguments on the causes of the obesity epidemic are those that take up more social and environmental issues, such as the rise of the fast-food industry, the lack of safe sidewalks and other means of engaging in physical activity, the consumption of soft drinks, and the demise of school lunch programs across the nation. Despite the popularity of these explanations, a great many of the interventions—and some of the most harmful ones at that—occur at the level of individuals' bodies.

Specifically, those believed to be most at risk (usually children) and most capable of changing future generations (usually women) are subject to the most interventions on their bodies. Perhaps because they are so defined by their bodies and thought to be vulnerable to the whims of their bodies, women and children have historically been subjected to intense medicalization and interventions; consider the proposed mandatory testing of pregnant women for drug use and HIV status and the host of physical fitness and antidrug campaigns aimed at children. In short, their bodies are often constructed as troublesome, in need of surveillance or correction, and the sites of crises. The fight against fat has proven no different in this respect, with the language of crisis and epidemic identifying the enemies as women and children and spawning "treatments" for obesity that act, first and foremost, on bodies rather than on the inadequate sidewalks and the food deserts, areas where affordable and nutritious food are difficult or impossible to attain, that are also blamed for obesity. This is a book about how the war on obesity is, in many ways, shaping up to be a battle against women and children, especially women and children who are also marginalized via class and race.

PLOTTING A NEW COURSE

Currently, most conversations about obesity operate on one of two axes: fat is beautiful versus fat is ugly and fat can be healthy versus fat is always unhealthy.

In his newest book, *The End of the Obesity Epidemic*, Michael Gard writes about the reception given his previous book, *The Obesity Epidemic*, which he coauthored with Jan Wright. He provides examples of reviews and opines that those who reviewed the book seemed to garner from it either that he was "pro-fat" or that he was completely "anti-science."[12] He states that both lines of thinking about the work missed the point because he was actually engaging in a wholly different kind of conversation, as he and his coauthor aimed to look at the ways conversations about the obesity epidemic were ideological rather than purely scientific.[13] In other words, Gard and Wright were working on a different axis.

Like Gard, I hope to initiate a different kind of conversation. This book plots the discussion about obesity on a different axis, examining who is blamed for the obesity epidemic and the interventions that occur because of that blame. This is not, then, a book about whether obesity is healthy or unhealthy or ugly or attractive; regardless of whether obesity is healthy, attractive, ugly, or lifeshortening, the ways women and children are blamed for obesity and the ways interventions aimed at preventing obesity are affecting women and children are problematic in and of themselves. From bariatric surgeries performed on children to women being positioned as responsible for carrying to term a generation of thin children, this book looks closely at the stories of real people whose lives are drastically altered by interventions that are supposedly for their own good. The argument is not necessarily that we shouldn't be at all concerned about obesity but rather that the nation seems to be in the grips of a panic that fosters engaging in rash and poorly researched practices to supposedly curb obesity, practices that are often ineffective at best and downright damaging at worst. This is not a book that offers definitive truths about the obesity epidemic; instead, it is a work that offers readers a different way of thinking about obesity, particularly about how public discussions and policies around the obesity epidemic deeply affect private lives.

In attempting to outline a discussion of obesity on a different axis, I'm aware that some readers will, as Gard notes, still misunderstand my argument because "moral and ideological predispositions shape the way they read, think, and advocate when it comes to human body weight."[14] As a scholar, I also have my own framework for understanding body weight. As Gard writes in his introduction, "I take it for granted that many of my own biases will be more obvious to others than to me, that others will see things that I am too myopic to see, but that this fact does not disqualify me (or anyone else) from speaking or attempting to critique received ways of thinking."[15] I believe his perspective about offering a different kind of voice in the conversation—in spite of that voice being critical of well-received ways of thinking—is especially vital given how the lives of so many people, especially those of women and children, are negatively affected by interventions to stop obesity.

As is the case with so many practices and interventions surrounding bodies and health, including dieting, people are often simultaneously blamed and empowered through policies and interventions, particularly those that appear to offer them choices. An individual who is blamed for his or her obesity may feel empowered by making the choice to have bariatric surgery. A mother who knows she may be blamed for having an obese child may feel empowered by making what she feels are the best choices for her fetus by monitoring and regulating her own weight during pregnancy. My aim is not to strip away all claims of agency, but I do want to acknowledge the pressures people may feel to be empowered in specific ways and the manner in which some choices may have the illusion of being empowering when, in fact, they are not.

The focus of this project, then, is on fat blame and the way that women and children—who are, in many respects, just everyday people—are pushed, pulled, and sometimes even victimized by interventions such as bariatric surgeries and having their families broken up by the courts. Their victim status is highlighted here so that, as Karen Zivi argues in her book *Making Rights Claims,* we can challenge that same status.[16] If we think about this in terms of a social issue such as sexual assault, it is clear that those who are sexually assaulted must necessarily understand themselves as victims of a kind of violence and inequality and be understood as victims before any kind of structural analysis or reclaiming of power can occur. In other words, you must understand yourself as a victim before you can even begin to understand yourself as a survivor and reclaim agency. If you are not a victim, after all, then what have you survived? Likewise, before policies can and will change, the public must understand members of a particular group as being victims of discrimination. This project hails women and children as victims with the aim of eventually helping to provide a fuller and richer kind of agency for them.

ENEMIES OF THE STATE

By now, I dare say it would be impossible to find an American who isn't aware that the United States has declared a war on obesity.[17] In doing so, the country has said that fat is one of the most serious enemies it faces, an enemy formidable enough to warrant a war. When Surgeon General David Satcher announced America's "war on obesity" on December 13, 2001, he and Health and Human Services Secretary Tommy G. Thompson held a press conference. To motivate those watching, Thompson declared that "all Americans—as their patriotic duty—[should] lose 10 pounds."[18] As his call to action suggests, "fitness" often signifies more than a healthy body: it also marks who is and who is not a worthy American. For such a call to go out only a few months after the attacks of September 11 suggests that the problem of obesity was deemed critical. Curiously, at the same time that other leaders were telling Americans that consuming was the way to defeat the terrorists, by moving forward with a normal way of life and keeping the economy strong by shopping, Tommy Thompson was urging people—at least some people—to scale back on their consumption. Perhaps Thompson's call was about the fear of war, especially war on American soil, in the same way that John Kennedy's Presidential Fitness tests were designed to make sure that young people were "fit" for civic duty. According to Greg Critser, one prominent figure in the discussions of the Presidential Fitness tests was quite blunt about the national investment in fit children, saying, "Why was a pull-up so important? Ask any soldier who had to pull himself out of a foxhole, or any fireman who had to hang from the window of a burning building."[19] Yet, such standards became applied to everyone in society, not just those who would need to perform such tasks. In short, all Americans were expected to be in the fight, and it was their individual responsibility—and this applied even to children—to fulfill these goals.

There is a long historical trajectory for such discussions. In fact, historians of fat, such as Peter Stearns and Hillel Schwartz, have documented that concerns about food and weight have flourished especially during times of national angst or war. For instance, during World War I, "healthy eating became part of a patriotic duty, with one influential doctor saying that 'any healthy, normal individual who is now getting fat is unpatriotic.'"[20] Some of the concerns that drove conversations during World War I about overconsumption being unpatriotic were based on fears of food shortages, but of course, this belies an assumption that fatness necessarily manifests as a result of the overconsumption of food. Schwartz notes that concerns about food during World War I didn't start out being about fatness or about fat in foods but later came to be projected onto fats as a food category and fat people as a demographic. As many people began to consider it criminal to waste rationed foods such as fats, meat, and sugar, overweight people were targeted because they were assumed to be excessively consuming these rationed goods. The assumption seemed to follow the logic of "you are what you eat." According to Schwartz, "a woman overweight by 40 lbs was to be accounted as hoarding 60 lbs of sugar in her excess flesh."[21] From there, the jump to thinness equaling patriotism was short but devastating: "In such an atmosphere, reducing weight became civil defense," and in 1918, a member of "the Interallied Scientific Food Commission announced, 'There are probably a good many million people in the United States whose most patriotic act would be to get thin . . . and then to stay thin.'"[22] In short, "[the war] transformed gluttony into treason."[23]

In 2003, on the verge of the war with Iraq, Richard Carmona, the sitting US surgeon general, boldly declared that obesity was the most pressing problem facing contemporary America and scoffed at the idea that Saddam Hussein's weapons of mass destruction (WMDs) could even compare.[24] The most dangerous enemy was among us—on our very bodies. Since that time, little about the rhetoric of the war against obesity has changed. As the website for HBO's 2012 documentary series *Weight of the Nation* proclaims, "Obesity in America has reached a catastrophic level. Almost every aspect of our lives is threatened. The first step toward ending the damage is learning how to fight back."[25] As we all learned later, there were no weapons of mass destruction in Iraq, but the rhetoric of WMDs had already done a tremendous amount of damage because people were swept up in fears of what the future might hold, justifying extreme actions. The same appears to be true for the war on obesity.

This is not, of course, the first time that US health officials have declared war on an illness. Before the war on obesity, there was the war on HIV, a virus that struck fear into the hearts of millions of Americans and made gay men the scapegoats of the HIV epidemic. A similar kind of fear and penchant for blame now seems to have been mapped onto obesity, which Susan Sontag, perhaps best known for her analysis of how illness and metaphor work in societies, suggests is part of an ongoing historical process by which societies map various anxieties onto bodies and diseases. She writes, "It seems that societies need to have one illness which becomes identified with evil, and attaches blame to its 'victims,' but it is hard to be obsessed with more than one."[26] Certainly, numerous public health campaigns are running at any given time in contemporary America, ranging from awareness about heart disease to mental illness. But it is the concern about weight that drives national campaigns such as First Lady Michelle Obama's Let's Move! initiative, as well as the fervor around discussions of school lunch programs, whether soda companies ought to be allowed in schools, and programs that send letters home to parents about their children's body mass indexes (BMIs). It's difficult to imagine such widespread and concerted efforts taking place around, say, mental health, with letters being sent home about the importance of stress management or the surgeon general saying that mental illness is the nation's worst enemy (even though the number of people now taking medications such as SSRIs might indicate otherwise). It also seems unlikely that a documentary about another illness would make a claim like that made by HBO's *Weight of the Nation*—that America's whole way of life is threatened by a particular disease—and remain popular nonetheless. In short, obesity has arguably become the illness that US society is now obsessed with.

To be sure, a great deal of stigma still surrounds HIV, but it can reasonably be argued that the larger part of current public discourse about the most threatening disease facing Americans now revolves around obesity rather than HIV. Take, for example, an editorial from the *New York Times* that Sontag quotes as reading, "We all know the truth, every one of us. We live in a time of plague such has never been visited on our nation. We can pretend it does not exist, or exists for those others, and carry on as if we do not know."[27] The editorialist was writing about HIV in the 1980s, but the piece could just as easily have been written about obesity yesterday, illuminating the ways in which American society has now chosen obesity as its one illness and has mapped the evil and blame once associated with HIV and queer sexualities onto obesity and fat people. In fact, there is a surprising similarity to the claims made in *Weight of the Nation*. As Anna Mollow points out in her recent *Bitch* article, "In 1966, *Time* described homosexuality as a 'pernicious sickness.' Today, 'a deadly epidemic' is the cliché about 'obesity.'"[28] Further, descriptions of fatness and homosexuality share a great deal of turf, with theories about fat people's lack of control as the cause of their fatness now being as widespread as theories once were about overbearing mothers and absent fathers causing homosexuality.[29] And although Mollow doesn't pick up this thread, many of the theories about the cause of childhood obesity focus as much on absent or inappropriate parenting as those earlier theories about homosexuality did.

In what I think may be the best example of how the fear once attached to HIV is now projected onto fatness, Greg Critser, author of the popular *Fat Land: How Americans Became the Fattest People on Earth,* equates fast-food restaurants with San Francisco bathhouses when he paints a picture of those he thinks most likely to be counted as "victims" of the obesity epidemic. He writes, "Places like McDonald's and Winchell's Donut stores, with their endless racks of glazed and creamy goodies, are the San Francisco bathhouses of said [obesity] epidemic, the places where the high-risk population gathers to engage in high-risk behavior."[30] In a few sentences, Critser artfully harnesses the fear and disgust many people felt about HIV and puts them to work on the obesity epidemic. The tie between McDonald's and Winchell's and San Francisco bathhouses and between obesity and HIV establishes obesity as a correlate to a disease many Americans consider to be the punishment for engaging in high-risk (read sinful and immoral) behavior.[31]

Fat Studies scholar Natalie Boero asserts that the obesity epidemic is represented as a national crisis that has individual solutions,[32] and the same was true for the HIV epidemic. In the end, both fat people and those with queer sexualities are blamed for not being able to control their urges and appetites. In her ethnographic study of Overeaters Anonymous, Boero found that the organization actually uses the term *abstinence* when referring to not eating trigger foods,[33] which I would argue echoes ties to sexuality and suggests that it's all about an individual controlling urges. No one, after all, is really forced to go to a bathhouse. It's a place one chooses to go, and Critser's rhetorical strategy of aligning bathhouses and fast-food joints puts volition at the forefront, which is one of the ways the "victims" of the disease of obesity end up being blamed for their own condition. Sontag notes that illnesses that elicit fear are often tied to "spoiled identities," as Erving Goffman calls them.[34] Part of the reason such illnesses and identities spark fear is precisely because they are read as being the result of deviance. Bioethicist James Childress writes of HIV: "Many of the actions that lead to the exposure of HIV are not considered 'innocent,' and the associated lifestyles are sometimes viewed as a threat to dominant social values."[35] The premise seems to be that people ought be able to resist the "endless racks of glazed and creamy goods" and the bodies of attractive men—and when they don't, they have no one to blame but themselves.

Interestingly enough, the practice of blaming individuals for obesity among so-called at-risk populations, such as African American and Hispanic communities, comes from both the Right and the Left. Both sides ultimately suggest that fat people are harming themselves and the nation, and they again echo previous fears about queer sexualities and HIV. As Mollow writes: "According to the right wing, queer sexualities are a threat to our children, a risk to our national security, and a blight on our future. Similar claims are routinely repeated about 'obesity,' on both the Left and the Right: Fat people are charged with 'eating themselves to death,' weakening our military, overburdening our healthcare system, and promoting disease among children."[36]

In the comments section for Mollow's *Bitch* article, the vitriol against fat people themselves—regardless of any environmental causes of overweight and obesity—was explicit. One person wrote, "Maybe [fat people] could stop using excuses and just lose the Weight [*sic*], because it is nobody's fault but your own." Another commenter declared that "fat people irresponsibly trash their own body [*sic*] and expect doctors to fix everything for them." Finally, dismissing structural causes for obesity and putting the blame squarely onto the shoulders of individuals, one person wrote, "If you have 30 minutes to watch tv, you have enough time in your day to take a walk and improve yoyr [*sic*] weight.

If you can afford McDonald's for lunch, you can afford to pack a salad and hummus instead."[37] The comments left on Mollow's piece were not so different from the recent tweet by New York University psychology professor Geoffrey Miller in the sense that weight was seen as an individual flaw with an individual solution in all of these remarks. Miller's tweet stated: "Dear obese PhD applicants: if you don't have the willpower to stop eating carbs, you won't have the willpower to do a dissertation. #truth."[38]

Sontag asserts that "one feature of the usual script for plague" is that "the disease invariably comes from somewhere else."[39] In the case of obesity, the somewhere else apparently is the bodies of those who are already marginalized via their gender, race, class, or immigrant status. For Professor Miller, it seems that it's also the bodies of people who don't have Ph.D. degrees and people who, according to him, will never attain that level of education. Adding obesity or childhood obesity to those already "spoiled identities" by portraying obesity as primarily a problem of race and of individuals—as campaigns such as Let's Move! arguably do when they acknowledge structural problems but intervene primarily at the level of the individual by promoting healthful eating and exercise as solutions—potentially provides new avenues for racism and classism, especially in light of arguments about obesity contributing to the rising costs of health care. Writing about the changing face of America and its growing immigrant population, American Studies scholar George Lipsitz maintains that new avenues of racism often appear in response to changing demographics and the resulting anxieties. He observes, "Competition for scarce resources in the North American context generates new racial enmities and antagonisms, which in turn promotes new variants of racism."[40] As Boero found in her study of people attending weight-loss programs, many individuals opt to lose weight in order to fit in—to avoid discrimination—rather than to be more healthy.[41] It hardly seems a coincidence that at a time when medicalized or biologically based accounts of race or poverty or both have fallen out of vogue, arguments about the classed and raced nature of obesity have gained popularity, allowing accounts that front-load personal responsibility and prompt blame to find fresh footing because they focus on obesity and supposedly are for the benefit of those who are fat.

None of this is to deny that some groups of people may be heavier than others on average or that access to nutritious food and exercise are not without importance or are not influenced by socioeconomics. It is to say, however, that the fear of fatness and what Robert Crawford has called the construction of "unhealthy others" may rework "existing class, race and ethnic prejudices into public health issues."[42] Bodies and what in Critser's case are presumed to be people's regular diets have become a way to mark difference: "In a society that likes to discuss equal opportunity and resists class labels, the United States has used dieting as a marker among groups."[43] The result is that negative attitudes about fatness easily map onto already existing negative attitudes about minorities, and because diets and fatness are seen to be artifacts of personal responsibility, people may feel justified in holding a host of problematic beliefs about minorities and blaming fat people regardless of other mitigating factors. In fact, studies have shown that people with strong antifat attitudes are also more hostile toward minorities and the poor.[44] For instance, Mollow asserts that "the slur 'fat, ugly dyke,' used to police women of all sizes and sexual orientations, exemplifies the deeply rooted intersections between fatphobia and homophobia."[45] According to American Studies scholar Amy Farrell, understanding this complex interplay among fatness and other stigmatized categories is paramount. She writes, "If we want to think clearly about health issues within this national and international anxiety regarding the 'obesity epidemic,' we had better work to strip away the cultural baggage that has fueled a fat-hating perspective."[46]

Examining the obesity epidemic and the hatred of fatness necessarily entails understanding how fatness intersects with troublesome attitudes about race and other social categories that organize US society. At first glance, Critser, whose book was met with a great deal of critical praise and was even reviewed in the *New York Times* by Michael Pollan, in some ways appears to follow the good liberal explanation that obesity rates in communities of color aren't the result of personal failures. He argues that many poor blacks are almost forced to eat at McDonald's and therefore become obese. In fact, at several points in his book, Critser maintains that the obesity epidemic is driven by a fast-food industry that traded in its desire to be associated with a white, family atmosphere for a growing inner-city, poverty-stricken, and captive market. In short, he contends that fast-food industries exploit populations who are hungry, need food, are short on cash and time, and often lack transportation—arguments that are, by now, quite familiar to most people.

Even though Critser staunchly argues that we must recognize these social and economic causes of obesity and understand why they affect poor people of color more than others, he also clearly retains the right to criticize obese people in (de)moralizing ways and to suggest that they are to blame:

Although open around the clock, the Winchell's near my house doesn't get rolling until around seven in the morning, the Spanish language talk shows frothing in the background while an ambulance light whirls atop the Coke dispenser. Inside, Mami placates Miguello with a giant apple fritter. Papi tells a joke and pours ounce after ounce of sugar and cream into his 20 ounce coffee. Viewed through the lens of obesity . . . the scene is not so feliz.[47]

Regardless of his intentions, Critser's description reads much more like an anthropological description of obesity as a result of poor parenting skills and misguided role modeling than as an argument about racial or socioeconomic injustices beyond an individual's control.

Critser might argue that if the Winchell's wasn't there, the people he describes might not have such easy access to fritters, coffee, and sugar, yet his descriptions imply that obesity remains largely volitional and particularly a problem for weak people of color, especially weak mothers of color who "placate" their children with large portions of sugary, fattening foods. Although Pollan heaps a great deal of praise on Critser's book, even he concludes his *New York Times* review by pointing out that "instead of seriously entertaining any public solutions to what he has so convincingly demonstrated is a public problem, Critser ends by imploring us to eat less, get off our duffs and, incredibly, bring back gluttony as a leading sin."[48] In the end, Critser firmly places the blame on the parents in the scene he describes, and his conclusion is not so different from the one reached by the social worker who essentially blamed Adela Martinez-Regino for her daughter's obesity, telling her that she understood "it's hard to say no."

THE LANGUAGE OF WAR

The targeting of specific people in what is supposedly a public crisis may be an unfortunate consequence of the rhetoric of war so often used to talk about fatness in the United States. Writing about the US government's war on AIDS, Michael Sherry insists that wars require a recognizable enemy, in part, because the emotions that such rhetoric inspires can't readily be directed at something as ephemeral as a virus: "Since the most obvious enemy—the viral agent—was faceless and invisible, [HIV] served poorly as the object of those intense emotions that war . . . arouses; instead, it located the disease within and on the bodies of the disease's victims."[49] Surely, the war on obesity, with its constant references to bankrupting the United States and ruining the nation's future, must also require a recognizable enemy. Nameless, faceless adipose tissue doesn't provide a clear sense of one's enemy any more than a virus does—nor does it address the lack of sidewalks or the poorly planned school lunch programs. As Boero puts it, fat bodies absorb the criticism instead of structural inequality.[50]

The use of war imagery to talk about obesity, particularly the elimination of obesity, runs the risk of producing as many problems as it might resolve, especially when that rhetoric is so often used to discuss people who are already on the margins of US society. As Sontag points out:

> In all-out war, expenditure is all-out, unprudent—war being defined as an emergency in which no sacrifice is excessive. But the wars against diseases are not just calls for more zeal, and more money to be spent on research. The metaphor implements the way particularly dreaded diseases are envisaged as an alien "other," as enemies are in modern war; and the move from the demonization of the illness to the attribution of fault to the patient is an inevitable one, no matter if patients are thought of as victims.[51]

Those who are already considered "others" in society via being people of color, poor, and/or working-class are often the individuals most closely associated with the obesity epidemic. And as a consequence, many people may well become social pariahs with the continued use of the war metaphor.

There is a long history of such cultural wars being visited on particular groups. Take the war on poverty that ultimately ended up looking much more like a war on poor people, since those receiving public assistance became subjected to increased surveillance. For women in particular, the war on poverty was waged on their bodies because states began to enforce "family caps" that limited the number of children a woman could have and still receive assistance. Historically, the use of the war metaphor has often meant that a group of very specific people rather than a large social problem became targeted.

One need only think of nightly news reports about fatness, which almost always include footage of fat bodies without heads, to understand that even though the individual identities of fat people may be camouflaged, the group identity is not. As Sontag says, this is part of what enables fault to be attributed to the patient, and it happens even when those said to be the victims of obesity are children. The point is clearly exemplified by two magazine covers that heralded the downfall of the nation's children due to obesity. A photograph for the cover of a July 2000 issue of *Newsweek* featured a young boy whose face was partially hidden behind a double-scoop ice-cream cone while his larger-than-average body was totally visible (Figure 0.1). *Time* followed suit with a strikingly similar cover shot nearly eight years later (Figure 0.2). Both covers also included headlines about the childhood obesity epidemic. The

Figure 0.1: *Newsweek* cover from July 3, 2000

How Obama Is
Fighting Internet
Innuendo

Inside China's
Gold Medal
Machine

TIME

**SPECIAL
HEALTH ISSUE**

Our
Super-
Sized
Kids

It's not just genetics
and diet. An in-depth
look at how our lifestyle
is creating a juvenile
obesity epidemic—
and the scoop on
how to cure it

www.time.com

Figure 0.2: *Time* cover from June 23, 2008

message they sent was clear: this is what a child who is a problem looks like. People may not have been able to pick the *particular* little boys out of a crowd because their faces were either cut off or obscured by their ice-cream cones (thereby allowing both magazines to exploit these boys with a clear conscience), but the audience had surely gotten the message about identifying children who looked like these little boys, rather than ubiquitous fast-food outlets or nonexistent sidewalks, as "problems."

THE CULTURE OF FEAR

In the midst of an epidemic or crisis, everyday objects can come to inspire fear. During the AIDS epidemic, many people came to fear commonplace objects such as public drinking fountains and restaurant cutlery. Similarly, the use of ice-cream cones on the covers of *Time* and *Newsweek* served as an important rhetorical device that located the danger of childhood obesity close to home, a tactic that has been common to other domestic, issue-based "wars," such as the war on drugs. Without doubt, one of the most infamous images from public service announcements during the war on drugs was the image of the frying pan and the egg. The image of the egg sizzling in the hot pan came with the message "This is your brain. This is your brain on drugs."[52] In an instant, the war on drugs was moved into America's houses by using, according to rhetorician William N. Elwood, "an object found in almost every American kitchen and a common breakfast item to convey the message that 'the drug problem' [was] as close as [the] viewer's home."[53]

In the case of obesity, even ice-cream cones become dangerous, and these items may be in the hands of our children. At the very least, such items are, as Cultural Studies scholar Charlotte Biltekoff points out, on grocery shelves, and they are common objects that are being represented in the war on obesity in ways that both suggest immediate danger and promote fear.[54] According to Elwood, during the war on drugs, President George H. W. Bush noted that the "American people would achieve 'victory over drugs' . . . 'neighborhood by neighborhood, block by block, child by child.' Although there was a great deal of discussion about the socioeconomic features of the drug trade and drug use, it was still the individuals who were blamed for using drugs."[55] The war on drugs also focused on volition, with Nancy Reagan's famous tagline "Just Say No" being her best advice about how to fight the battle. The war against obesity also seems to be positioned as a "child by child" battle, but now it is also cone by cone, and it is still the sort of war where individuals who appear not to be able to "just say no" are blamed.

Given that the discussion of obesity has historically been used as a way of talking about and working through fears regarding the demise of American culture, the current war on obesity may not be entirely about obesity but rather may be, at least in part, about other social tensions for which fatness is a convenient replacement. Because obesity is medicalized, it is convenient to be outraged at fat people because the outrage is supposedly *for their own good*: "Americans love to moralize about fat because, among other reasons, fat has become a convenient stand-in for various characteristics that have been traditionally associated with the pariahs of the moment."[56] Rather than arguing that women ought to be in the home because they belong there and not at work, it's now convenient to say that their being in the home will alleviate childhood obesity. And rather than saying that people of color and/or poor people don't deserve respect because they're not hardworking, people can now say that they don't deserve respect because their fatness is bankrupting the nation and is an obvious sign of both their laziness and their overconsumption of resources.

SAVE THE CHILDREN

The statistics about childhood obesity are so commonplace in daily discussions that most Americans probably know them by heart: "Childhood obesity has more than tripled in the past 30 years";[57] "16% of children age 6–19 years are overweight";[58] "today, about one in three American kids or teens is overweight or obese."[59] Just as ubiquitous is the long list of side effects said to accompany childhood obesity, including everything from depression and sleep apnea to heart disease, type 2 diabetes, and various forms of cancer. Nearly everyone has heard that children today are likely to have shorter life spans than their parents due to the prevalence of childhood obesity. [60]

After hearing about the complications, illnesses, and premature death associated with obesity in children, many people undoubtedly want to help. It's difficult for them to think about children suffering in such ways without wanting to do something. Even more gut wrenching may be the fact that children are usually seen as innocent victims, which is likely why so many charities focus on "saving" the children—both abroad and at home. Whether it's children in Appalachia who need dental care or starving children in the Sudan, images of suffering children motivate people to care about populations who might otherwise be forgotten. Surely, fewer people would be likely to contribute to campaigns that featured seemingly able-bodied adults who needed food or dental care because they would probably think that adults were capable of helping themselves.

Obesity coupled with childhood, however, presents its own set of specific challenges, especially given the omnipresence of "fat talk"[61] in US society. Some people may want to "save" fat children because they think it's terrible that youngsters would suffer type 2 diabetes at an early age. But I would guess that just as many people want to end childhood obesity simply because they don't like fat and/or because of the cost they think each and every American—in spite of his or her weight—will have to take on for those overweight and obese children. Some campaigns that aim to end childhood obesity actually encourage people to adopt the perspective that childhood obesity should be ended because it's expensive. At the launch of her Let's Move! campaign, First Lady Michelle Obama declared that because of childhood obesity, "the physical and emotional health of an entire generation and the economic health and security of our nation is at stake."[62] Rhetorically, she asked that people care about obese children, yes, but one of the reasons she offered for doing so was because they were about to bankrupt the country and ruin what many might refer to as "our way of life," as HBO's *Weight of the Nation* might put it. Even if her strategy proves effective and people begin to care about fat children, they may do so not because they see children as inherently worthy of care but because *not* caring about them may mean that everyone else must sacrifice their health care dollars and their country.[63] In this case, I'm not convinced that the ends justify the means, particularly when the attitudes toward fat children and the interventions into their lives so often involve placing blame and responsibility on the youngsters and their mothers.

Beyond hearing that the costs of childhood obesity are more than $3 billion a year,[64] Americans are also being told that the costs of adult obesity are skyrocketing out of control and that the best way to control those costs is to prevent obesity as early as possible in the life cycle.[65] It's not just that fat children are costly as fat children but also that if they grow into fat adults, they become even more expensive, for it is believed that their risk factors for diseases such as diabetes will go up (contributing to direct costs) and their productivity at work will plummet (contributing to indirect costs).[66] Studies show that children who are obese are likely to become obese adults, and even those who are obese at very young ages (as early as two years old) are thought likely to grow up to be obese.[67] These data are used to bolster claims that obesity in children is threatening and needs to be stopped before the United States is left penniless. And that is one of the reasons why children such as Anamarie Regino are sometimes removed from their homes.

A POUND OF FLESH

Since obesity is so often framed as an individual medical issue in American society and since, as Abigail Saguy argues in *What's Wrong with Fat?*, how issues are framed exerts a tremendous amount of influence over how solutions are imagined, it shouldn't be too surprising that individuals are the targets of most interventions. Although there's a great deal of talk about food deserts and unsafe sidewalks, even campaigns such as Let's Move! still ultimately suggest that it's up to individual families and children to overcome the obstacles and produce thin youngsters. The changes most expected are actually changes to individual bodies. In short, the commonsense solution to the obesity epidemic is really thought to be for people to just lose weight. Just say no to the carbs, as Miller might say.

In spite of the fact that blaming fat people for their own condition is likely to spawn more discrimination against them as a group, including children, some people contend that weight-based discrimination may actually be helpful. Critser, for instance, argues that targeted weight-based discrimination can help stem the tide of obesity by helping individuals control their weight—in spite of all other factors. Contrasting statistics about black and white women's average weights, Critser opines that "social stigma may serve to control obesity among white women."[68] And citing the rising number of overweight children and adolescents, he finds the prospect of young black women *not* being teased about their weight problematic.

Recently, Daniel Callahan, a prominent bioethicist and cofounder of the Hastings Center, made waves when he also argued that weight-based discrimination could be helpful. Calling for "discrimination lite," Callahan believes that strategies similar to those used to stigmatize smokers—by making their behavior socially unacceptable—should be applied to overweight and obese people. After several individuals reminded him that those working in public health have repeatedly indicated stigma is not an appropriate treatment, Callahan continued to insist that such measures were reasonable and indeed necessary, in part because he believes that many fat Americans aren't aware of their fatness. According to Lindsey Abrams, when responding to critics who consider stigmatizing obesity is an overreach of government into the lives of individuals, Callahan argues, "Whatever they may think about the power and excess of government, it [government intervention] is inescapable in this case, as much as with national defense."[69] His choice of comparison is telling. By using the language of war and national defense, he has, as Sontag argues, suggested that all is fair in the war against obesity.

When a child isn't thin or doesn't become thin and family intervention is judged to have failed, the child is sometimes removed from his or her home with no apparent regard for the fact that there may be little the parents can do about the child's weight or that there may be different styles of parenting. As scholars who study public health campaigns, among them Lisette Burrows, have noted, the concept of valued or valuable cultural "difference" seems to fall by the wayside when body size, food, eating, or parenting around these issues are being discussed. Even in the United States, a country that openly acknowledges the multicultural nature of its society, "health" and a "good diet" are assumed to be without context and value neutral.[70] Critser paternalistically dismisses the notion that "health" or "wellness" might vary or should be allowed to vary within communities, and he proposes opening up yet another avenue of discrimination, all in the name of equal opportunity—equal opportunity stigma, that is. In suggesting that the African American community is behind the times in terms of its role models for young women, he pathologizes African American culture, just as "much of the conversation among experts about why people of color and the poor are more likely to be obese . . . entails pathologizing cultural preferences, such as foodways, parenting styles, and beauty standards."[71] As I discuss in several of the following chapters, a similar kind of pathologizing of difference—be that difference in race, class, or even marital status—is visible in cases where obese children are removed from homes, supposedly for their own good, or when parents are prosecuted because their child's obesity is understood as a sign of neglect.

BLAME THE WOMEN

In a recent editorial about McDonald's being sued for using toys to entice children to eat Happy Meals™ and the ways such practices have led to the epidemic of childhood obesity, the author squarely places the ultimate blame and responsibility on parents rather than on the fast-food chain, remarking that "kids can't drive themselves to McDonald's."[72] Regardless of how flawed such thinking might be (because surely not all fat children eat at McDonald's and not all thin children refrain), the commonsense notion that parents are responsible for giving their children unhealthy food remains powerfully entrenched. Further, because food practices are still so gendered in the United States—and are expected to be—it's more likely that the mother is blamed for giving her children foods such as Happy Meals™ or, alternatively, for causing a father to have to take his children to McDonald's because mom is working outside the home or just doesn't cook. After all, when people bemoan the demise of the homecooked meal, their concern is that women, not men, aren't fulfilling their role in the kitchen. Americans may talk about "deadbeat dads" who don't meet their financial responsibilities, but they don't tend to talk about men who are "bad fathers" because they fail to cook meals or change diapers.

A political ad paid for by psychiatrist and presidential hopeful Mark Klein, which appeared in 2006 in the *Washington National Times Weekly*, a conservative news magazine with nationwide circulation, firmly placed the blame for the childhood obesity epidemic on women. The ad featured a photo of a woman in a business suit moving swiftly away from her children—so swiftly, in fact, that her image was blurred for effect. Behind her trailed two cartoon children, one of them yelling for her "momma." In the text of the ad, Klein blamed "feminist careerism" for the divorce rate, low wages for women, a decrease in buying power, emotionally starved children, and finally the epidemics of both adult and childhood obesity and diabetes. He claimed that the "obesity driven" epidemic of diabetes among children has resulted from "mothers working" and "too few adults and children eating balanced, nutritious, portion-controlled homecooked meals."[73]

The idea that working mothers specifically are a primary cause of childhood obesity is also prevalent in many parenting manuals about children and weight. One particularly strong example of this trend of blaming obesity on food that isn't homecooked by mom comes from J. Clinton Smith. He cites research from 1994–1995 claiming that "57 percent of Americans of all age groups—71 percent of teenage boys—consumed meals and snacks away from home on any given day."[74] Smith adds that many of these snacks and meals were based on fast foods, and he asks, "Is this trend likely to continue, given the fact that 75 percent of American women work outside the home?" He responds to his own query with a resounding, "Yes, because with many working parents, preparation of any meal, much less a healthy one, can constitute a major time commitment."[75] Although Smith acknowledges larger cultural issues, such as both parents working and the desire to provide for one's family by having two incomes, his statements still suggest that the increased consumption of fast foods (and therefore the increase in childhood obesity) is tied to mothers working and not preparing more meals at home.

Some authors posit that the lack of family meals is at the heart of both the childhood obesity problem and the general decline of America. Paula Ford-Martin, in one of several sections of her parenting manual about overweight children, cries, "Alert! Up to 40 percent of American families seldom eat together," and she goes on to cite a 2003 study that found children who ate "meals with their families four or five times weekly were significantly more likely to eat more vegetables, fruits, and dairy products."[76] Claims about the lack of mothers in the home to cook meals, the greater reliance on fast food, and data that suggest family meals are key to children eating fruits and vegetables may all have some truth behind them and be relevant to discussions about childhood obesity. Yet, even though authors such as Ford-Martin speak more frequently than, say, Smith, about family meals rather than mothers' particular responsibilities, the role of the mother is likely more linked to preventing childhood obesity due to the expectation that women are the ones who cook and gather families around the dinner table. According to Gard and Wright, Mary Eberstadt goes even further in her article "The Child-Fat Problem" when she argues that "America is in deep social decline and that at the heart of the problem are absent mothers."[77] Writing specifically about the problem of overweight children, Eberstadt notes, "There would appear to be an obvious relationship between absentee parents— meaning particularly . . . mothers—and overstuffed children."[78] Nowhere does Klein or Eberstadt, both of whom directly blame women, suggest that men could also cook dinner or that men's careers might be causing problems.

Looking at a series of articles from sources such as the *New York Times* and the *Sacramento Bee,* Boero argues that analyses of family dynamics that may contribute to childhood obesity (such as eating out or the lack of homecooked meals) often do not "explicitly mention mothers, but when 'both parents work,' it is mothers, whose paid work is often seen as unnecessary, who are to blame for children being home alone."[79] Again, it might be true that Americans are eating more fast food or that a significant portion of American families no longer eat meals as a family unit. The leap, however, to the claim that such factors are solely, primarily, or even partially responsible for childhood obesity is often not based on sound evidence but rather on a nostalgia for a particular lifestyle, a lifestyle that places mothers at home rather than at work. Because the problem is framed as an issue of women being out of the home, the solutions imagined focus primarily on getting women back into their traditional roles.

The cover of Critser's *Fat Land* also makes clear the assumption that women are responsible for feeding children the kinds of food thought to cause obesity (Figure 0.3). The subtitle of the book, *How Americans Became the Fattest People in the World,* rests right below an image of a spoon full of ice cream, syrup, and sprinkles being offered to a child who is already holding a piece of pizza and wearing a donut as a bracelet, a hamburger as a cummerbund, and whipped topping, nuts, and a cherry as a hat. The hand holding the spoon is decidedly a female hand, as indicated by the red-polished nails. Authors don't always have control over the art used for book covers, of course, but publishers certainly do,

Figure 0.3: Cover of Greg Critser's *Fat Land: How Americans Became the Fattest People on Earth*

and Houghton Mifflin knows that what sells books are images that are visually arresting but also familiar in terms of the ideas and values they portray. As part of her study on mother blaming, Paula Caplan surveyed 125 articles published in nine mental health journals from 1972 to 1984. She found that "mothers were blamed for seventy-two different kinds of problems in their offspring," including everything from bed-wetting to "homicidal transsexualism."[80] In other words, blaming women is a familiar tactic in confronting what are often complicated and vexing social problems or stigmatized identities among children.

In current discussions of childhood obesity, however, it's not just that women are blamed for children not having homecooked meals or eating fast food; it's also that they are blamed for literally reproducing childhood obesity. Various studies, such as those positing that even children who are obese when under two years of age still have a good chance of growing up to be obese adults, have prompted discussions about what is now referred to as "fetal overnutrition."[81] This theory hypothesizes that women being heavy may contribute to their future children being fat. Women who are overweight or obese during pregnancy—and even before pregnancy—are now thought to predispose their fetuses to obesity throughout their lives. Although fetal overnutrition has been studied for more than ten years, researchers and scientists still haven't reached firm conclusions about its veracity, as is so often the case with research into obesity. In a recent Canadian study of siblings born to women who gave birth both before and after bariatric surgeries, researchers noted that the children born after bariatric surgeries seemed to be thinner than older siblings who had been born presurgery. Reporting on the story via the Associated Press did, however, point out that the study was not conclusive: "Clearly diet and exercise play a huge role in how fit the younger siblings will continue to be, and it's a small study. But the findings suggest the children born after mom's surgery might have an advantage."[82] Though much of the buzz surrounding the study was about the genes of the children born to moms after bariatric surgery being positively affected by a different uterine environment, as the Associated Press reporter astutely notes, other environmental factors—including diet and exercise—may have been at play as well. Such studies are still inconclusive, suggesting only that there might be an advantage.

No doubt, we've learned a great deal about how the uterine environment may affect children, but thanks to the field of epigenetics, which seeks to understand how traits are passed along and how certain genes may be turned off or on, researchers also know that men are just as likely (and perhaps more likely, in some cases) to pass along traits to a fetus. Nonetheless, much of the data is ignored or certainly not considered mainstream because American culture focuses much more attention on women's bodies, in particular the parts of women's bodies that involve future children. As Rebecca Kukla notes, American culture has a long history of portraying women as merely vessels for carrying children. She cites a *Time* cover from November 11, 2002, which features the title "Inside the Womb" and depicts a free-floating fetus, as a prime example of how discussions of what happens in the womb often occur as if the womb is distinctly separate from the woman.[83]

The mother blaming that involves women's bodies and the childhood obesity epidemic, then, represents a deeply gendered and fatphobic cherry-picking among a vast field of influences on fetuses. Yet, whether by virtue of poor feeding practices, role modeling, or their own bodies, women are the ones most consistently blamed for the childhood obesity epidemic—even when the evidence is still being debated and effects on fetuses are poorly understood. As for the study about children born to mothers who had bariatric surgeries being better off, reporter Lauren Neergard rightly concludes, "Only time will tell if these youngsters born after mom's surgery really get lasting benefits."[84]

Because we don't know the answers to so many of the questions raised by the panic surrounding the childhood obesity epidemic, including what causes obesity and what the best solutions for it might be, we need to slow down and take a step back to carefully examine the collateral damage. As Gard and Wright point out in the epigraph to this introduction, how we move forward from this point isn't necessarily—and perhaps shouldn't be—based on finding out how we've arrived here. Rather, the most important decisions to be made are about how the real people caught in what has become a political, moral, and ideological debate should be treated. The search for scapegoats that leads to the blaming of women and children and to hasty interventions into their lives and on their very bodies doesn't improve their existence.

HOW IT ALL COMES TOGETHER

In chapter 1, I discuss how recent conversations in the war against obesity position women's bodies, in particular, as among the most strategic sites in the battle of the bulge—in ways that affect their broader lives and, in some cases, even their reproductive choices. The basic thinking is that if women remain thin during pregnancy, childhood obesity will be prevented. On the surface, some people may find this to be a reasonable recommendation, but the ways in which concerns about maternal obesity and obesity in women are tied to concerns about childhood obesity have led to discussions and policies that may end up undermining all women's reproductive rights. For example, there are now new weight guidelines for pregnancies, certain restrictions on fertility treatments for women whose BMIs are above a set level, and other policies and practices that position women as mere vessels for carrying pregnancies that will result in a generation of thin children. Thus, concern about women's weight stems not necessarily from concern about their health but rather from concern about the trouble their bodies might bring to others, namely, the children they bear and the nation that believes it will have to pay for obesity-related expenses.

As I show in chapter 1, the focus on maternal obesity and its effects on children represents a serious culling from all possible influences on a fetus, especially since new work in the field of epigenetics suggests paternal obesity could exert as much—if not more—influence on the future weight of a fetus. Perhaps even more disconcerting is that the practices now being proposed, such as counseling *all* women about their weight and advising *all* women to maintain an ideal weight (even if they don't currently plan to get pregnant) and limiting heavy women's access to fertility treatments, may drive many women away from medical care, simply because they fear being lectured or facing further interventions. Political scientist Karen Zivi argues that, historically, marginalized women have suffered the most under such interventions but that the values underpinning the recommendations and policies harm all women because they suggest that women's rights are ancillary to fetal and child rights. She argues that this "ideology . . . comes to function as a regulatory norm that authorizes the disciplining of women's lives and bodies that results in the subordination of women's interests to those of children in ways that often jeopardize the well-being of both."[85]

When children are judged to be too fat, one of the remedies currently used is removing them from their home environments, which are often thought to be the cause of their obesity. In chapter 2, I discuss what have become three touchstone cases of children being removed from their homes because of obesity. Like the Regino case, these cases underscore the complexities of how fat is constructed and how fat on a child's body comes to symbolize poor parenting. Although many conversations about childhood obesity mention the struggles parents face in today's food and social environments, the final blame is still often laid at the feet of the parents, who are expected to make their children thin no matter what. When children remain fat, parents are almost always imagined to be uncooperative with authorities, dismissive of social conventions, and a danger to their offspring.

These three touchstone cases also suggest that there are gendered expectations for who is doing the parenting and that parents' bodies often serve as indicators of their ability to care for a child. In all three cases, the mothers are expected to be the primary caregivers—even when the fathers could also provide care. Thus, this chapter continues to show how mother blaming features in the war against obesity. I also argue that in these cases, being fat—in and of itself—literally removes women from the realm of good parenting, partly because their bodies are thought to be evidence of their ability to contaminate their children with their bad eating and exercise habits. Repeatedly, the courts have insisted that a mother's weight is evidence of her inability to care for herself and therefore to care properly for her child, at least as far as weight loss is considered proper child care. In the court documents, any other good parenting that may be taking place is ignored, as the focus is only on making the child thin and on the mother's failure to do so. I argue that by taking such an approach, courts are doing harm to children and to families by failing to account for the psychological consequences of removing youngsters from their homes.

Chapter 3 examines the ways in which fat children's very bodies have come to symbolize failure—of the children, the parents, and even the nation. Here, I turn my attention to recent representations of children in several public health campaigns and argue that the shame these campaigns engender shouldn't be understood as a treatment for obesity; in reality, they are likely to make children less healthy by encouraging them to be too focused on their weight. When children see other children who look like them being held up as examples of disease and as warnings of future demise, they may come to understand their own bodies as their enemies. I use studies from experts on children and body image to make this point but also offer an analysis of the writings by one of the children who was featured on Georgia's Strong4Life billboards with a literal "warning" sign across her stomach. Her writings suggest that she feels guilt over eating even one piece of a graham cracker, and I question how fostering what many experts would consider disordered eating behaviors can possibly lead to healthier children.

In this chapter, I widen my scope to investigate what happens to children featured in such ads and also to question the broader cultural effects of these kinds of representations. I consider what it means for children's bodies to be used as public message boards in these ways and how doing so may not only encourage fat children to see their own bodies as the enemy but also prompt other children and adults to see fat children as adversaries. Teasing is often said to be one of the most painful experiences fat children endure, yet people working on public health campaigns that use children as evidence of an epidemic don't seem to give much thought to the ways these representations may actually encourage the teasing of fat children. Looking at studies about peer-to-peer teasing and parental teasing, it's clear that teasing has a profound negative impact on children's lives. Many children who are regularly teased, especially by parents, suffer depression and develop eating disorders. The campaigns I examine explicitly aim to raise awareness about childhood obesity among parents, but they fail to take into consideration the harmful effects of having parents focus on a child's weight. I argue that these campaigns are both shortsighted and harmful and that a better choice would be to work toward establishing a culture in which all children are supported, regardless of their body weight or shape.

When all else fails—and obesity can't be stopped before it ever starts by counseling women or intervening in their pregnancies—there are surgeries that can be performed on children's bodies, some literally excising a pound of flesh as sacrifice and payment for being obese. In chapter 4, I discuss bariatric surgeries that are now being performed on children and what it means to alter youngsters' bodies so drastically. Gastric-banding procedures performed on adolescents are on the rise, but so is the virtually irreversible Roux-en-Y procedure, which surgically reconstructs a smaller stomach pouch and bypasses a large portion of intestine. Both gastric banding and Roux-en-Y come with serious side effects attached, including nausea, vomiting, diarrhea, and malnutrition (all of which are intended side effects meant to stop patients from over-eating or from eating certain foods) as well as more severe and unintended side effects, such as internal bleeding, slippage of bands and pouches, malnourishment to the point of disease, and even death. Currently, the accepted guidelines allow for performing these procedures on boys as young as fifteen and girls as young as thirteen,[86] but some surgeons take on much younger patients.

I question what it means to perform such drastic procedures on children, supposedly with the aim of making them healthier. I look closely at the physiological and psychological effects of these surgeries, especially since they reinforce the notion that children ought to change their bodies in order to alleviate what are ultimately social problems, such as teasing. Looking at postbariatric narratives from adults and studies about their compliance with required eating and vitamin regimens, it's clear that many grown people don't necessarily understand that having these procedures will drastically alter their lives and that almost all patients struggle with the rigid routines the surgeries require. And all of this raises serious doubts as to whether children and adolescents can comprehend the gravity of these operations or commit to the required follow-up care.

In the end, what I'm suggesting is that we needn't engage in a separating of the wheat from the chaff in terms of who is fat because of structural inequities and who is fat because of overeating. Nor am I suggesting that we parse out who is a good mother and who is a bad mother based on the cause of a child's obesity. As Kathleen LeBesco suggests, concentrating on why people are fat almost always entails a kind of "will to innocence" model in which some fat people become okay (because being fat is not their fault) whereas others become blameworthy (because they've brought on their own condition).[87]

Regardless of how someone comes to be fat, removing children from homes, undermining women's reproductive rights, performing poorly studied surgeries on young bodies, and representing children and parents as social pariahs aren't helping to make anyone's life better. And none of these approaches appear to be real solutions to what is supposedly an epidemic; after all, not all children can be given surgeries. In the end, it's likely that fat women will continue to become pregnant, and it's likely that there will still be children who eat well and exercise and remain fat. It's also likely that women will continue to work outside the home, and there certainly aren't enough foster homes for all the fat children in the United States. Given these very real limits to the interventions now being proposed and implemented, some of the most vexing and lingering questions about the childhood obesity epidemic would appear not to be about its cause but rather about why, in spite of their limitations, these interventions persist and even appear reasonable to so many people today.

CHAPTER ONE

Children First

Maternal Ideology in the War on Obesity

Maternal ideology . . . comes to function as a regulatory norm that
authorizes the disciplining of women's lives and bodies that results in the
subordination of women's interests to those of children in ways that often
jeopardize the well-being of both.
    —Karen Zivi, "Contesting Motherhood in the Age of AIDS"[1]

Most women who become pregnant have fears and worries. What vitamins
should I take? What about that glass of wine I had before I knew I was pregnant? Is it okay to eat shellfish? Will my child be fat because I am? Similar to
admonitions against drinking, smoking, and consuming certain foods while
pregnant, concerns about childhood obesity have now brought new pressures,
recommendations, and warnings for women. In her advice manual, *The Everything Parents' Guide to the Overweight Child,* Paula Ford-Martin advises
women to breast-feed in order to minimize the possibility of obesity.[2] Recently,
cesareans have become suspect, with doctors warning that delivering a child by
C-section may significantly increase the risk of childhood obesity.[3] In another
parenting advice manual, *Understanding Childhood Obesity,* J. Clinton Smith
cautions women to maintain a careful watch of calorie intake while pregnant
because consuming too many calories is likely to lead to having an obese child.[4]
Of course, we now know that breast-feeding has many advantages for children, and for many years, doctors have been advising women against gaining
too much weight during pregnancy because of the potential for complications
during delivery. There has also been a movement back toward vaginal births
whenever possible, as people have become wary of too many interventions
during pregnancy. Yet, in recent years, the mounting cautions about maternal
body weight and what is now referred to as "fetal overnutrition,"[5] in particular,
signal a turning point in the discussion about childhood obesity: increasingly,

women's bodies are seen as receptacles for pregnancies, and mothers as the foot soldiers in the battle of the bulge.

The concern over the childhood obesity epidemic continues to produce fast-moving, dynamic discussions and sometimes recommendations and policies that may not be based on evidence that they foster well-being. Some of these discussions and policies are now leading to what many may consider the ultimate "treatment" for childhood obesity by seeking to prevent pregnancies that even have the *potential* to produce fat children. This particular set of strategies for preventing childhood obesity necessarily undermines women's reproductive rights, routinely represents certain women as bad mothers, and calls forth visions of the eugenics movement because the conversation seems to suggest that some people are worthy of reproducing (or being reproduced) but others are not. Though seeking to prevent fat children by preventing fat women from reproducing certainly affects fat women more immediately, the conversations occurring and policies being put in place potentially affect *all* women—regardless of their body size and regardless of whether they intend to have children.

MATERNAL IDEOLOGY AND MOTHER BLAMING

Arguably, women are subjected to a set of standards pertaining to their mothering practices that constitute a type of ideology. In her work on women and motherhood during the AIDS epidemic, Karen Zivi argues that the meaning of motherhood was renegotiated by the presence of AIDS, which she says shaped a kind of "maternal ideology" against which women's mothering practices were judged. She writes, "Maternal ideology [was], in other words, used to judge women, to determine if they [were] engaging in acceptable mothering practices, and to decide whether the regulation of their lives and the circumscription of their rights [was] warranted."[6] In this particular maternal ideology, motherhood became "inextricable from public health and rights arguments," at least in part due to the idea that a public health crisis involving children was afoot.[7] Women who were HIV-positive were almost automatically slotted as "bad" mothers according to this maternal ideology, an ideology that suggested no logical woman could possibly want to have a child because of the risk of passing on the virus. Women with HIV who wanted to have a child or who actually had a child became caricatured as uncaring and reckless rather than represented as complex, rational decision makers who had the ability and also the right to make choices regarding their bodies and reproduction. In short, as

Zivi shows, the framework of maternal ideology distilled HIV-positive women down into "conduits of contagion" and suggested they "had an allegedly deficient 'moral universe' that compromised their ability to be good mothers."[8]

Against the narrative backdrop of HIV-positive women as bad mothers carelessly risking passing HIV to their fetuses, many policy makers sought to intervene by recommending mandatory HIV testing for *all* pregnant women. Their thinking was that "if women could not be 'responsible' or 'logical' enough to keep from putting infants at risk, then it was the state's duty to intervene. Women who posed a threat to the health of their children because of their morally irresponsible behavior, should, they argued, be the subject of regulatory public health policies such as mandatory testing. That was the duty of the state in the time of crisis."[9]

The rhetoric of "crisis," "epidemic," and "war" tends to spawn and validate policies and interventions that might otherwise seem extreme. Further, the fight against fatness in children has drawn the interest of the state in ways that are similar to those of the "war against HIV." In fact, several antiobesity campaigns have recently intensified their focus on the role of maternity and, in particular, on maternal weight gain in an effort to wage what they think will be a more effective battle against obesity in children.[10] The idea seems to be that the best course of action is to stop obesity in children before it ever starts by preventing pregnancies deemed "at risk" for obesity. One such campaign is Shape Up America! (SUA), a nonprofit effort founded by former surgeon general C. Everett Koop in 1994 that now maintains close ties to Michelle Obama's government-sponsored Let's Move! campaign. On the front page of its website, SUA offers a link to (and a downloadable version of) a 2012 article entitled "Severe Obesity: The Neglected Problem," which was published in *Obesity Facts: The European Journal of Obesity*. The authors, John G. Kral, Ruth A. Kava, Patrick M. Catalano, and Barbara J. Moore, essentially argue that in order to stem the tide of obesity, interventions are especially important for people of reproductive age:

> To stem intergenerational transmission of obesity, there is an urgent need to i) prevent obesity and SO [severe obesity] in people with reproductive potential, ii) prevent pregnancy in those already obese and severely obese, and iii) effectively treat people currently affected with SO to minimize the risks of gestational obesity and optimize healthy outcomes for mother and offspring. If Society [sic] is willing to prosecute drug-abusing mothers, and warn of alcohol and tobacco use during pregnancy, should we not be serious about preventing obese pregnancies?[11]

As is often the case with discussions of childhood obesity,[12] the authors begin by talking about *people* of reproductive age, but as they move forward, it becomes apparent that it's *women* of reproductive age who are actually their focus—as evidenced by their references to "pregnancies" and "drug-abusing mothers."

As in conversations about HIV, in discussions of obesity and pregnancy the welfare of fat women themselves becomes secondary to concerns about what they may pass along to their children. Regarding how women with HIV were talked about during the AIDS crisis, Kimberly Mutcherson observes, "To the extent that women found themselves mentioned in discussions of the growing plague, it was as vectors of disease transmission . . . to innocent newborns."[13] She goes on to show that the construction of women as the source of contagion contributed to troubling policies regarding women and mandatory testing: "In part, because women have been viewed as transmitters of HIV, they have been targets for adverse HIV/AIDS policies and legislation."[14] The authors of the article featured on the SUA site similarly justify their focus on women of reproductive age by claiming that when SO women "carry to term [they] are more likely to have fatter babies, who are more likely to be obese by the age of 4 and remain so through adolescence and into their reproductive years."[15] They go on to note that the "intergenerational transmission of obesity is stronger for maternal than paternal obesity, implying an important role in the uterine environment."[16] Kral and his coauthors maintain that recent evidence points to "metabolic imprinting on developing susceptible neural circuits during gestation and infancy" and that "the data suggest that parental obesity, by whatever mechanism(s), predisposes the offspring to obesity."[17] Thus, even though these authors acknowledge both that paternal obesity may play a role and that the data remain a bit unclear as to why parental obesity in general matters, they nonetheless insist that parents and especially mothers play a crucial role in passing obesity along to their children. The emphasis on mothers persists in the authors' choice of language as well as in a great many of our cultural representations—in spite of the fact that some studies find that paternal BMI may exert as strong of a correlation to a child being overweight or obese as maternal BMI.[18] And as was true of women who were HIV positive, the concern appears not to be for the women themselves but rather for the effect that their weight will have on others.

Fat women's bodies are often portrayed as problems for others. In her article entitled "Normative Imperatives vs. Pathological Bodies: Constructing the 'Fat' Woman," Samantha Murray takes readers back to what she considers a key moment when fat women became depicted as a source of trouble and anxiety for others. Citing Dr. James McLester's 1924 article about fatness in women, which was published in the *Journal of the American Medical Association*, Murray contends that McLester "casts the fat woman as less-than-woman, less-than-human, unable to truly access her 'inner self'; or perhaps she does not even have a core, but is merely an assemblage of the worst indiscretions and shortcoming of women."[19] McLester's account was not centered on fat women's health itself but rather on how their fatness affected others around them, primarily by being an affront to accepted aesthetics of female embodiment, leading Murray to conclude that "medical opinion of the 'fat' female body is not that it is a suffering body but rather that it is a *source* of suffering for *others*."[20] The idea that fat women's bodies bring suffering to others seems to also be present in an article by John Kral from 2004. According to Megan Warin and her coauthors,

> Writing in the prestigious journal *Pediatrics* in 2004, [Kral] argues that all women, even "newborn girls," have the potential to become "doubly damaging," both polluted and polluting, since fat is passed on through the female body. Accordingly, the only way to curb the obesity epidemic is to "urgently" target young girls and young women; from birth to menarche, behavior modification in mothers and children should be the first choice in obesity prevention.[21]

Thus, although fat women may be particularly targeted, all women are constructed as representing the possibility of contagion because the specter of motherhood is so closely tied to being female. As Martha Fineman puts it:

> As an institution with significant and powerful symbolic content in our culture, motherhood has an impact on all women—independent of the individual choice about whether to become a mother. It comes from the durability and tenacity of the assumptions made about any individual woman that are forged in the context of cultural and social forces that define the "essential" or idealized woman. For this reason, all women should care about the social and cultural presentation of the concepts of motherhood that are part of the process that constructs and perpetuates a unitary, essentialist social understanding of women. "Mother" is so interwoven with that notion of what it means to be a woman in our culture that it will continue to have an impact on individual women's lives.[22]

Fineman describes something that most women have experienced and that a great deal of feminist scholarship has commented upon. Regardless of whether or not a woman is a mother or has desires to be a mother, the cultural expectation is that she will behave in "motherly" ways by adopting culturally idealized attitudes toward children and caring for others. The idea that the words *woman* and *mother* are essentially interchangeable in the culture and that all women are possible sources of misery for others is certainly reflected in Kral's arguments that women in general—not just those who wish to become mothers—must be counseled from "birth to menarche" in order to best curb the obesity epidemic and not be "doubly damaging."

All women are subject to the kind of maternal ideology that so closely ties being female to motherhood, but in a political climate where fatness represents a moment of crisis, fat women in particular are at risk for facing judgments and interventions because their bodies are believed to signal a kind of failure. Much like the bodies of women with HIV are thought to indicate moral failings and desires run amok, so, too, the fat body is seen as unruly and a source of danger and anxiety. Women with HIV were often portrayed, according to Zivi, as "vaginas waiting to infect men and uteruses waiting to infect fetuses" because they were believed to be engaging in a "freely chosen" and "unrestrained" sexual life where they were "in denial [and] not using condoms."[23] In other words, the popular narrative about HIV-positive women was that they refused to heed medical advice about the transmission of AIDS and were out of control.

AN INSATIABLE APPETITE

The fat female body has been represented similarly in the sense that fatness is believed to be volitional and to visually announce an unwillingness to curb one's appetite. As Susan Bordo makes clear in her work, within US culture, obesity is understood as "an extreme capacity to capitulate to desire."[24] Showcasing popular media's inclination to equate unrestrained eating with unrestrained sexuality, Bordo analyzes numerous commercials for high-fat, taboo food items, such as ice cream and cake, and builds a convincing argument that food advertisements regularly play upon the idea of unrestrained female desire. Her analysis of the movie *Flashdance* is perhaps her best example of representational conflations of eating and sexual desire. The movie, featuring the thin and athletic Jennifer Beals, is a 1980s cult classic about Alex, an aspiring dancer working as a welder to make ends meet, hustling her way to the top by pushing herself to literally dance until she drops.

Her fiery desire for her dance career is matched only by her desire for her male lover, who also happens to be her boss. In one of the more risqué scenes in the movie, Alex and her boss are at dinner when she removes her tuxedo jacket and reveals that she is wearing only a vest and cuffs underneath—no shirt.

Her back is completely exposed, and the curves of her breasts peek seductively from the sides of the vest. At that moment, she picks up a piece of lobster, dips it in butter, and proceeds to suck the butter off the meat, repeatedly sliding the piece of lobster across her lips while staring at her boss and lover. With a face filled with anticipation and a raspy voice, he asks, "Is that lobster good? I guess you're really hungry, huh?"[25] The message is clear: "Unrestrained delight in eating operates as sexual foreplay, a way of prefiguring the abandon that will shortly be expressed in bed."[26]

Although Beals is thin, as are most of the women featured in the advertisements Bordo analyzes, the idea that unrestrained eating symbolizes unrestrained sexual desire still attaches to fat women. Given that the cultural narrative about fatness is that it always results from unrestrained eating, it stands to reason that fat women are often seen as hypersexual.[27] During her investigation of fatness in America, sociologist Marcia Millman discovered that many men who attended dances hosted by the National Association for the Advancement of Fat Americans (NAAFA) did so in order to meet fat women they assumed would be both "easy" and "orally fixated."[28] Apparently, the logic is that if a woman is fat, she is orally fixated on food; if a woman is orally fixated on food, she must be orally fixated in other ways as well. Women who are HIV positive and women who are fat are believed to be motivated by their own personal desires for satisfaction—even when those desires may put others at risk—which places them outside the coconstructed norms of womanhood and motherhood.

As more emphasis is placed on the female body as a reproductive chamber and as concern about the obesity epidemic is heightened, women who are both fat and pregnant live under scrutiny. That is, as the "interiority of women's reproductive bodies is brought sharply into the media limelight as a causal agent in the obesity 'epidemic,' but also as the potential solution,"[29] "women who are obese and pregnant are thus all the more visible, and doubly grounded in biology as reproductive, and as fat."[30] Put another way, in a society where the fat body is already stigmatized and women's bodies are already under scrutiny, fat and pregnant female bodies are under a microscope of sorts. In part, the scrutiny results from the belief that there's no excuse for being fat, especially since our world is overrun with advice about how to lose weight and media accounts and advertising that make losing weight seem as simple as making the choice to do so. Similarly, media reports became one of the key ways HIV-positive pregnant women were positioned as purposefully harming fetuses: "By suggesting that women had the information and resources to make different choices and take different actions and simply refused to do so, the media presented HIV-positive pregnant women as willfully and knowingly engaging in irresponsible behavior" and "needlessly and recklessly exposing their children to harm."[31] Representations of being able to choose against fatness and easily lose weight are ubiquitous in the culture, despite evidence showing that very few people can actually lose weight and keep it off,[32] and fat and pregnant women are likely to also be seen as choosing to expose their children to harm.

In the same way that HIV-positive women were seen as "morally reprehensible" because they were believed to be "knowingly and willfully expos[ing] others to the risk of a lethal disease,"[33] headlines about the influence of overweight and obesity on fetuses characterize heavy women as morally lacking. Thus, one headline from *Mail Online* proclaims OBESITY LEGACY OF MUMS-TO-BE: CARRYING TOO MANY POUNDS IN PREGNANCY MAY GIVE YOUR BABY A LIFE OF WEIGHT PROBLEMS. And in case the headline wasn't explicit enough, that particular article ran with the subhead OVERWEIGHT MOTHERS-TO-BE COULD BE CONDEMNING THEIR UNBORN CHILDREN TO DECADES OF ILL HEALTH.[34] To speak of "condemning" a child to a "life of weight problems" or "decades of ill health" leaves little room for understanding fat, pregnant women as anything other than irresponsible.

The very language of *fetal overnutrition,* a phrase that is common in literature about pregnancies, suggests that it is, in fact, women who are the "conduits of contagion" during the obesity epidemic. The woman's body is the pathway for nutrition to the fetus, and the word *overnutrition* makes it seem as if a woman eating too much is the primary means by which a child may end up obese. As a result, more physicians than Kral have proposed that *all* women of childbearing age should receive prepregnancy counseling so that even unplanned pregnancies can be safe from the threat of obesity,[35] proving yet again that the notions of "mother" and "woman" are so tightly coconstructed as to be nearly interchangeable.

In terms of guidelines for weight gain during pregnancy, the recommendations for heavy women have now been lowered from the standard 20 pounds to between 11 and 15 pounds.[36] Perhaps even more concerning, some health care providers have suggested that for obese women in particular, "no weight gain, or even *weight loss,* during pregnancy might be the optimal weight change to minimize adverse birth outcomes."[37] Of course, it's not a secret that the ways many women might maintain a steady weight or lose weight during pregnancy could involve poor eating habits or excessive exercising, which could lead to health problems for them and their fetuses. The health care field also knows that a woman being underweight can cause problems for her fetus, such as a lack of amniotic fluid or a baby that is born underweight.[38] In short, data suggest there may be complications on both sides of the weight spectrum. Yet, it's the fear of obesity in children that drives recommendations for women of childbearing age.

Blaming mothers for vexing social problems is, of course, not a new strategy. In her book *Don't Blame Mother,* Paula Caplan tells readers they must "start with this fact: in our society it is acceptable to blame Mom."[39] In her study of 125 articles published in mental health journals, Caplan found that "mothers were blamed for 72 different kinds of problems in their offspring," including "aggressive behavior" and "learning problems."[40] Recommendations based primarily or solely on preventing obesity actually create a climate where mother blaming can begin at the earliest possible stage. Natalie Boero asserts that "this focus on the fetus is now front and center in the discourse of mother blame surrounding childhood 'obesity.'"[41] The assessment, then, of whether one is a good mother begins with the fetus and sometimes reaches even further back to what is now referred to in the medical community as preconception care. This, in turn, provides even more opportunities for the monitoring of reproductive-age and pregnant women under the assertion of what have come to be called "fetal rights," rights that now seem to center on a child's right not to be fat.

My aim here is not to contend that assertions about mothers' health and effects on fetuses are without merit but rather to point out that these claims are gender loaded because—obviously—it's women who carry children to term. This physiological fact does not, however, have to mean that women's bodies become viewed as mere vessels in which a perfectly thin child must be safeguarded and produced. As Bordo notes, "Woman-as-fetal-incubator" discourse is "most likely to emerge in the context of issues concerning the 'lifestyle' of pregnant women."[42] In an era when being obese is often seen as a "lifestyle choice," claiming that the war on obesity begins in utero and that mothers must vigilantly guard against obesity from the moment of conception (or even before) positions women's bodies as a serious source of cultural anxiety in the war against obesity: "Fat pregnant bodies are constructed as bio-cultural anxieties, distilling biological and social causes into one embodied location."[43] Women and in particular pregnant women are simultaneously represented as those most able to stop the obesity epidemic and those most at fault for it.

The blaming of women and mothers is especially troublesome in light of the field of epigenetics, the study of the mechanisms that are thought to turn genes on and off, so to speak, because epigenetics suggests that paternal lineage may have more effects on an individual fetus's health and more of a continued influence across generations than was previously thought. Overeating for even one winter, smoking at the time of puberty, and even eating specific kinds of foods known to affect metabolic functioning may all predispose a man's children (and even his grandchildren) to being obese.[44] In her *New York Times* article about the recent interest in such studies, Judith Shulevitz asserts that in what is the "best-known example of the power of nutrition specifically to affect the genes of fathers and sons," a study from "a corner of northern Sweden called Overkalix" suggests that paternal influence is, in fact, profound.[45] The Overkalix data focused only on times of feast and famine from 1799 forward. Since the area was so isolated, children literally either feasted or starved, providing a unique sort of petri dish for observing the effects of paternal under- or overnutrition:

> When the study appeared in 2002, a British geneticist published an essay speculating that how much a boy ate in prepuberty could permanently reprogram the epigenetic switches that would govern the manufacture of sperm a few years later. And then, in a process so intricate that no one agrees yet how it happens but probably has something to do with the germline (the reproductive cells that are handed down to children, and to children's children), those reprogrammed switches are transferred to his sons and his sons' sons.[46]

Considered a landmark study of epigenetics, the Overkalix study concluded the influence is so strong that in the case of men, "a single winter of overeating as a youngster could initiate a biological chain of events that would lead one's grandchildren to die decades earlier than their peers did."[47] In mainstream discussions, so much emphasis is placed on women and the role of the uterine environment that the role men and sperm may play in human development is at least overshadowed and sometimes almost erased. Nonetheless, Shulevitz states, "what a man needs to know is that his life experience leaves biological traces on his children. Even more astonishingly, those children may pass those traces along to their children."[48]

One can hardly imagine men being depicted the way women are in conversations about the causes and cures of childhood obesity, conversations that extend out of medical literature and into popular culture. In their article entitled "Framing the Mother: Childhood Obesity, Maternal Responsibility and Care," JaneMaree Maher, Suzanne Fraser, and Jan Wright include a photo that recently ran on a website called Topnewsonline; the photo underscores the level of visibility women have in discussions of passing along obesity via reproduction.[49] In this image, the representation of a woman, who appears to be in the last trimester of her pregnancy and who is lovingly cradling her midsection, is juxtaposed with that of a young boy whom many would read as overweight or obese. In case one were to miss that point, the boy is holding an ice-cream cone, complete with two different kinds of toppings, that obscures part of his face. Juxtaposing the image of a woman loving her unborn fetus with the image of a young boy who is being obscured by a large cone emphasizes that both the womb and the ice-cream cone are dangerous, marking both as sources of anxiety and perhaps even as taboo. The parts of the woman's body that are visible and dramatized are her uterus and her hands, suggesting that the hands that cradle the fetus may later prepare food or buy food, perhaps even troubling food such as an oversize ice-cream cone. Maher and her coauthors argue that the photo neatly ties together pregnancy and a child's eating habits and assumed weight later in life.[50] As Megan Warin, Tanya Zivkovic, Vivienne Moore, and Michael Davies write, "Pregnancy is a biological process but exists within socio-cultural, economic, and political realms,"[51] and representations of pregnancy like the one from Topnewsonline literally leave men out of the picture, ignoring any role they may play and suggesting women alone bear the responsibility.[52]

The invisibility of men in such discussions makes an even stronger argument that women are treated as a special case where pregnancies and possible influences on a fetus are concerned. Think back to the article on the SUA website by Kral et al. Although many people may find it commonsensical that women would be prosecuted for using drugs while pregnant, opponents of such measures have argued that prosecuting women means they are not receiving equal protection under the law. As legal scholar Nancy Kubasek states, "By failing to treat all individuals similarly, fetal-abuse prosecutions violate the equal protection clause."[53] This means women are being targeted and not simply because the uterine environment has an influence on a fetus. After all, in addition to the possibility of paternal influence that epigenetics now highlights, fathers of children may smoke or be abusive in myriad ways that represent a potential threat to a fetus, but "fetal-abuse laws are directed at only the mother."[54] In many people's minds, "pregnant women have become a special class of people that should be treated differently from every other citizen"[55] who might also influence the well-being of a fetus.

Fat women are likely to be subject to even more targeting given the hypervisiblity of obesity in our society and the invisibility of fat women as rights-bearing subjects. At first, this may seem like a contradiction. How, after all, can a group be both invisible and hypervisible? In the case of fat women, this contradiction exists because stereotypes of fat women as slovenly, morally bankrupt, and stupid are omnipresent in our society whereas the real experiences of fat women and their lived realities are often invisible. In her book *Invisible Woman: Confronting Weight Prejudice in America*, W. Charisse Goodman writes about the invisibility of fat women in this way:

> A big woman is neither seen nor heard in our thinness-obsessed society, and is defined purely in terms of her weight and other people's prejudice. Instead of being treated like an authentic human being who just happens to be heavy, she is forcibly transformed by cultural assumptions into an almost mythically unnatural and repulsive figure consumed by physical and emotional problems.[56]

Similarly, Terry Poulton writes that "when you're noticeably overweight, you suffer the double whammy of disappearing, as far as your real identity is concerned, yet remaining all too visible as an object of disgust."[57] Thus, Goodman and Poulton rightly point out that even though fat women exist throughout society, the ways in which they are represented and thought about are often not reflective of their lived realities or their humanity but rather are much more in keeping with social stereotypes about their slovenliness and lack of moral fortitude.

UNFAIR INFLUENCES

In the midst of the hysteria about obesity, the idea that women pass obesity on to children through their bodies nearly guarantees both surveillance of and interventions upon women's bodies that may go far beyond recommendations about weight gain during pregnancy. Consider again Kral et al.'s article featured on the SUA website and the rhetorical question the authors pose: "If Society [*sic*] is willing to prosecute drug-abusing mothers, and warn of alcohol and tobacco use during pregnancy, should we not be serious about preventing obese pregnancies?"[58] No doubt, when many people think of drug-abusing mothers, the image that comes to mind is racially loaded. Popular media accounts and cultural imagination call forth a particular image associated with drug abuse and motherhood, and this image is overwhelmingly of women of color who, like women with HIV, are thought to recklessly endanger their fetuses in order to satisfy their own needs. Most likely, the image called to mind is a woman of color using crack cocaine. To employ such a racially and morally loaded image as a comparison to obesity situates obese women in the same constellation of recklessness and immorality.

The history of prosecuting drug-abusing mothers is actually a history of devaluing women of color and their motherhood. In what has often been called a battleground of the war on drugs, several states have seen skirmishes over whether pregnant women should be prosecuted for everything from drug trafficking (because they technically transmitted drugs to a child after birth but before the umbilical cord was cut) to child abuse if they were found to be using drugs while pregnant.[59] The first of such convictions in the United States took place in July 1989 when a crack-addicted twenty-three-year-old named Jennifer Clarise Johnson was found guilty of "exposing her baby to drugs while pregnant."[60] Yet, the criminal prosecution and conviction of women for using drugs during pregnancy remains hotly contested—for good reason. As legal scholar Dorothy E. Roberts convincingly argues, the prosecution and conviction of *certain* women for *certain* abuses makes visible the inequities and prejudices of US society.[61]

Much of the argument against such policies has centered on the ways sifting through all possible influences on a fetus to prosecute only a few disproportionately affected women and women from certain groups both echoes and adds to existing inequities. Consider that only 3 percent of women use illicit substances during pregnancies but that approximately 54 percent "use legal substances that could be harmful to a fetus, including alcohol and tobacco."[62] Further, many scholars have shown that women of color, in particular black women, are more apt to be investigated and prosecuted for drug abuse or other forms of child abuse or neglect.[63] In short, *certain* women, primarily black women and/or poor women, are being prosecuted for using *certain* kinds of substances because they are unfairly stereotyped as bad mothers and visibly marked in our society. They are marked via their race, their socioeconomic status, and/or their use of state aid, making them easy targets for both criticism and interventions. Thus, the full context of the interventions must be considered rather than distilling everything down to harms that may come to a potential child.

Maternal ideology, however, has a tendency to be unequally applied. As Mutcherson argues, there is an "unequal valuing of mothers" that "defines good motherhood in terms of race (white) and class (anything but poor)," placing some women "outside the rarified circle of good motherhood."[64] In short, maternal ideology works to construct some women as always already bad mothers who need to be monitored as "special cases" and all pregnant women as potentially dangerous. As Bordo contends about the ways in which pregnant women are treated differently from anyone else who may influence the well-being of a fetus, "There are no legal justifications for the discrepancies between the treatment accorded pregnant women and that given to non-pregnant persons. Rather, to explain such contradictions, we must leave the realm of rationality and enter the realm of gender ideology (and, in many cases, of racial prejudice as well). These decisions, clearly, are mediated by normative conceptions of the pregnant woman's appropriate role and function."[65]

Drug use and possible effects on a fetus are not the only issues at play here. There are also underpinning cultural values and expectations about what it means to be a good mother, who can use drugs, and what kind of drugs may be used without prosecution or without the fear of prosecution. As legal scholar Krista Stone-Manista points out in her work on the inequities of drug-abuse prosecutions of pregnant women, there is little evidence that crack cocaine is worse for a fetus than tobacco.[66] Yet, the very choice of language in the SUA-featured article is telling: we *warn* of alcohol and tobacco use but *prosecute* drug abuse, even though the evidence of harm to a fetus doesn't necessarily support such a differentiation.

After all, it's now widely acknowledged that the supposed epidemic of crack babies never really materialized. The fear was that an entire generation of babies born to mothers who were using crack during their pregnancies would be permanently damaged by in utero exposure, and as a result of these fears, many women were prosecuted. But scientists, now looking back on twenty years of having tracked children who were exposed, have found that "the long-term effects of such exposure on children's brain development and behavior appear relatively small."[67] A slight increase in learning difficulties and/or behavior problems has been reported, but scientists have had a difficult time teasing out the influence of being exposed to crack from the influence of factors such as living in poverty and under stress. To put it another way, the influence of crack doesn't seem to have been any greater in these children's lives than a host of other factors, including socioeconomic class and racism—factors that most people never consider when they think about child development and whether anyone ought to be prosecuted.

It appears, therefore, that the concern about crack cocaine during pregnancy is not exclusively health related. In explaining why crack cocaine attracted so much attention and elicited so much concern, family physician and medical journalist Susan Okie says the following: "Cocaine use in pregnancy has been treated as a moral issue rather than a health problem."[68] Deborah Frank, a pediatrician at Boston University, believes that "society's expectation of the children [born to women who used crack during pregnancy] . . . and reaction to the mothers are completely guided not by the toxicity, but by the social meaning of the drug."[69] The point Okie and Frank make is that in the case of crack cocaine, the evidence about what the drug would or would not do to children wasn't the most salient factor, especially considering that alcohol is widely known to have a greater effect. Rather, the social meanings attached to crack, a drug associated primarily with poor, black women who supposedly cared nothing about themselves or their babies and were often on state aid, drove the push toward stigmatizing and prosecuting women who used crack during pregnancies. In some sense, they were punished and devalued for being seen as bad mothers as much as they were punished for causing harm to children.

Certainly, in contemporary US society, fat people are also devalued. There is overwhelming evidence that they are discriminated against in health care, housing, employment, and virtually every other arena where one might expect to see a marginalized group face discrimination.[70] Perhaps it's no coincidence that people who may be devalued due to their race or class are also the most likely to be fat. According to current statistics from the Centers for Disease Control (CDC), Mexican Americans are most likely to be obese, followed by blacks and nonwhite Hispanics, and whites.[71] The CDC also notes that among women, the incidence of obesity decreases with both a college education and a higher income.[72] Treating women, particularly fat women, as special cases may conveniently lash together not only problematic ideas about women but also negative attitudes about heavy people (and again, attitudes about people of color and/or poor people who are more likely to be fat). Though it may now be politically unpopular to target women due to race or class, interventions due to weight are often seen as helpful rather than discriminatory. That is, many of the same attitudes and actions toward women of color and/or poor women that would be called discriminatory in another situation can be couched as justified—or even helpful—when read through the lens of fatness because such claims are supposedly about health.

But the emphasis on weight can also be understood as unfair. The potential effect that a woman's weight will have on her child represents a winnowing of all the possible influences on a fetus. The concern about maternal weight, in and of itself, showcases a certain kind of bias against fatness and fat people. As Dorothy Roberts notes, there is a "universe of maternal conduct that can injure a fetus."[73] Although she looks only at drug abuse among poor, black women, her arguments regarding the range of behaviors and exposures that may also affect the fetus are important to keep in mind because they illuminate the social decisions about what kind of influences will be tracked and who will face interventions and/or prosecutions. As she argues, lead, secondhand smoke, sexually transmitted diseases (STDs), and even living at high altitudes can all affect the fetus, yet we do not intervene in such cases,[74] indicating that concern about possible effects on the fetus are not always solely based on harm to the forthcoming child.[75] Again, the focus on maternal weight gain represents a serious culling among a wide field of possible influences on a developing fetus—in much the same way critics of prosecutions against women using drugs while pregnant have argued that punitive policies represent an investment in moralizing as much as an investment in better health outcomes.

One result of the moralizing is that when a woman's role as "life support" for a fetus is in conflict with her desires, that role is deemed more important, making her choices "expendable."[76] Women are expected to put their wishes or desires aside, and those who don't appear to do so are often understood and portrayed as selfish and unmotherly. Yet, there are good reasons to question this scrutiny and the caricature of women as uncaring "conduits of contagion." In her work with women who were HIV positive, Zivi found that despite the stereotype of recklessness, many HIV-positive women struggled a great deal with whether to become pregnant or what to do once they realized they were pregnant.[77] A recent *Allure* article by best-selling fiction author Jennifer Weiner makes it clear that fat women share similar concerns, as she writes about holding her newborn daughter in her arms and wondering what the child's future would be like: "I'm far too embarrassed to ask my doctor the only thing I want to know: Will she be normal, or will she be [fat] like me?"[78] Of course, women don't *have* to struggle with these questions in order to see their rights to reproduce upheld or to avoid being targeted. Rather than suggesting that it's the worrying that makes one a good mother or the absence of that worrying that makes one a bad mother, I would argue what is worrisome is that women who have the potential to pass a trait along to a child overwhelmingly are portrayed as stock, flat characters rather than complex individuals.

Ultimately, the choices surrounding what warrants interventions and conversations about maternal influences can help us to better understand the perceived value (or lack of value) of individuals in our society and what it means to place so much attention on members of particular groups and on particular influences. Roberts notes that our country's long history of reproductive policies and interventions in the lives of people of color suggests that "the value we place on individuals determines whether we see them as entitled to perpetuate themselves in their children."[79] The devaluing of women of color (and of people of color in general) spawned a terrible history of forced sterilizations and other policies that stripped women of control over their bodies and reproductive freedoms. The devaluing of fat people has, at times, taken on similar-sounding rhetoric amid fears that fat people will proliferate.

A prime example of such beliefs playing out is a comment left on an article from the United Kingdom about the fetuses of fat women being treated in utero to "cut the risk of having a fat child."[80] A commenter named black_and_loud had this to say about the use of the drug metformin in fat women as a means of treating obesity in utero:

> If you can't look after your own body, you can't look after a gift as pre-cious as a child. FACT. Overweight people breed overweight kids. I'm all for forced sterilsation [sic]. If you stop them being able to have kids in the first place, then public health will be better just in one generation, the pressure on the NHS [National Health Service] would come down, and we'd have more money to spend on diseases that aren't the fault of the people being treated[,] like heart and lung cancer.[81]

Setting aside for a moment that both heart disease and lung cancer may also be caused by behaviors that one chooses, I would add that sentiments like those expressed by black_and_loud were pervasive in the comments section for the article.

However, black_and_loud's comment spotlights a willingness to appro-priate a slogan usually used by those who are trying to protect reproductive freedoms (If You Can't Trust Me with a Choice, How Can You Trust Me with a Child?) in the service of making an argument about limiting the choices of fat women because the assumption is that they're not taking care of their bodies and therefore would be bad mothers. As Zivi explains, "'Bad mothers,' by implication, are those women who put their children in harm's way either through a willful disregard for their maternal instincts or perhaps because they lack such instincts."[82] And "good mothers" are those who "engage in acts of self-sacrifice and self-abnegation, always putting the interests of their children before their own."[83] For black_and_loud, self-sacrifice and self-abnegation are defined as not having children because doing so may cause harm to the off-spring and may compromise the National Health Service's ability to pay for those who are believed to be more deserving of treatments. In these ways, the rights and desires of individual women are swept aside in favor of the rights of the unborn and of society in general.

A NEW KIND OF EUGENICS?

In addition to comments such as those from black_and_loud that take on what can arguably be called a eugenical tone, consider Greg Critser's very successful

Fat Land: How Americans Became the Fattest People on Earth, in which he argues that "fat attracting fat" (fat people being stigmatized and therefore ending up in relationships with one another because thin people are not attracted to them) and creating fat children is a serious problem.[84] Citing a study by German psychologist Johannes Hebebrand, Critser contends that "assortative mating" causes heavy parents to "influence their children's fatness both through genetics and environment."[85] According to Critser, Hebebrand measured people's current heights and weights along with their recalled weights from the time at which they were most likely, as he assessed it, to be marrying and mating—between twenty and thirty years of age. After Hebebrand examined his data against that of the general population, he determined that his findings weren't evidence that fat attracting fat had caused the rise in obesity, but he nonetheless felt confident in asserting that such findings are vital in understanding why obesity rates are increasing. Critser says that Hebebrand explained his findings in this way:

> It is not exactly a straight line. . . . There are all kinds of other factors going on here. Take the case of the thinner person marrying the fatter person, who soon drags the thinner person down into his or her habits. He watches ten hours of TV and she begins to do the same, and over time she becomes obese too. In this case it wasn't the genetics of assortative mating that makes for fat kids. It's the environment that both parents produce.[86]

Essentially, whether due to fat attracting fat, genetics, or lifestyle, fat people are to blame; they can even contaminate thin partners with their poor habits.

Critser follows Hebebrand by noting that he's aware the ideas he's presenting may spark memories of eugenics for some readers. Yet, he insists that "acknowledging such a dynamic ['stigma causing assortative mating'] might help prevent a eugenic reality."[87] That reality would be a nation of fat people assumed to be unhealthy and unfit, a reality that HBO's recent series *The Weight of the Nation* showcases by opening each segment with the claim that the obesity epidemic threatens the survival and well-being of the United States as a nation.[88]

With such claims, one can hardly help remembering eugenical arguments about who was deemed fit and unfit to breed and how the nation would be affected in the future. In fact, Kathleen LeBesco argues that the search for the "fat gene" and the deep desire to find the origin of fatness call to mind immediate and disturbing associations with eugenics. In examining the papers of Charles Davenport, a man many consider the father of the eugenics movement, LeBesco suggests that even though Davenport doesn't make direct reference to fatness, his statements about whose ability to reproduce ought to be limited are nonetheless instructive. She quotes him as saying: "In the first place, the perpetuation of a defective strain of human beings tends to thwart all future progress, and cannot be defended by either reason or charity. Secondary reasons are the need for reducing the enormous public expense as present involved in the care of defectives."[89] According to one source, "Concern about the issue is so high that British doctors have started to medicate babies in the womb. In an NHS trial, overweight mothers-to-be in four cities are being given the diabetes drug metformin in a desperate attempt to stop their babies being born obese."[90] Like LeBesco, I find it hard to read sentiments such as those expressed by Davenport, Hebebrand, Critser and news stories about doctors who are now treating obesity in the womb without seeing striking similarities. LeBesco investigates only Davenport in her work, but her argument that such statements and practices seem to "reveal . . . tactics employed in an effort to keep fatness from reproducing itself"[91] certainly seems applicable to more recent conversations about preventing fatness.

The history of the limiting of reproductive freedoms doesn't seem so remote when one listens carefully to contemporary conversations about fatness as an "epidemic." In discussing mandatory drug testing and treatments for pregnant women, opponents of such policies have often argued that "[these] policies [have] to be understood in the context of practices like the forced sterilization of poor women and, therefore, as reinforcing longstanding narratives about the danger of certain women's reproduction and contributing to the devaluation of poor and minority women's mothering."[92] In regard to fatness and who is most at risk for interventions, history and contemporary context are no less important.

Although a great deal of the conversation about overweight and obesity purports to be rooted in concerns for people's health, this segment of the conversation, in particular, seems to also be about a desire to limit the number of fat people in the world. At first blush, some might think that the limiting of fatness and fat people represents a neutral impulse—or even an impulse for the social good—by reducing the amount of money spent on health care and preventing children and adults from living what are believed to be miserable lives. Yet, as Disability Studies scholars have long pointed out, concerns about limiting or preventing certain kinds of embodiments should also be examined as moral issues. Worried about the implications of prenatal testing and parents selecting for or against particular disabling traits, scholars such as Christopher Newell have encouraged people to remember that "genetic conditions occur in a social context, and their meaning and impact are inherently social."[93] In other words, not only physiological conditions but also the social meanings of those conditions are being discussed. Whether fatness is considered genetic or not, society is at a point where most people see obesity as a condition; in that sense, Newell's claim that the meanings ascribed to conditions are inherently social should be taken seriously in discussions of obesity.

In light of the troubling history about the reproductive rights of marginalized women being undermined as well as current conversations about fat attracting fat, it's probably not all that surprising that concerns about the possible outcomes of pregnancies for fat women already seem to be influencing discussions and policies about fertility treatments. And this, in turn, underscores yet another way in which women's reproductive choices are being managed due to concerns about obesity in children. When such complex social situations arise, it's quite easy to posit that the problem (and possible solution) lies with women and their reproductive choices. In New Zealand, which has a national health care system, policies in place since 2001 have restricted women with high(er) BMIs from receiving in vitro fertilization (IVF) treatments paid for by national health care services; the argument is that these women have poorer results and that the scarcity of funds warrants curtailing their right to access these services.[94] Some health care providers in New Zealand have asserted that heavy women are not "too disadvantaged" by such policies,[95] but others have argued that women's individual rights to found a family are, indeed, violated when they are denied access to IVF until they've lost weight and achieved an acceptable BMI.[96]

Those opposing such restrictions contend that denying fertility treatments violates women's individual rights and that even though there is some evidence that being larger may make IVF less successful, maternal age is an even bigger factor to consider. Given how long it may take some women to lose weight (if they *ever* manage to do so), they may then be at an age where their chances of becoming pregnant are even further reduced.[97] Thus, age becomes a factor, and beyond that, perhaps not surprisingly, so does class, as "affluent women manage to bypass these draconian restrictions" because they are able to simply pay for the treatments themselves rather than having to rely on their health coverage.[98] Since many women put off having a family so they can advance their careers,[99] it's likely that some who seek out fertility treatments are older and may have less success with the procedures, yet their ability to pay for these procedures privately means they can easily access them. In other words, the restriction of fertility treatments can become another avenue by which women of color, poor women, or other women who are marginalized may be further disadvantaged.

Currently, there are no official restrictions on IVF treatments in the United States, at least not at the national level. As clinical embryologist Christine Leary notes, however, regional and specific clinic guidelines are being developed.[100] And because unofficial restrictions may already be in place due to the well-documented fat-based discrimination in our health care system,[101] these new guidelines may end up reflecting those very biases. Several scholars have already pointed out that women from other stigmatized groups face challenges when seeking fertility treatments. Writing about the ethical issues with "assisted reproductive technologies" (ARTs) in Australia, M. M. Peterson notes that in that country, women who are believed not to be good mothers or to lack appropriate family structures are sometimes denied ARTs because reproduction professionals have the power to choose individuals they consider to be appropriate candidates. As a result, poor women, lesbians, and single heterosexual women have sometimes been denied assistance with becoming pregnant. As Peterson states, "Many ART medical professionals feel entitled to exercise power over the reproductive autonomy of their referred potential clients, denying some women freedom of procreative choice by electing to re-inforce entrenched ideologies about the family unit."[102]

Decisions about BMIs and fertility treatments are made at more local levels in the United Kingdom, with England, Wales, Scotland, and Northern Ireland all participating in a national health care system (the NHS) but allowing practitioners to choose to limit treatment based on BMIs. Currently, only England specifically lists a high BMI as a factor that may disqualify one from coverage.[103] One survey of how weight is used to screen clients revealed that two-thirds of the clinics in the United Kingdom—even in countries that didn't necessarily have guidelines—"'actively' apply specific weight criteria for offering various fertility treatments." Further, "nearly all of the centers reported providing advice on lifestyle changes for weight loss."[104] Similarly, Peterson found that many IVF workers believe they need to employ their "common sense" about the appropriate use of IVF.[105] Ethically, however, one can only imagine the extent to which such "commonsense" approaches foster discrimination against women in the fatphobic environment that nearly covers the globe at this point. In the United States, where there are currently no published guidelines, "treatment decisions are made at the provider and/or clinic level,"[106] which suggests that supposedly commonsense approaches may also be put into practice in this country.

To be fair, health care providers working in IVF have voiced legitimate concerns about the complications that may be experienced by obese women during their pregnancies, such as more difficult deliveries or an increased risk of hypertension. Yet, those risks needn't govern whether fat women have equal access to fertility services any more than they govern whether fat women have access to other forms of medical care. As S. Pandey, A. Mahashwari, and S. Battacharya write of New Zealand policies that restrict heavy women's access to IVF treatments, "In other areas of healthcare, the risk of complications does not prevent overweight and obese women from receiving medical and surgical treatment."[107] Here again, women's individual rights seem to be compromised by judgments and fears surrounding obesity and the ways in which those judgments and fears affect the notion of who can be a good mother or who is worthy of becoming a mother. If weight isn't used as a justification for denying other kinds of medical services, it shouldn't be used for denying fertility services.

There's good reason to be worried about what it means to grant or deny health care based on volitional behaviors. In an article entitled "The War on Fat People: Time for a Truce," Vicky Allan writes,

> When access to healthcare is dependent upon compliance with a series of lifestyle ideals, we are entering perilous waters. . . . NHS starts to become like a Government-run insurance scheme in which the providers are allowed to sift out those who do not meet certain criteria of blamelessness. We start with smoking, obesity, and alcoholism, but where do we stop? So you went on a skiing holiday? In that case it's your own fault your leg broke and therefore you should pay for your treatment.[108]

Allan's example may seem extreme, but her point is valid. It should be troubling that certain behaviors that are clearly volitional—such as participating in sports—may result in injuries yet go without question when it comes to the expenditure of health care dollars. Allan is not saying that obesity never produces complications or that participating in sports always results in injuries but rather that, in general, we do not have health care systems where the litmus test for determining if a person deserves care is based on whether he or she is blameless for the condition needing treatment.

Given that a behavior such as smoking may also influence the efficacy of IVF, the policing of fat women in this arena looks like another case of fatness being hypervisible and the climate of panic and fatphobia affecting policies and guidelines for medical procedures. In short, it appears that obesity is so freighted with meaning as to trump smoking as a concern. Leary notes that because something such as smoking can't be as easily policed as weight, clinics don't tend to focus on making a woman stop smoking before receiving IVF— even though some clinics do have policies about patients being smoke free for three months before beginning treatments.[109] The ideology of motherhood and the notion that some women are just better mothers than others, which is a moral issue rather than a health issue, may also be heightened by the visibility and stereotyping of fatness. According to Annemarie Jutel, "It is upon the belief that the appearance of the body provides access to inner truths about an individual that the association between fatness and deficiency of character is grounded."[110] People may not like smoking, but smoking is seldom seen as a window into a person's inner character.

WHOSE HEALTH?

It's clear, too, that policies such as those in New Zealand are about more than the health of fat women or a concern for the outcomes of IVF or resulting pregnancies; these policies also offer an opportunity to advance a broader agenda of weight loss. In other words, they may represent another way in which the rights of women in general and certain women in particular are undermined in the name of tending to the needs of others, reinforcing the notion that women and mothers should be self-sacrificing. In a moment of candor while writing about whether high BMIs should exclude women from fertility treatments, C. M. Farquhar and G. R. Gillett assert that "lifestyle changes such as weight reduction and exercise are firmly in the control of patient [sic]."[111] A few paragraphs later, they note that the restriction of IVF for heavy women is a means of delivering a message about weight loss to many people, adding, "This is an important public health message for women and their families in the reproductive years. . . . Fertility services have an opportunity to promote that message."[112] In this instance, restricting access to fertility services uses fat women to broadcast a public health message to the whole nation, compromising these women's rights for the sake of supposedly promoting the good of the whole. According to Anjel Vahratian and Yolanda R. Smith, the CDC in the United States has made a similar claim, saying that it's good to use the "preconceptional and interconceptional period as an opportunity to improve one's personal health as well as that of a future child."[113] The trend in health care, then, seems to be to use contact with women seeking fertility treatments—or all women who wish to have children—to promote what is seen as a more important health message: women should lose weight not only for themselves but also for others.

Using any opportunity to speak with women about their weight and its potential effect on others is not, in the end, likely to encourage better health for women. In fact, it may mean they avoid medical care altogether—much as women with HIV or women who use drugs may choose to avoid medical care. The omnipresence of discussions of obesity and the hypervisibility of obesity may lead some women to feel that they would not be welcome in a medical office. The fear of being unwelcome in such a setting is not unreasonable, especially given several recent studies conducted on the attitudes of health care providers. In 2001, in what is considered one of the landmark meta-analyses of bias against overweight and obese people, Kelly Brownell and Rebecca Puhl discovered that antifat bias is quite common among health care providers, with some of them even saying that caring for obese patients "repulsed" them.[114] Further, of 586 nurses surveyed, 63 percent said they believed that obesity could be prevented by self-control, 43 percent stated that they believed obese persons were overindulgent, 33 percent stated that obese persons experience "unresolved anger," and 22 percent characterized obese persons as "lazy."[115] As Natasha Schvey argues in her recent article in the *American Medical Association Journal of Ethics,* "Health care professionals are common sources of stigmatization for individuals who are overweight," and because studies have found that one way of coping with stigma may be to overeat, "despite their best intentions, health care professionals who display weight bias may, in fact, be helping to perpetuate our nation's obesity crisis."[116]

The situation doesn't seem to be improving, even though one might think the statistical normality of overweight and obesity would foster comfort with and understanding of larger people. In 2008, Rebecca Puhl, T. Andreyeva, and Kelly Brownell found that weight-based discrimination was nearly as common in America as discrimination based on gender or race.[117] Much like the punitive measures against women who use drugs during pregnancy, antifat bias in US society in general and in health care settings in particular seems to ensure that women will both be discriminated against and be apt to avoid health care. Recent studies aimed at consumers of health care find that fat women, in particular, are prone to avoid medical care because they fear the reactions of health care providers. A study of 498 overweight and obese women conducted by researchers from several California medical centers concluded that obese women are more likely than nonobese women to delay Pap tests, pelvic exams, and mammograms, even when they clearly understand the risks of cancer and self-report that they are at least moderately concerned about those risks.[118] The researchers found that women who had tried five or more times to lose weight were the most likely to delay cancer screenings.[119]

Although the majority of the women in the study had insurance that would pay for such routine cancer screenings, they reported that they encountered numerous barriers to receiving appropriate care, ranging from harassment about weight to blood pressure cuffs and waiting room chairs that didn't accommodate their body size.[120] Given these concerns as well as the potential for undergoing moral judgment due to the possibility of reproducing obesity, it seems likely that even more women—fat and thin—will find medical offices unwelcoming and avoid routine self-care and prenatal care. It's difficult to fathom that these pressures lead to better health for anyone. In fact, as Zivi claims in the epigraph to this chapter, such a climate is likely to jeopardize the health of both women and children.

CHAPTER TWO

There's No Place Like Home

Fatness and Families in the Courts

*Sometimes it is easier to take a child out of the home than take the time
and resources to provide the right solution to the problem.*
—Dr. David Orentlicher, ABC News[1]

In 2011, physician David Ludwig and lawyer Lindsey Murtagh made national
news when they teamed up for a commentary in the *Journal of the American
Medical Association* entitled "State Interventions in Life-Threatening Childhood Obesity." In the piece, Ludwig and Murtagh contend that in certain
cases, the best course of action is to remove obese children from their homes.
Describing what they see as problems that may necessitate state intervention,
they write: "Inadequate or unskilled parental supervision can leave children
vulnerable to . . . obesigenic environmental influences."[2] They also note that
"even relatively mild parenting deficiencies, such as having excessive junk food
in the home or failing to model a physically active lifestyle, may contribute to
a child's weight problem."[3] Although they allude to obesigenic environmental
influences, a phrase that has become code for everything from an industri-
alized food system to a lack of neighborhood sidewalks to the popularity of
video games, Murtagh and Ludwig ultimately believe that parents should be
able to overcome those influences and produce a thin child. To make their
case, they cite a 2009 article from *Pediatrics* entitled "Childhood Obesity and
Medical Neglect." In that piece, Todd Varness, David B. Allen, Aaron L. Carrel,
and Norman Fost outline specific criteria for removing obese children from
homes: "high likelihood that serious imminent harm will occur," "a reasonable
likelihood that coercive state intervention will result in effective treatment,"
and "the absence of alternative options for addressing the problem."[4] Varness
and his coauthors admit there are factors related to weight that a parent may
not be able to control, but they still suggest that fat children should be removed
from homes:

In some cases, contributors to a child's obesity may be poverty (which limits access to healthy foods and space for exercise) and inadequate insurance coverage (which can hinder access to weight loss programs). It may seem unfair to charge these families with medical neglect for their child's obesity. It is important to note, however, that charges of medical neglect should not be moral judgments but rather are a means to protect children from harm.[5]

Their means of protecting children from harm is to remove them from the home rather than taking care of poverty or insufficient insurance, perhaps because the battle against childhood obesity demands flesh-and-blood targets rather than systemic targets such as poverty and the insurance industry.

Nonetheless, by implying that parents are responsible for producing a thin child, regardless of surrounding circumstances, these authors help to solidify what Gaia Bernstein and Zvi Triger call norms of "intensive parenting," the belief that parents should monitor and regulate nearly every aspect of their children's lives. Bernstein and Triger argue that intensive parenting means *preferred* parenting behaviors are made into policies that then *require* such behaviors in order for one to be considered a good parent.[6] The regulation of children's bodies via eating and exercise is no exception; indeed, according to recent polls, public opinion holds that despite any sociocultural issues such as poverty or lack of insurance, parents are ultimately responsible for obesity in their children. On July 12, 2012, Australian-based TheAge.com ran a piece called "Is This Child Abuse? The Courts Think So." In the piece, Adrian Lowe reported that Australian courts are also dealing with childhood obesity by removing children from homes. At the end of the article, readers were given an opportunity to respond to a poll consisting of one simple question: "Should obesity be a reason to take children from their parents?" Out of nearly 8,000 people who responded to the poll on the one day it was open, 62 percent said yes.[7] Public discussions of childhood obesity acknowledge environment as a problem but frame parents as the responsible parties, and increasingly, so does the US court system, as evidenced by a number of cases in which children have been removed from their homes.

MAKING THE CASE AGAINST WOMEN

The concern about childhood obesity has, therefore, been depicted as concern about poor parenting and abuse. As Rogan Kersh asserts in his article "The Politics of Obesity: A Current Assessment and a Look Ahead": "How issues are framed, or presented in public discussion, is important to which policy approaches are adopted."[8] Perhaps no better example of how childhood obesity is framed as child abuse exists than the statement made by Meme Roth, from the Association for Action against Obesity, on *The Morning Show with Mike and Juliet*: "If you have an overweight child, that is America's most pleasurable form of child abuse."[9] Courts seem to agree. In the process, so-called intensive parenting is being constructed as parenting practices that prevent and/or ameliorate obesity in children—and not just as preferred practices but as required practices.

As is the case with most social norms and expectations, how those expectations are constructed and applied raises questions about whose values have been taken as the norm and who may be unfairly subjected to such expectations. JaneMaree Maher, Suzanne Fraser, and Jan Wright argue that mothers are most often blamed for their children's obesity because mothers are still believed to be "carers with special responsibility for children's health and well-being."[10] Despite what some might try to claim, in the United States, caring for the home and children is still seen as a woman's domain. The amount of child care done by women today is the same as it was in the 1960s; in fact, women do 80 percent of the work of caring for children.[11] Further, Bernstein and Triger note that "the public discourse on parenting tends to focus on 'bad mothers' and not 'bad fathers.'"[12] And even "'community' programs designed to abate or prevent obesity" choose to "focus on women and mothers as significant points of intervention."[13]

The idea that women should monitor every aspect of their children's lives is one of the most problematic aspects of the new standards of intensive parenting. Attorneys defending women who have been prosecuted for child neglect and/or have had their obese children removed from their homes have fought to expose the unfairness of this expectation. According to a newspaper report by Ron Barnett, the attorney Grant Varner, who recently worked on a South Carolina case where a fourteen-year-old boy was placed in foster care due to his obesity, was quick to point out that there are times when children are out of a mother's care: "There's a strong likelihood that this kid is going to school and could eat whatever he wanted at school. . . . The big question is: What is this kid doing when he's not in Mom's care, custody, and control?"[14] Unfortunately, the point of intensive parenting is that a child is never supposed to be out of a mother's care or control, which is not a standard most mothers can possibly meet.

Although some standards for the care of a child may be necessary, many cultural and legal standards in the United States are based on *preferences* for how a child should be cared for, and preferences are often loaded with cultural values that represent the mainstream and status quo rather than the margins. Bernstein and Triger assert that "even desirable intensive parenting norms may be unsuitable as legal standards" because "intensive parenting is a culture, race, ethnicity, and class specific practice of parenting."[15] In short, they suggest that intensive parenting is "an American middle class parenting trend" and that the "legal enforcement to standardize parenting styles carries the risk of cultural coercion and is detrimental to minorities, historically disenfranchised communities, women, and people whose child rearing philosophies differ from the prevailing one."[16] Given that those most likely to be obese are also most likely to be the very people Bernstein and Triger name as most at risk under rubrics that standardize parenting, these families stand little chance of being judged adequate.

In their germinal work, *The Obesity Epidemic: Science, Morality, and Ideology*, Michael Gard and Jan Wright state that the age of the childhood obesity epidemic has produced two kinds of children: those who are already fat and those who might become fat.[17] I would add that the age of the childhood obesity epidemic and the panic about all children being at risk have also created several kinds of mothers: those who are expected to guard against children becoming fat, those who are urged to treat children who are already fat, and those who are punished if they have a child who remains fat. Thus, in addition to the usual responsibilities heaped upon mothers to provide daily care and basic necessities for their offspring, the obesity epidemic and the norms of intensive parenting have given mothers a new set of responsibilities and charges—and new ways to "fail" at all of them. Women are becoming the scapegoats of the obesity epidemic, and as is often the case with scapegoating, those who are marginalized in other ways (such as being fat, disabled, or single) appear even more at risk for being blamed for a child's size, all of which can be seen in the court documents from several key cases.

METHODS AND CASES

Many court documents involving children and charges of neglect and/or abuse are difficult to locate and examine because of obvious concern for the anonymity of the children involved.[18] Those that are widely available are instructive in the sense that they record not only the court's judgment about a particular case but also what appear to be opinions about much deeper issues, such as norms of gender, embodiment, and mothering. As is often seen with interventions into family life, prevailing cultural norms and ideals seem to exert powerful influences over the decisions that are made, as Bernstein and Triger argue, and court decisions pertaining to obesity in children are no exception.

In this chapter, I examine three court decisions involving children being removed from their homes due, at least in part, to obesity. These cases span fifteen years and three states: *In the Interest of L. T., a Minor Child* from 1992 in Iowa; *In re D. K.* from 2002 in Pennsylvania; and *In the Matter of Brittany T., a Child Alleged to Be Neglected* from 2007 in New York. I chose these cases because the court opinions on them are easily obtained by doing a basic search in a database such as LexisNexis, and as a result, these cases have been cited widely in the literature about the removal of obese children from homes in a variety of fields and by scholars with a range of opinions about family law, obesity in children, and parental responsibilities. Unless otherwise indicated, the information included here about these cases comes directly from court records. In each of the cases, constructs about what constitutes appropriate parenting and mothering in particular, as well as troubling stereotypes about fat people and fat women in particular, pervade the written decision of the court. Ultimately, the court documents showcase both anxieties about fatness and what Paula Caplan names "momism," a kind of "mother-blam[ing] and mother-hate" that is a "form of prejudice as virulent as the other 'isms' are acknowledged to be."[19]

The 1992 case known as *In the Interest of L. T., a Minor Child* deals with a female minor child from Iowa, known as L. T. or Liza T., who was diagnosed with "severe infantile personality disorder and morbid obesity caused by overeating as a method of coping with strife between her parents."[20] The parental strife resulted when Liza's mother, Natalie, divorced Liza's father for what the court notes was his drunken and abusive behavior. "Liza had witnessed the domestic violence," causing her, according to her doctors, to "still [be] angry about her father's behavior."[21] She was removed from her mother's care and was "placed in a residential treatment facility to address [her] problems of morbid obesity, depression, and personality disorder."[22] Prior to the order placing her in the residential facility, Liza had been hospitalized for a month at the recommendation of her psychologist.

In re D. K. centers around a male minor in Pennsylvania who was previously removed from his mother's care and placed into a foster home because of his morbid obesity and complications such as hypertension and sleep apnea. In this case, he was revisiting the court to ask that he be allowed to return home to live with his mother. At the time of the hearing in 2002, D. K. was sixteen years old and weighed 451 pounds. When he was removed from the home, he was being raised by his single mother, and she was still a single mother when he asked to be returned to her care and to their home. The court's opinion in this case was ultimately that the sixteen-year-old should still be considered a minor child in spite of his advanced age and that he should remain in a foster home despite his wishes to return to his natural mother.[23]

In the Matter of Brittany T., a Child Alleged to Be Neglected addresses the 2007 case of a female minor in New York who was removed from her home due to her parents' failure to "take steps to properly treat the child's morbid obesity" and "ensure that the child attend school on a regular basis and on time."[24] Brittany T. lived with both her mother and her father at the time of removal, and the court opinion cited here provides an overview of the three years that the court system and child services were involved with the case. Although the court recognized that both of Brittany T.'s parents had physical limitations (her father used a wheelchair, and her mother was reported to be obese and suffering from gallstones), it maintained that the parents willfully violated orders to treat Brittany T.'s obesity.

MAKING A SPECIAL CASE

Long before lawyers such as Murtagh and physicians such as Ludwig began making recommendations that obese children be removed from their homes, each state or county had its own codes regarding what constituted neglect or abuse and when a child could be removed. This is still the case, and even though there are some differences from municipality to municipality, there is generally a stated agreement that obesity *alone* should not be read as a sign of neglect or abuse and that the child's life must be threatened in some way before removal is attempted. For example, in the case of Liza T., the code referenced in the court's opinion states that she was considered a "child in need of assistance," defined by the state of Iowa as "an unmarried child who is in need of medical treatment to cure or alleviate serious mental illness or disorder, or emotional damage as evidenced by severe anxiety, depression, withdrawal or untoward aggressive behavior toward self or others and whose parent, guardian, or custodian is unwilling or unable to provide such treatment."[25] Using this litmus test, Liza T. was judged to be a child in need of assistance because she was "suffering from morbid obesity and depression."[26] In other words, obesity alone was an insufficient reason for removing her from the home.

Likewise, in the case of D. K., the court notes that "certainly [child services] would not be justified by intervening simply because a child was overweight, or did not engage in a healthy lifestyle. Rather, the obesity must be of a severe nature reaching the life threatening morbid state, which has also manifested itself in physical problems . . . or mental problems."[27] Similarly, in the case of Brittany T., the court asserts that in New York, "state intervention will generally not be justified simply because a child was overweight, or simply did not engage in a healthy and fit lifestyle. However, where there are clear medical standards and convincing evidence that there exists severe, life-limiting dangers due to parental lifestyle and persistent neglect, removal is justified."[28] In all three of these cases, the courts declare that obesity alone does not warrant a child being removed from a home; the child must also be in imminent harm and reside with a parent or parents who are neglectful regarding that harm.

Yet, it is the child's visible obesity rather than any sense of imminent harm that likely prompts at least the initial inquiry. Historically, women mothering children who look "different" have been particularly targeted for blame and judgment. This brand of mother blaming—judging a mother based on a child's appearance—has been most thoroughly explored by scholars in the field of Disability Studies. In her germinal piece on mothering disabled children, Gail Landsman asserts that in the case of a visibly different child, the mother is often held accountable for her failure to produce a "normal" child.[29] Put another way, mothers are often blamed for their child's atypical embodiment. Jane Taylor McDonnell, the mother of an autistic child, notes that having a marked child has meant that people, from doctors to school nurses, have felt entitled to ask questions about "what happened" to her child, questions that she believes suggest her mothering skills and lifestyle might be the cause of her son's autism.[30]

Landsman echoes McDonnell's experience when she states that many conversations about her own child's disability turn on the notion that she, as a mother, did something improperly, thus causing the disability.[31] With obesity, people may also believe that a mother either did something improperly or didn't do something that she should have. A quick search on Amazon.com alone yields nearly 100 advice manuals about how to prevent obesity in children,[32] and cultural conversations about how to lose weight or prevent obesity are infinite. In the age of the advice manual and the concern about childhood obesity, mothers who have access to expert advice on how to have a thin child but who still have a fat one are likely to be scrutinized because of the sheer volume of available information. Many people would ask how a parent *couldn't* know how to make a child thin. Even though a fat embodiment may have become much more the statistical norm in recent years, it is certainly not the socially accepted norm; as a result, parents of fat children are apt to face the same sorts of interactions as parents of visibly disabled children because their children are also embodied in ways that are considered undesirable.

Since a great deal of what is described as the rationale for removing fat children could also be said of thin children, it seems even more clear that obesity functions as the trigger. For instance, Deena Patel, who thinks obese children should be removed from homes, claims in her article "Super-Sized Kids: Using the Law to Combat Morbid Obesity in Children" that "only one in 100 children eats a balanced diet as described by the United States Department of Agriculture's (USDA) Food Guide Pyramid."[33] In making this claim, Patel isn't speaking about obese children but children in general, which means there are many youngsters in the United States who are not being adequately nourished, regardless of their body weight. Patel goes on to say that "all children take in fats and sugars in excess of recommendations."[34] Aside from the fact that such a sweeping claim can't possibly be supported, she is again talking about "all" children, meaning that both fat and thin children would be eating in ways that are less than ideal, thereby making nearly every parent in the nation culpable in some degree of child neglect. The same is true for certain claims made by Murtagh and Ludwig; remember their claim that keeping "excessive junk food in the home or failing to model a physically active lifestyle" are also "mild parenting deficiencies."[35] Certainly, many parents of thin children have junk food in the house and don't exercise, but because their children remain thin, no one intervenes. Arguably, the lack of intervention stems, in part, from the belief that obesity is the way poor eating habits and lack of exercise manifest.

This emphasis on obesity rather than other aspects of overall health may also lead to children being treated for what should ultimately be secondary concerns. Take, for instance, the way the court reacts to the body of Liza T.: "Liza's physicians diagnosed her as having severe infantile personality disorder and a problem with morbid obesity caused by overeating as a method of coping with the strife between her parents."[36] The court record shows that Liza weighed 290 pounds upon entering the hospital and 266 pounds at the end of her month-long stay. No mention is made of any progress she made or any treatment she received regarding her personality disorder or her anger about her father's behavior. It's only her body weight that is tracked and recorded. Commenting on the court's written opinion on the case, legal scholar Sondra Solovay notes that Liza's weight is mentioned "seventeen times in the two-page decision. By contrast, the court pointed to her 'other' psychological problems (the alleged cause of her extreme weight) only eleven times."[37] In essence, it was Liza's weight and weight loss that seemed to garner the attention of the court rather than her psychological issues—even though weight alone should not have been enough to remove her from her home and doesn't appear to be the primary health issue.

It may also be that fat children's embodiments stigmatize them because they are not seen as the "right" size for their gender or as performing gender "correctly." For example, one billboard from Georgia's Strong4Life campaign against obesity,[38] which comprised a series of billboards that were eventually pulled but were up long enough to spark a good deal of debate about their depictions of fat children,[39] featured a black-and-white photograph of a young girl with the caption "It's Hard to Be a Little Girl When You're Not." This caption can be read as being about a child having to face "adult" health problems due to her size. But it can also be read as a "little girl" who is violating gender norms; specifically, she may be seen as violating the norm that females take up as little space as possible in the world. As scholars such as Iris Marion Young have pointed out, being appropriately feminine means making oneself as small as possible through gestures such as crossing the legs while sitting and taking small strides while walking—all in an effort not to claim too much space.[40]

The reference to not being a "little girl" might also evoke images of little girls playing princess and a fat girl not being able to participate, either because she is shunned by other children or because she can't find a princess dress that fits. Such an image may also cause panic about a little girl's burgeoning sexuality, which is likely assumed and expected to be heterosexual. What if she is shunned by males as a potential mate—in childhood games and in her future? Feminist scholar Angela Stukator argues that fat women are sometimes seen as asexual because they're not deemed appropriately feminized in their gender expression.[41] Because their bodies may not "fit" within the idealized construct of large breasts sitting atop narrow waists, fat women are sometimes read as gender atypical, which leads to panic not only about gender but also about sexuality. Think of the character Pat on *Saturday Night Live,* played by Julia Sweeney. Sweeney was not a large woman, but when she was in character as Pat, the costume she donned rounded her body in ways that confused people about whether Pat was male or female and, as a result, whether Pat was gay or straight. Gender and sexuality are closely tied together in these ways; it's impossible to label a person as gay or straight if gender is unclear.

Fat boys also potentially violate norms of gender expression and what is assumed to be heterosexuality. The perceived "softness" of the fat body stands in direct opposition to the hardness required of ideal masculinity, thus violating the gender norm of little boys developing and showcasing muscle on their way to adulthood. Fat usually connotes femininity, as body fat is often associated with the fleshy hips, thighs, and buttocks of women. Speaking of Al Roker's substantial weight loss and his account of how it changed his life, Amy Farrell asserts that his weight loss moved him into adulthood in the sense that losing weight meant he was no longer seen as "cuddly," an adjective much more appropriate for a small child than a man and reminiscent of a teddy bear or a child's toy.[42] Even at young ages, of course, little boys are not really expected to be cuddly but rather are expected to begin acting out—through their very embodiments—norms of masculinity. Further, "for overweight boys, the description of 'gay' or 'fag' is often added to the taunts."[43] Thus, as with little girls, when a little boy's gender seems to be inappropriately expressed through body size or type, his heterosexuality is also questioned. For parents of fat children, having a child whose very body violates or calls into question so many assumptions, values, and norms about bodies, gender, and sexuality inevitably also calls one's parenting skills into question.

To fully understand how fatphobia may be the key element in cases of removing children from homes, try to imagine a world in which a very thin teenager is removed from her home due to her low body weight. Writing about the differences drawn between parents of thin children and those of fat children, Ron Barnett asks, "What about the parents of every 16 year old in Beverly Hills who's too thin? Are they going to start arresting parents because their child is too thin?"[44] We don't have a public outcry to prosecute the parents or mothers of children and teens who suffer from anorexia. Parents have been prosecuted for willfully starving their children,[45] but parents of anorexics are not prosecuted for their children's refusal to eat. In a world where parents may have children at either extreme of the weight spectrum, thinness doesn't trigger the same response.

In fact, on the website for the National Association of Anorexia Nervosa and Associated Disorders (ANAD), one of the featured articles is a *Newsweek* piece called "Fighting Anorexia: No One Is to Blame." In the article, a Mayo Clinic eating disorder specialist, Dr. Julie O'Toole, says, "Most young anorexics . . . have wonderful, thoughtful, terribly worried parents."[46] She adds that to comfort parents, she explains anorexia to them this way: "I tell them it's a brain disorder. Children don't choose to have it and parents don't cause it."[47] The article notes that O'Toole "then gives the parents a little pep talk. She reminds them that mothers were once blamed for causing schizophrenia and autism until that so-called science was debunked. And that the same will soon be true for anorexia. At the conclusion of O'Toole's speech, she says, parents often weep."[48] Imagine the same talk being given to the parents of a fat child, a child whose size may be caused by overeating. Imagine Marlene Corrigan being given such a pep talk after her 680-pound daughter, Christina, died. In reality, she was vilified, prosecuted, and convicted for being a neglectful mother, even though she'd repeatedly asked for help with Christina.[49] The disparity in the treatment of parents highlights many of the ways in which parental responsibility for a child's body size is contingent upon fatphobia; it also reflects a rigid set of beliefs about what causes fatness and how parents, especially mothers, can and should prevent a child from becoming fat but can't prevent a child from becoming too thin.

The case of Liza T., in which a mother was blamed for her daughter's eating as a means of coping with the stress of her parents' divorce, also showcases how differently the mothers of heavy children may be treated. Legal scholar Sondra Solovay opines that in cases of children using another coping mechanism besides food to handle depression or stress, parents wouldn't be expected to control the behavior. As she observes, "If a child blinks furiously as a means to deal with depression," he or she would not be removed from the home because the parent couldn't control that blinking.[50] Yet, because Liza T. used food, her mother was expected to exert control. Given all the possible aspects of a child's embodiment or eating habits that parents can't and don't control, the concentration on obesity as something that parents can and should control involves picking among innumerable factors and speaks to the culture's investment in thinness and moralizing about fatness.

It's difficult to imagine that all this concern and action is only about a danger posed to a child. Anorexia doesn't get nearly as much press, but anorexia kills children. In fact, it is a serious threat to health and causes a great deal of familial and financial stress. As the ANAD website acknowledges, "Anorexia is a killer—it has the highest mortality rate of any mental illness, including depression. About half of anorexics get better. About 10 percent of them die. The rest remain chronically ill—exhausting, then bankrupting, parents, retreating from jobs and school, alienating friends as they struggle to manage the symptoms of their condition."[51] As is often argued about obesity, anorexia also affects increasingly younger children:

> Recently researchers, clinicians and mental-health specialists say they're seeing the age of their youngest anorexia patients decline to 9 from 13. Administrators at Arizona's Remuda Ranch, a residential treatment program for anorexics, received so many calls from parents of young children that last year, they launched a program for kids 13 years old and under; so far, they've treated 69 of them. Six months ago the eating-disorder program at Penn State began to treat the youngest ones, too—20 of them so far.[52]

In spite of what look to be anorexia's apparent similarities to obesity in children—such as the accompanying depression and risk of death as well as the fact that the number of sufferers is rising and the affected population is getting younger and younger—anorexia prompts a very different reaction, with parents typically receiving resources, pity, and forgiveness rather than scorn and prosecution.

Another reason why parents of anorexics may be treated so differently is that having a child who is drastically thin, especially a female child, may signal that the norms of gender and sexuality *are* understood and being appropriately passed on to the children. The common feminist understanding of the anorectic body is that it becomes so thin that, especially in the case of young women, it thwarts gender norms by not presenting the kinds of hips and breasts normally associated with femininity and a heterosexual identity.[53] But the more common and popular understanding of anorexics is that they are trying too hard to embody social norms. Outside of academia, arguably the most common understanding of anorexia, especially in young women, is that it arises from extreme and misguided aspirations to meet the idealized cultural expectations of femininity and therefore of heterosexuality. In other words, the common understanding is that young girls want to look like the women in magazines and other media representations. Of course, people aren't necessarily comfortable with having young women die of anorexia, but having a child who suffers from the disorder may garner more sympathy because the child still appears to be trying to embody social norms and what are considered ideals. Moreover, children suffering from anorexia may well be thought of as innocent victims of the mass media's representations of unattainable physical perfection.

These differences in reactions between parents of children at both ends of the weight spectrum (and of children who may all be suffering from some sort of disordered eating or other challenge) suggest that parents of fat children are being unfairly blamed and prosecuted. As Solovay argues, "It is simply inappropriate for the state to put the force of law behind the regulation of weight in childhood, absent actual abuse like *forced* feeding or *forced* starvation."[54] I imagine that Solovay's claim appears reasonable to many people when applied to thinness, but as the public polls about obesity and children show, it may not appear so sensible when applied to fatness.

LIKE MOTHER LIKE CHILD

In a court case that focuses on a child's weight, one might expect that the youngster's body will be discussed, but having the body of the mother considered as a piece of evidence reveals biases against fatness, particularly fatness present in women who are also mothers. In the cases of D. K. and Brittany T., the fatness of the mothers' bodies is cited in the court documents as a kind of evidence of their inability to appropriately parent. Both of Brittany T.'s parents were in the household, but her father was "confined to wheelchair and, he testified, suffer[ed] from cardiomyopathy, muscular dystrophy, arthritis and scoliosis."[55] No mention of his weight is made in the court documents, even though seemingly all details about why he used a wheelchair are included. The court's opinion apparently considers the father's weight literally unremarkable; in other words, readers are left to assume that the father was of average weight because the court documents don't mark him otherwise. Brittany T's mother, who is referred to as Shawna T. or Mrs. T. in the court's decision, is described quite differently and with much more detail regarding her weight: "The court has observed throughout the past four years that Mrs. T. herself is very obese (the April 6, 2006 [. . .] 30-day report to the court indicated that her weight at the nutrition clinic on April 5, 2006 was 436 pounds). Moreover, at least fairly recently, the court has observed that the mother suffers from some very audible breathing difficulties."[56] The juxtaposition of two bodies that both arguably fall outside social norms—the physically disabled body in a wheelchair and the fat female body, which may also be physically disabled—provides a glimpse into the ways a fat body can become more of a liability.

In terms of failing to live up to social norms, Mrs. T. is certainly held more accountable for what the court considers the troubling aspects of her daughter's life, likely because mothers are expected to be role models in ways fathers may not be. Although Mr. T takes responsibility for some problems in his daughter's life, Mrs. T. draws much more of the court's ire. While discussing Brittany T.'s absences from school, which the court decision cites as one of the reasons for intervention, the court notes that the father took ownership of his daughter's tardiness "because he thought school started at 8:15, not 8:00."[57] But even though the father claimed to be responsible for Brittany having been late on twenty-five of the sixty-eight days she attended school prior to the hearing, the mother's weight and her failure to have Brittany follow a diet receive the most attention, especially because Mrs. T. is positioned as the person who should be her daughter's role model. In summarizing the testimony of Dr. William J. Cochran,[58] the court opinion reads:

> [Dr. Cochran] testified that it is important that the parents be role models regarding lifestyle and weight. Typical of his concerns was an incident he described in November of 2004. He testified that he had just spent a long session with Brittany and Mrs. T. regarding Brittany's health, including appropriate eating and foods, regarding which the mother said she understood. Right after the appointment, he went to an eating establishment

across from the hospital. There he saw Brittany eating french fries and a "hamburger or something of that nature."[59]

Although the opinion begins by discussing the importance of "parents" (plural), it soon turns toward the mother and her role in Brittany's life. Nowhere does the court's decision indicate that the father should be responsible for understanding the diet that his daughter is supposed to follow, nor does the court ever suggest that the father is an inappropriate role model. His eating habits and knowledge of his daughter's diet—recommended or actual—are absent from the record. When Dr. Cochran asserts that Brittany's problems are "the result of poor parental modeling and control of food intake"[60] and expresses his disappointment that other taboo foods (besides those he witnessed them eating) were recorded in Brittany's food logs, it's Mrs. T. who is positioned as the poor role model, presumably due to her own obesity and what appears in the documents as "evidence" that Brittany T. has sometimes eaten forbidden foods. Mrs. T.'s body dovetails with the consumption of and recording of certain foods to serve as proof that, as Murray argues, "fat people's bodies . . . tell of their failure to understand, to take seriously, or commit to 'common sense' principles for health and normalcy."[61] In this way, Mrs. T.'s "failure" appears not as a momentary misunderstanding by an individual (as her husband's misunderstanding about the start time for school is presented) but rather as a result of fatness being associated with pathology and a tacit understanding that mothers are responsible for children's eating. All of this means that a fat mother must be responsible for a fat child's overeating.

Although both parents in the case have some physical challenges (it's also noted, for instance, that Mrs. T. recently had a hospital stay due to gallstones), Mrs. T.'s body is positioned as being more transgressive and problematic than that of Mr. T. The details of his medical history suggest that he uses a wheelchair through no fault of his own, as conditions such as muscular dystrophy and scoliosis are deemed to be out of one's control. In American culture, however, excessive weight is almost always read as volitional and a sign of a person being irresponsible. Anna Kirkland argues in her book *Fat Rights* that "most ordinary people do not consider fat people to be victims of a disease . . . instead, most people think that getting fat is primarily caused by bad behaviors like eating too much and failing to exercise."[62] In this instance, the description of Mrs. T.'s weight becomes a way to define her as resistant to normalization, both in terms of her own body weight and in terms of the court orders about her daughter. Fat Studies scholars posit that much of the hostility fat people face in contemporary US culture can be traced back to the belief that fat people are, in essence, thumbing their noses at social norms: "In the case of the obese ... what is perceived as their defiant rebellion against normalization appears to be a source of the hostility they inspire."[63] In other words, Mr. T.'s body may be understood as less than ideal through no fault of his own, but Mrs. T.'s body is seen as a purposeful act of resistance against social norms and expectations.

A NARROW DEFINITION OF "PARENT"

The court opinions suggest that the term *obese*—at least for the mothers in these cases—is code for a variety of shortcomings and failures to meet the norms of mothering practices. In the case of D. K., his mother, Donna K., is described as "homebound as the result of her own obesity, allegedly in the 600-pound range."[64] D. K.'s father had passed, so Donna K. is his primary care-giver and the only parent discussed in the court's decision. Much like in Mrs. T.'s case, the court in the *In re D. K.* case is quite clear that the mother's body is being read as evidence of her inability and/or unwillingness to control her own weight and is at least part of what makes the court cautious about returning custody to her. When contemplating D. K's desire to return home and his belief that while he was in foster care, his new eating habits had become "ingrained," the court cites medical testimony by a nutritionist who reported that "he did not believe that the mother ... with her limitations as noted above would provide the necessary help and support the minor needs in order to avert a return to his former lifestyle."[65] The "limitations ... noted above" are that Donna K. is obese and homebound, presumably as a result of her size.

The court document suggests that *obese* signifies much more than just body weight. The court eventually decides that returning home is not in the best interest of D. K., since his mother will likely cause him to backslide, which can be interpreted as another of the "limitations" of Donna K. The decision reads, "[Donna K.] has been unable to maintain her own health by addressing her own obesity problem, and therefore it is highly unlikely that she will now be able to do so with regard to her son's identical problem."[66] In this instance, the mother's body is not described as a conduit of contagion to a fetus as I discussed in chapter 1, but it appears no less potent as a kind of contaminating agent to a sixteen-year-old son—or at least it is read as evidence of the *potential* for her to contaminate her son with what are assumed to be her own bad habits that have resulted in her obesity.

Clearly, Donna K. is seen as having limitations because of her own inability to lose weight, but beyond that, her fat body serves as evidence that she is also limited in terms of her "natural" ability to parent. The court decision reviews prior case law, noting that "even where there are inadequacies in the child's home, the court should first consider ordering CWS [Child Welfare Services] to take the steps necessary to instruct the parents in the skills needed, and to provide follow-up supervision in the home, where feasible."[67] To further make the point that a child should stay in the home if at all possible, the decision cites two cases: one case in which a nine-year-old child who had been diagnosed with psychosocial dwarfism was left in the care of the parents even though "there was conflicting expert opinion as to whether specialized institutional care was required" and another case involving a child who had severe burns that apparently required specialized care.[68] The court notes that in each of those cases, "it was determined that the parents, with proper training and supervision, could adequately and properly care in their own home" for the child.[69]

Writing about Donna K., however, the court denies her ability to provide D. K. with the necessary care: "Unlike those parents [of the child with psychosocial dwarfism and the child with severe burns], the mother here [Donna K.] does not have the *natural abilities* typical of *any* parent, as she is limited by her own extreme obesity. Her *own problems* interfere with her ability to meet the special needs of her son."[70] Setting aside for a moment the issue of what constitutes so-called natural abilities, the use of the word *any* seems to remove Donna K. entirely from the category of "parent." She may be the child's biological mother, but she is positioned as unable to be a parent, a rhetorical move reminiscent of the popular idea that any woman can be a mother but it takes someone special to be a mom.[71]

Another reason Donna K. is judged as inadequate is the belief that, in her case, abilities to parent are related to able-bodiedness, as the court asserts that being homebound contributes to why Donna K. does not have the supposedly natural abilities of other parents. The decision asserts that being homebound "prevented her from even attending her son's medical appointments, so as to be fully advised as to the seriousness of his condition."[72] This description, which immediately follows the sentence about natural parenting abilities, suggests that a mother's natural ability to parent is tied to not only thinness but also able-bodiedness. The contrast between this and the case of Brittany T.'s father, who is described as "confined to a wheelchair" yet not explicitly labeled as incapable of being a good parent because of his disability, is troubling, not because being disabled should automatically discredit one's parenting abilities but because the contrast indicates a parent's disability may be judged differently depending on gender and how that disability manifests. Certainly, many people who are disabled and/or homebound are exemplary parents. In the case of obesity, however, it seems that the moral judgment attached to fatness is so strong as to taint everything else. Body weight, which is believed to be volitional, is so stigmatized in the culture that the court's opinion of Donna K.'s being homebound may be overdetermined in ways that another kind of disability may not be. Given the assumption that a mother will be the parent who takes a child to the doctor or, in the case of Mrs. T., the parent who is expected to understand a child's medical and dietary needs, Donna K. may also be judged inadequate for failing to do what a mother should.

Of course, Donna K. isn't explicitly described as disabled in the court record but only as homebound; however, even fat people who are not physically disabled are often perceived as such and assumed to be incapable of performing certain tasks.[73] The power of being perceived as disabled is such that the Americans with Disabilities Act acknowledges the perception of being disabled as warranting protection. In other words, under current US law, one does not have to be disabled in order to be discriminated against as disabled; a person may be discriminated against because he or she is *perceived* as disabled.[74] In the case of Donna K., being homebound constructs her as disabled, at least in terms of her mobility, and although Mrs. T. is not described as homebound, her able-bodiedness is called into question by the stressing of her breathing difficulties and fatness. Many people may wholeheartedly disagree with discriminating against a person due to a disability, but when the disability is thought to be caused by fatness, a different response is often evoked because of the moral issues attached to fatness. As Kathleen LeBesco and Jana Braziel note, the 1990s brought a host of changes to our language, with denigrating jokes about and terms for women and people of color falling out of favor. Fat, they say, remained outside these changes: "Still, there is something about fat that escapes this change. People openly [and] disparagingly refer to themselves and others as fat. Perhaps it is because fat is a subject-making experience over which we are perceived to have some degree of control, unlike gender or race, which are commonly—though mistakenly—taken to be fixed, static identifiers, that fat continues to be so maligned."[75] Although some scholars have argued that disability, as a category, is also socially constructed and therefore no more static than gender or race,[76] it's certainly true that many people still also believe disability to be what LeBesco and Braziel refer to as a "fixed identifier." That is, many people still see disability as being out of an individual's control—even though any number of preventable accidents may have caused the disability. Think, for example, of someone who is now disabled due to having had an accident as a result of driving while intoxicated.

Because fatness is believed to be volitional, however, both Donna K. and Mrs. T. are likely not going to benefit from any positive changes to our language and culture regarding disability. In reality, they may be even more maligned because they are seen as not *really* being disabled, in the sense that they are thought to be able to control their weight. Put another way, they could choose to be thin and able-bodied; that they do not make that choice means they may be read as purposefully choosing to be fat and therefore choosing to be disabled, another instance of resisting social norms.[77] Of course, it's reasonable to point out that a person who now uses a wheelchair as a result of a drunk-driving accident also made a choice to drink and drive, but such a choice is more often seen as an isolated incident—the one time that the person made the mistake and suffered a consequence. With fatness, people are frequently believed to have made the poor choice (presumably, to eat too much food or food that is too fattening) over and over again, and consequently, they are blamed for their disability in ways that other people with disabilities may not be.

Donna K. strikes the court as so flawed, in part because of being homebound, that she is virtually excluded from the category of "parent." Of all the possible comparisons that could be drawn to Donna K.'s situation, the court chose the case of a child with psychosocial dwarfism and the case of a child with severe burns. Psychosocial dwarfism is a complicated condition but is generally understood as a stunting of growth directly due to a reversible absence of growth hormone, an absence linked to some kind of altered emotional state. In most instances, children diagnosed with psychosocial dwarfism are experiencing some type of significant stress in their home environments that causes their pituitary gland not to function as it otherwise might. Human's emotional states influence the release of hormones, and in cases of psychosocial dwarfism, children stop growing in their home environments. In a different environment, however, they begin to grow again.[78] The first cases of psychosocial dwarfism that were documented by Dr. Robert Blizzard occurred among children who had come from brutal home environments,[79] but scientists now understand that children need not be brutalized in order to have the condition; in fact, psychosocial dwarfism is now recognized as being caused by a continuum of home environments. That is, in some cases, it may just be a lack of nurturing that causes a child to develop the disorder. Regardless, a less than optimum home environment triggers the condition in the child.[80]

By citing the example of psychosocial dwarfism, then, the court draws a parallel to Donna K. by suggesting that she is also the primary cause of her son's body size—his "condition," as it were. Yet, the court asserts that parents who almost certainly had inadequacies that caused their child to develop psychosocial dwarfism *could learn* to provide a proper home for their child whereas Donna K. cannot. Showing that such a comparison is purposeful and not merely a fluke in the literature, Murtagh and Ludwig also compare obesity in children to psychosocial dwarfism. When they call for obese children to be removed from homes, they actually go so far as to suggest that the comparison of obesity to psychosocial dwarfism is *the* most appropriate comparison to be drawn: "Psychosocial dwarfism, in which growth arrests from a complex interplay of biological, psychological and domestic environmental factors, provides a better comparison [than osteogenesis imperfecta]."[81]

Even conceding that, whether a child is of small stature or obese, a parent may have *something* to do with the child's size and even conceding that both a small body that results from psychosocial dwarfism and an obese body may indicate some kind of emotional trauma, the question of why the parents of a child with psychosocial dwarfism are thought to be able to learn to care for the child whereas Donna K. is said to be incapable of doing so lingers. The statures of the parents of the child with psychosocial dwarfism aren't mentioned, but psychosocial dwarfism is not an inheritable condition. Because those parents aren't mentioned explicitly, it is fair to assume they are of average height. It appears, then, that Donna K.'s obesity brands her and further indicates that her own embodiment causes her to lack supposedly natural abilities; it is part of what disqualifies her as an appropriate parent.

In this way, Donna K.'s fat body signifies both lack and presence—a lack of natural caring abilities and a presence of characteristics that make her a less than ideal mother. LeBesco and Braziel describe the fat body's simultaneously signifying lack and presence in this way: "Frequently, the fat body is read as the corporeal presencing of other, presumably more intrinsic, incorporeal qualities or characteristics—the signifying of latency and lack. Fat equals reckless excess, prodigality, indulgences, lack of restraints, violation of order and space, transgression of boundary."[82] In the court's estimation, the more "intrinsic, incorporeal qualities or characteristics" exemplified by Donna K.'s weight are a lack of parental responsibility and a lack of caring, which are thought to come naturally to any *but* a fat parent. Returning to the second example the court cites, the case of a child with severe burns, learning to care for the child in a way that minimizes pain and the chance of infection is undoubtedly a difficult task that requires specialized knowledge and extreme care. Yet, the parents of that child are believed to be capable of learning how to dress wounds and care for their child whereas Donna K. is declared incapable of parenting hers, presumably because she doesn't currently know and can't learn how to properly feed her son.

Arguably, Donna K.'s perceived inability to learn stems, at least partially, from the court inferring from her obesity that she can't—or won't—understand how to make herself thin, much like Mrs. T. may be seen as resistant to norms of female dieting for herself and resistant to imposing those norms on her daughter, Brittany T. Several problematic beliefs may join here to disqualify Donna K. as a parent: the widespread belief that being thin is a simple choice that one can and should make, the belief that fat people are too stupid to understand how to stick to a diet and exercise plan or even to understand that they *should* stick to such a plan, and the belief that fat people are simply too lazy to stick to a diet and exercise plan.

Perhaps one of the most utilized images by the dieting industry and America's cultural iconography in general is the makeover show, which depicts the thin person stepping out of the fat person, as if leaving the fat body behind is that simple a choice. "Just push yourself away from the table (and from your fatness)," the old saying goes. Rhetorically, this sentiment is echoed in books such as the popular series *Eat This, Not That!*, which also suggests that thinness is but one easy choice away: it's as simple as substituting one food for another. The message of choice extends beyond food and becomes about parenting more broadly, as is made clear in Georgia's Strong4Life campaign, a campaign proclaiming that all parents need to do to prevent childhood obesity is to "choose parenting."[83] In such a climate—where thinness is portrayed as so simple to achieve—it should come as no surprise that fat people are often characterized as dumb, irresponsible, and lazy and that the parents of fat children are seen as being too lazy to choose parenting.

The mothers in the three court cases discussed in this chapter may also be stigmatized via their embodiments: that is, their fatness and any physical limitations they have may also mean that they, like their children, are transgressing the bounds of gender norms by failing to embody idealized femininity, thereby lessening their value. As Susan Wendell argues in *The Rejected Body: Feminist Philosophical Reflections on Disability*, "Physical 'imperfection' is more likely to be thought to 'spoil' a woman than a man by rendering her unattractive in a culture where physical appearance is a large component of a woman's value."[84] Donna K. and Mrs. T. both seem to be judged guilty of having transgressed a cultural standard of parenting that implies mothers should look and behave in a certain way in order to be models of acceptable femininity and of diet and exercise. Of course, in American culture, it's increasingly difficult to separate acceptable femininity from diet and exercise. The *In re D. K.* opinion, in fact, states that for the court to entertain any future request that her son return home, Donna K. must "address her own health concerns and well-being."[85] Given that the opinion fails to list any other health concerns, it seems that what is being requested is that Donna K. lose weight in order to prove that she is capable of caring for her child, in part because the norms of gender, femininity, and motherhood are so closely bound.

Another way in which Donna K. seems to defy conventional femininity is by being a single mother. In the opening paragraph of the opinion, the court asserts that "[her son] was in the unfortunate circumstances where he was being raised alone by his mother."[86] The sentence continues with the court expressing concern over Donna K.'s weight and her being homebound, as I've already discussed. But the mention of single motherhood here can be read as indicating another way in which Donna K.'s parenting abilities and/or her ability to take care of herself may be judged inadequate and both her femininity and the stability of her home questioned. As a single mother, she may also be viewed by the court as failing at heteronormativity and failing to provide her son with an appropriate model of a family or of a heterosexual relationship; perhaps the court reads her status as a single mother as another kind of "unfortunate" behavior in the sense that she is behaving inappropriately by raising a child alone. Because she's raising a male child on her own, some of the concern may also be rooted in a fear that she can't teach him how to be a "man," especially since fat boys are often feminized and not considered to embody the norms of masculinity. Thinking back to the Strong4Life campaign and its claim that "It's Hard to Be a Little Girl When You're Not," I wonder if the panic and concern about childhood obesity also couches a kind of panic about gender and heteronormativity. As Fat Studies scholar Samantha Murray argues, "Western culture's current panic over obesity is underpinned by a moral anxiety about the preservation of fixed gender identities and normative female sexuality and embodiment."[87] I would suggest that the concern is about normative sexualities and embodiments in general.

BACK TO THE FUTURE

Although the courts claim to focus on imminent harm, much of the concern about what will happen to fat children is based on imagined and hypothetical futures, in terms of their abilities to embody norms of gender and sexuality and even health. Lisette Burrows, a prominent figure in the study of children's health, has noted that television shows such as *Honey, We're Killing the Kids* may indicate that parents literally feel as if they're killing their children when they fail to make them thin(ner).[88] Certainly, such shows also teach the viewing public that parents are responsible for children's weights. *Honey, We're Killing the Kids* was popular enough that there was both a BBC version and a US-based version that ran on TLC,[89] and I would argue that because it uses hypothetical time-lapse photography to turn children into patently unattractive obese adults, wearing dowdy clothing and eyeglasses that were stylish in 1952, the show also suggests that parents may be killing their children's chances of growing up to be in relationships and/or have families.[90] The show aims to paint a bleak future for these children, one in which they are unattractive, seemingly unhappy, single, and unloved. They're never shown as vibrant adults with families or careers but only as lonely parodies, taking the focus away from the issue of imminent harm to a child.

This emphasis on a hypothetical future is not limited, however, to television shows. Legal scholar Melissa Mitgang questions whether courts have truly looked closely at the imminent harm they say is required for removing an obese child from the home or instead have been guilty of considering the child's potential future in their decisions. She argues that in the cases of L. T., D. K., and Brittany T., the children seem to have been taken out of their homes due to a concern for future problems rather than their current states of health. She notes that in D. K.'s case, "the court emphasized that without continued intervention the minor would have a 'guarantee' of a short life span of only reaching his thirties," suggesting that the court was not just looking at an immediate threat or immediate limiting of life for D. K. but also at his hypothetical future.[91] Mitgang goes on to argue that in the case of Brittany T., the court claims to be invested only in issues of immediate danger related to obesity but nonetheless gives a great deal of credence to her physician's statement about her future. In the court documents, the doctor cautioned that unless Brittany T. received the needed medical care, she "'would . . . have continued weight increase and her health would deteriorate further.'"[92] The court's opinion on L. T. reveals a similar tendency to focus on future weight gain or future effects of weight, according to Mitgang, as the court states that L. T's "obesity was 'a *potentially*' life-threatening condition which will likely result in a significantly increased risk of hypertension and a decreased life expectancy."[93]

If courts wish to emphasize future harms, they should also consider the future emotional damage that might occur from removing children from their homes. Although depression is often noted as a problem for obese children,[94] there is a paucity of clear thinking about how a child removed from his or her home or how a mother who has her child removed might suffer psychologically, as was clearly the case with Anamarie Regino and her family.[95] To their credit, Murtagh and Ludwig admit that there may be serious psychological consequences for removing a child from a home, noting that after removal, "substantial psychosocial morbidity may ensue."[96] In short, they understand that it is entirely possible the psychosocial consequences for a child will be serious enough to negatively affect both the child's immediate health and his or her longevity. But despite such concessions, as Solovay points out, distinctions are often drawn between how courts may think about psychological consequences to thin and fat children: "With a thin child, the courts would consider the parent's actions and the emotional and psychological consequences to be a priority. With a fat child it can be tricky to get a judge to see past the number on the scale."[97]

Some advocates of removing children from homes dismiss the possibility of negative psychosocial effects on the youngsters because they believe that these children are likely to be separated from their families anyway due to health problems or even death. Law professor Cheryl George believes anyone arguing that obese children suffer psychologically from being removed from their homes only does so because an argument about psychological health "appeals to the emotions." She writes, "If judicial and state intervention were not allowed the child would perhaps be deprived of the privilege of being with her family because of hospitalization or even death due to obesity."[98] The logic of such an argument is that since the child is likely to be away from the family anyway, state intervention is justified. Aside from making the assumption that any or even all obese children will be hospitalized or die, George also implies that family isn't really important to a child's health.

Law and public policy professor Susan Brooks takes a different stance, arguing that removing children from homes—even when a parent is judged to be neglectful—is at odds with society's stated goals. She believes what is best for both parents and children is to educate and help parents and to keep the family together because to do otherwise harms everyone involved: "Our legal system purports to care about children. . . . Yet, in our efforts to help children, we often condemn their parents. . . . What we fail to recognize is that by these same actions, we deprive children of something they also cherish and need— their families."[99] D. K., for example, desperately wanted to go home, and his mother wanted him to return as well. But because of his weight and his mother's weight, both were deprived of living together as a family.

The American Medical Association has long opposed the prosecution of pregnant women for drug abuse because it recognizes that punishing women is ultimately damaging to their lives and those of their family members, including their children.[100] Yet, as Alyssa Newcomb points out, it was the *Journal of the American Medical Association* that published Ludwig and Murtagh's piece

the best that can be done, if something must indeed be done, is to remember a guiding principle of medicine that ought to extend to social policies as well: First, do no harm. And in this instance, not doing harm most likely means leaving obese children in their homes and with their families.

CHAPTER THREE

Public and Private Shame

Using Children as Message Boards

Congratulations! It's an Obesity Time Bomb!
—Grizelda

As cartoon artist Grizelda's words make clear, in some recent depictions of the childhood obesity epidemic, children are being labeled as time bombs rather than bundles of joy. Even children who are not fat are portrayed as dangerous, with the implication being that their bodies are just waiting to blow up. It doesn't necessarily matter whether Grizelda is poking fun by suggesting that people have become so unreasonably obsessed with obesity in children that the birth of a child is anxiety producing rather than merely joyful; nor does it matter if the artist is pointing to what she sees as the realistic and expected outcome of obesity for any child born into today's world. The cartoon in Figure 3.1 still captures the general sense that, in contemporary America, children's bodies are ominous reminders of the constant risk of the obesity epidemic and that the nation is at war.

Cartoons are not the only places where children are depicted in these ways, as several public campaigns have used real children and their bodies as literal warning signs. Take, for example, ads produced by Children's Healthcare of Atlanta as part of Georgia's Strong4Life campaign to end childhood obesity.[1] The ads featured black-and-white photographs of children looking directly at the camera and were captioned with lines such as "It's Hard to Be a Little Girl When You're Not"; "Warning: Childhood Obesity Has Increased 300% in the Last 30 Years"; and "Some Diseases Aren't Just for Adults Anymore."[2] Interestingly enough, the ads positioned the children looking back at viewers. Unlike in medical photographs and so many news stories about obesity, there were no black bars across their eyes and their faces weren't obscured in any way.

There was no attempt to hide the youngsters' identities or "protect" them, which is often the cited rationale behind obscuring people's faces. Many

'CONGRATULATIONS! IT'S AN OBESITY TIME BOMB...'

Figure 3.1: Artist Grizelda's *Obesity Timebomb,* Cartoonstock.com

scholars have written about the dehumanization caused by placing black bars across people's eyes in medical photography and using bodies without heads in news media accounts about obesity.[3] In this respect, one might think that featuring the children looking back at the audience actually empowered them in some way and kept them from being seen as objects, and I think this may have been the aim of the campaign—to humanize the issue of childhood obesity. In her examination of the social aspects of staring, Rosemarie Garland-Thomson explores the work of artists who have, either through photography or painting, sought to depict figures who, "refusing to wilt under another's stare," found a way to "insist on . . . dignity and worth."[4] Discussing Doug Auld and his paintings of burn victims, portraits that often feature subjects in postures and poses described as "regal," Garland-Thomson argues that these paintings create an atmosphere where viewers are "more likely to accept [the subjects] as fellow human beings, rather than grotesques to be gawked at or turned away from."[5]

Garland-Thomson's argument is spot on for artwork such as Auld's, but I would argue that the Strong4Life ads operate quite differently. As Garland-Thomson contends, "Staring bespeaks involvement, and being stared at demands a response."[6] Taking her point that a kind of response or action is demanded, what do the Strong4Life ads, with their starkly featured children, demand of viewers? One ad shows a large African American girl, Maya, with a big, red-fonted WARNING emblazoned across the advertisement (Figure 3.2). She is staring directly at the camera and viewer. The warning is placed across Maya's midsection, both emphasizing her width and staking a claim that her midsection is the source of the problem—literally where the danger supposedly resides. The positioning of the label also draws attention to her breasts, perhaps suggesting that she's a child in terms of her age yet not a child because she's developed early and is dealing with "adult" health problems. This is a common refrain within public discussions about children and obesity and certainly within this campaign (consider the slogans "It's Hard to Be a Little Girl When You're Not" and "He Has His Father's Eyes, His Laugh and Maybe Even His Diabetes").

Maya's stare back at her audience is stripped of any potential liberatory power by the fact that she is a child who has been labeled as a warning to others, a child who is not supposed to exist—at least not in that body. Auld's work focuses on people who have been burned, in events many viewers would see as accidental even though they don't know the circumstances surrounding the burns. The Strong4Life campaign hinges on the cultural assumptions that obesity is neither an accident nor an embodiment one can be proud of (much as a survivor of a fire or of breast cancer might feel); rather, the message is that obesity is preventable and that it's a shame that anyone, especially a child, has to live "that way." Auld's work is successful, at least in part, because the narrative of the "damaged" body that can become a source of strength is possible for those who have been burned. In mainstream American culture, the fat body, which is almost always imagined as a failure and seen as a source of disgust and hardship, doesn't hold that same possibility.[7]

Maya's stare, then, serves more to confront her audience with the supposed harsh reality of the childhood obesity epidemic than to reverse or rework any sort of power dynamic between this child and her audience. Work such as Auld's is meant to "make . . . an extraordinary sight ordinary,"[8] but viewers are surely accustomed to seeing children who look very much like Maya. She's

Figure 3.2: Maya Joi featured in the Strong4Life campaign

really quite ordinary looking. The aim here seems to be the opposite of Auld's work in that Strong4Life seeks to make the ordinary extraordinary, which is in keeping with both the concern over parents and society not *seeing* childhood obesity as a real problem and the rhetoric of the wake-up call. According to Children's Healthcare of Atlanta, "75% of parents of obese children don't think they have a problem on their hands."[9] Part of the concern is that parents tend to brush off their children's excess weight as merely being "chubby" or having "baby fat," and therefore, they see the weight as a mundane part of growing up instead of a medical, cultural, and parental crisis.

Rather than offering empowerment, the ad featuring Maya does what James Elkins discusses in his book *The Object Stares Back: On the Nature of Seeing.* Elkins understands seeing as always enmeshed in cultural constructs and contexts and notes that, although looking can sometimes seem like an innocent act, "just looking" isn't possible. He posits that there can be a "violent side of seeing, where the mere act of looking—an act that can also be the gentlest, least invasive way to make contact with the world—becomes so forceful that it turns a human being into [an] . . . example of a medical condition."[10] Thus, the "question for starers is not whether we *should* stare, but rather *how* we should stare."[11] In the case of Maya, it seems that viewers are invited and encouraged to stare at her as a warning; she is a child gone awry, and her looking back at us is a call to action for us both to see her (or at least her waistline) as the problem and to help fix it. Those involved in the campaign seem to acknowledge this is how the children featured in the ads are being used, for Linda Matzigkert, the chief administrative officer for Children's Healthcare of Atlanta, said in an interview about the campaign, "We felt that because there was so much denial [of obesity] that we needed to make people aware that this is a medical crisis."[12] The aim of the campaign, then, is to use images of what many people might consider ordinary-looking children with extraordinary captions to jar an audience into action and to hold up children's bodies as evidence of crisis.

SHAME ISN'T A TREATMENT

There's no doubt that shame plays a part in how many public health ads about obesity work. One advertisement by Strong4Life features a fat boy asking his mom why he is fat. The mother, a fat woman herself, responds by hanging her head down silently, an action and posture normally associated with being ashamed. Similarly, in recent Blue Cross and Blue Shield of Minnesota television commercials, produced as part of its "Today Is the Day"[13] campaign to end obesity, heavy parents see their behavior reflected in their children, also evoking a kind of silent shame. In one commercial that seems to have disappeared from all the sites where it was originally posted,[14] a young, chubby girl pushed her own miniature grocery cart through the store behind her fat mother. As they rounded a corner, the mother glanced into her daughter's cart and saw that it was full of convenience foods. With her daughter looking up at her lovingly, the mother realized that she was negatively influencing her daughter's eating habits, and her own face fell. In the other commercial produced for the campaign, which is still being aired, two young boys (who most people would say are chubby) are arguing over whose father can eat more and boasting about the day when they will be able to eat 1,000 corndogs. The father in the commercial, who is a fat man, walks toward the boys with a tray of fast food and then overhears their conversation. He looks mournfully down at the plastic tray that's holding orders of french fries and neon-colored slush drinks. Both commercials close with the tagline "Today is the day we set a better example for our kids."[15]

Although Blue Cross and Blue Shield of Minnesota insists that the ads target parents so that they can better understand how their food choices affect their families,[16] fat children are also very much a part of this campaign. I would argue that children also become targets of these ads. Lindy West makes this point in her piece "It's Hard Enough to Be a Fat Kid without the Government Telling You You're an Epidemic." Recounting her own struggles with growing up as a fat kid, West says she can't even imagine what it must be like for fat children today, who see "bodies that look like [theirs] with their heads chopped off" regularly featured in news stories and in commercials such as those from Blue Cross and Blue Shield of Minnesota. In short, she says, these commercials and similar representations send the message that fat children are a "'problem' that needs to be 'fixed.'" Researchers who study how media representations affect children agree that youngsters pay close attention to how children who look like them are represented in media and that seeing negative portrayals affects not only their understandings of themselves but also how they imagine others must see them, all of which makes it nearly impossible for them to ignore the messages: "If children believe that others (e.g., peers, family) use such messages to evaluate them . . . children cannot simply ignore mass media messages as a comparative referent."[17]

Also writing about the ways the commercials trade in shame, Lindsey Abrams notes in her piece for the *Atlantic* that the Minnesota campaign bears a striking resemblance to Georgia's Strong4Life campaign. Abrams interviewed

Marc Manley, who worked on the Blue Cross and Blue Shield of Minnesota campaign, and he told her that one of the reasons fat adults and children were chosen was precisely so people could "recognize themselves in the commercials in order to effect what he hopes will be an 'aha' moment."[18] West wonders, however, about what kind of aha moment the Minnesota-based campaign is supposed to elicit. Writing about the commercial featuring the little girl and her mother, she notes that the contents of the mother's and daughter's shopping baskets include ice cream, sugary cereals, and something called "pizza poppers." Of the moment when the mother notices the contents of her daughter's basket, West sarcastically writes, "Then the mom turns around and looks at the child and is like, "Holy shit, MY GROSS CHILD IS FAT BECAUSE OF PIZZA POPPERS!!!"[19] The mother's realization isn't only about her own behavior; it is also a realization about her *child* being a problem. Regardless of *why* the child is a problem, the little girl in the commercial is still portrayed as troubling—even as dangerous to others—a message that's telegraphed again at the close of the commercial when, under the Blue Cross and Blue Shield of Minnesota logo, the following appears: "Obesity affects us all."

In a National Public Radio story about the Minnesota ads, Rebecca Puhl, whose work on public health advertising about obesity is considered a touchstone of sorts, argues that shame doesn't make people want to change and that being made to feel shameful actually causes people to have "lower intentions to improve their health behaviors."[20] In other words, shaming tactics make people care so little that they don't even want to bother trying. Perhaps this is why shame isn't used as a tactic for treating other conditions—even those that may also be, at least partially, under an individual's control. Apparently, the individual isn't expected to have an aha moment caused by a shameful realization. Writing in the *Yale Law Journal*, Lucy Wang points out: "For no other chronic illness do we encourage discrimination as an incentive. There are no campaigns, for example, to stigmatize people with heart disease or high cholesterol. Heart disease is the number one killer in the United States. As with obesity, personal choice plays a role in prevention and management of heart disease. Unhealthy lifestyles are indeed a serious problem, but not one unique to obesity."[21] Even though I think personal choice may not always play a role in obesity (many people are still what our society would call fat after every attempt has been made to lose weight), Wang's point here—that shame isn't used as an incentive in the cases of other supposedly preventable conditions with high mortality rates—still stands.

The use of shaming tactics where obesity is concerned likely occurs because obesity not only is seen as a preventable condition but also is understood to be a moral issue in ways conditions such as high cholesterol and heart disease are not. Other health campaigns that target entirely voluntary behaviors, such as smoking, often do so in ways that may shock or horrify, but they don't shame. At the same time Blue Cross and Blue Shield of Minnesota was running commercials about obese parents and children, another Minnesota-based organization called Still a Problem was running a public awareness campaign about underage smoking. In one commercial, two teens buy tickets for a roller coaster, only to find themselves trapped on the "ride of smoking" by a cowboy who is running the coaster.[22] As the cowboy, who bears a striking resemblance to the Marlboro man, puts the ride in motion, the teens begin screaming that they want off, but he pays them no mind. When the roller coaster completes its first cycle, the miracle of television presents viewers with the teens' once-fresh faces now haggard and aged, as a voice-over explains the health consequences of a lifetime of smoking. The cowboy looks at their drawn and gaunt faces and sends them on another cycle of the roller coaster. Adults are also implicated in this commercial, but the children seem blameless. The ad suggests that advertising (the Marlboro man) forces adolescents into the cycle in the first place, and because the teens are locked on the roller coaster and unable to free themselves, they apparently have no personal responsibility for smoking. Ultimately, it's a fairly sympathetic portrayal of teens who become addicted to cigarettes—even though every one of the teens must have chosen to smoke that first cigarette.

The reference to the Marlboro man in the commercial is telling in the sense that his presence incriminates advertising, a connection rarely made where obesity and food advertising are concerned, at least overtly in public health campaigns. Food advertising, especially if aimed explicitly at children, has been harshly criticized by Kelly Brownell, who runs Yale's Rudd Center for Food Policy and Obesity. Brownell doesn't mince words when he calls food advertising that targets children "pervasive, pernicious, and predatory."[23] A search in any academic database for "advertising effects on children" yields results almost exclusively about food advertising, with almost all of that research showing that such advertising is one of the most significant influences on the food choices made by children and teens.[24] The American Psychological Association reports food advertising operates both swiftly and powerfully in the lives of children: "Product preference has been shown to occur with as little as a single commercial exposure and to strengthen with repeated exposures."[25] According to Mary Story and Simone French, given that most children will see between 20,000 and 40,000 ads per year and that on any given Saturday morning, 11 of 19 ads shown will be for packaged foods, repeated exposure is nearly guaranteed.[26] Even children who might not watch television have little chance of avoiding food advertising because so many companies now market on multiple fronts, including at schools. In addition to directly advertising in schools via soda machines, companies also provide schools with free merchandise, such as textbook covers and bookmarks, that feature their products and logos. Some companies purchase space on school athletic wear, and others manufacture educational materials, such as the Oreo counting book.[27] If children manage to avoid the branding at school, there are other ways to capture their attention. As Story and French point out, even children's clothing has become a way to expose kids to logos and hopefully inspire brand loyalty, with Target producing "loungewear based on iconic cereal brands like Trix and Lucky Charms."[28]

Criticizing advertising has also become part and parcel of what are considered to be more just, true, and sympathetic explanations of the obesity epidemic, with many liberals explaining that parents simply can't compete with advertisers for their children's attention the way Trix the Rabbit™ can. The Berkeley Media Studies Group reports that in 2005, more than $12 million were spent on advertising that targeted children, with the bulk of that being for "packaged snack foods, fast foods, and sweets."[29] According to the American Heart Association, which has spoken out against advertising that targets children, Saturday morning ads for fruits and vegetables are nonexistent.[30] These agencies directly tie advertising to the childhood obesity epidemic, yet there is shockingly little movement to curtail the advertising or even directly implicate it in mainstream messages that are part of campaigns against obesity.

If people really believe that obesity is caused by eating too many calories and/or certain kinds of foods, if people are so convinced that food advertising for sodas, sugary cereals, and fast food preys on children and exerts a great influence over their food choices, and if people really think that childhood obesity is one of the greatest crises—if not *the* great crisis—facing the United States, then why *isn't* advertising targeted? Why aren't there public health campaigns that make it less than cool to be swayed by advertising, in the same way public health campaigns sought to make it less than cool to always give in to peer pressure? The answer, it seems, is twofold—because changing the food system, including advertising, seems too overwhelming a task and because our society takes a certain pleasure in "fat hating." Part of that fat hating seems inherently tied to fat shaming. Health campaigns such as the one launched by Blue Cross and Blue Shield of Minnesota use what West describes as "plan A," which is to punish *people* rather than criticize America's food system.[31] I would argue that even accounts of the obesity epidemic that acknowledge problems with the food system still ultimately blame individuals and suggest that they should overcome all obstacles to being thin or even that they are their own obstacles to thinness.

Even as the food system, in which the same company that produces Frosted Flakes with a Tony the Tiger™ logo also produces a line of Special K weight-loss products, remains safe, fat boys are portrayed as actually being invested in overeating by the Blue Cross and Blue Shield commercial. West posits that the portrayal of two boys bragging about whose father can eat the most and boasting about their future eating goals actually "invents" a problem where none exists, rather than addressing real public health issues such as the food system.[32] Even conceding that children like to take part in one-upmanship or that boys may be socialized to be competitive, it's hard to imagine that there are so many boys in today's world whose main life goal is to eat as much as possible that a public health campaign is warranted. This particular ad also implies that these boys are heavy because they made a concerted effort to be so, which seems especially unhelpful given that this is already a popular stereotype about fat people.

The most innocuous way of viewing this situation may be to see that obesity functions as a stand-in for the real problem of a lack of nutritious food, a problem that may affect *any* child regardless of weight. Brownell, who has arguably been one of the most visible figures in the war on obesity, has as much as admitted that the fundamental problem he sees isn't necessarily obesity. At a recent conference, sociologist Abigail Saguy "asked Brownell directly why he persisted in talking of 'obesity,' rather than, say, 'nutrition.' He responded that it was the only way to compete for scant public attention. He did not believe that an epidemic of junk food could attract as much notice."[33] In other words, Brownell admits that a game of bait and switch is being played with the public. The panic about obesity among children is, in this case, a useful shill for getting attention because "nutrition" just doesn't inspire people to act.

An important question, however, is how children will act in such a climate. Regardless of both campaigns' desires to concentrate on getting adults to recognize the problem of obesity and to understand their own behaviors as troublesome, it is likely that children will see themselves as damaged. In spite of the controversy surrounding the Strong4Life ads and their eventual disappearance from billboards,[34] Maya and her mother, Stormy, have remained some of the most vocal supporters of that campaign and have spoken openly about their choice to participate in it. Let me be clear that I don't want to demonize Maya Joi, as she's known on her blog, or Stormy. Parents and adolescents often choose to participate in problematic campaigns, dieting—or engaging in any number of activities or behaviors related to weight loss—because there's a great deal of pressure to do so. My aim here isn't to suggest that Maya or her mother should be blamed or shunned in any way but rather to examine how the campaign and what is known about their perspective on weight and bodies highlights a particular cultural moment and ways in which many parents and adolescents find themselves struggling.

Maya's mother was the first to see the announcement that the campaign was looking for adolescents to participate in a series of ads, and she asked Maya if she'd like to be featured in the program. When questioned in an interview about how she felt on being asked to participate, Maya responded, "I was a little bit hesitant but then when I thought about it, I was like well it'll be a good message to other kids like me. . . . What's the message? Being overweight is a problem, but you're not the only one dealing with it."[35] Given such statements and others she has made in different venues,[36] Maya seems to have consented to the use of her image, in the strictest sense, and to have had her own specific goal for appearing in the campaign. Yet, I'm left wondering if she fully understood the context of looking and staring that scholars such as Elkins and Garland-Thomson point out or what it means for her body to serve as a warning sign to others.

I also wonder how Maya's understanding of her weight may be influenced by the idea that she is primarily or even solely responsible for the size of her body. Although much of the discussion about childhood obesity centers on parental responsibility for acknowledging and treating children's weights, youngsters seem to be increasingly expected to "do something" about their weight and lauded for it when they do. For a while, Maya Joi maintained a blog where she posted results of her weigh-ins and talked about her struggles with her weight. The photo on her blog's home page was of Maya smiling and happy, a stark contrast to the image featured in the Strong4Life ad, which served as the blog's background.[37] Although the blog now appears to be inactive, what Maya posted illustrated her understanding of and thinking about her weight, her body, and people's responses to her postings. Almost as if she was at a twelve-step meeting, she introduced herself to her audience by writing, "Hi! I am Maya Joi, and I acknowledge that I am obese. Even though I want tot [sic] change it, I am not ashamed of my body. I have great self-asteem [sic]; sometimes, I have a little too much."[38]

It's difficult to fathom that the girl with too much self-esteem is the same girl who later posted this message: "The one thing I will admit is I had a *piece* of graham cracker. I feel guilty. But I'm gonna exercise so much tonight."[39] Maya's final post on the blog was a justification of her daily weigh-ins and going on a juice program, which she refused to call a diet and instead called a "reboot," echoing the language of the recent documentary *Fat, Sick, and Nearly Dead*.[40] After she apparently received some feedback from concerned readers about her focus on weight, she wrote, "I am not really even worried about my weight. Its [*sic*] way more about my health."[41]

Maya seems to think being healthy means being worried about one piece of a graham cracker and having too much self-esteem, even though many experts would consider worrying over a piece of a graham cracker evidence of disordered eating and would wish that teenage girls had more self-esteem. Maya has taken the onus, however, for her weight, indicating that she sees her eating and her attitude as flawed and warranting public confession.

In presenting her blog to readers, Maya clearly depicted her obesity not as a social problem resulting from a lack of access or education or any other sort of systemic inequity but rather as a personal problem. Philosopher and Disability Studies scholar Susan Wendell argues that disability, which is also often caused or heightened by social problems such as poverty or war, is similarly perceived as the personal problem of the individual. She writes, "The attitude that disability is a personal problem is manifested when people with disabilities are expected to overcome obstacles to their participation in activities by their own extraordinary efforts."[42] Wendell points out that in current American society, people often recognize that there may be social factors that lead to disabilities and that social decisions are made about how buildings will be constructed and for what kinds of bodies, for example; however, she also maintains that, for the most part, disabled people are expected to overcome these obstacles on their own. At most, disability is seen as a family matter. In other words, either the woman who uses a wheelchair or her family is supposed to figure out how to get her into a building without ramps. This is not so different from the situation facing fat children or the mothers of fat children who are expected— against all odds and in the face of all other obstacles—to make their children thin.

Maya is young girl of color, meaning she's from a population that the majority of experts would suggest is most at risk for obesity due to systemic factors, yet she appears to have internalized the message that she is responsible for her weight. And her focus on having eaten a piece of graham cracker is worrisome, especially in light of scholarship about eating disorders and marginalized women. For many years, eating disorders were thought of as a category of diseases that afflicted economically privileged white women, with the idea being that only women who were obsessed with their looks and sufficiently well-off to be able to refuse food or to binge and then purge food could suffer from eating disorders. I can't help but think, as well, that the idea that women of color don't experience eating disorders is fueled, in part, by the notion that some communities of color—the African American community in particular—are always more tolerant of larger bodies.

Becky W. Thompson's publication of her monograph *A Hunger So Wide and So Deep* marked the opening of a discussion about marginalized women and their concerns about fatness and experiences with eating disorders. Thompson asserts that eating disorders among women are not necessarily the result of frivolous concerns about appearance but can instead be complex reactions to any number of circumstances in which women may feel powerless. In short, her ethnographic work on eating disorders among marginalized women shows that these behaviors are often used as coping mechanisms and are the result of living with the stress caused by racism, heterosexism, classism, and sexual abuse.[43] In this way, Thompson's work opened new avenues for understanding eating disorders as related to traumas and as coping mechanisms, rather than only being about problems with body image caused by beauty ideals.

Yet, beauty ideals remain important in Thompson's framework, especially for young girls and women who may fall outside the traditional Western beauty ideal of being thin with long blond hair, pale skin, and blue eyes. Thompson recounts her work with one African American woman, called Joselyn, whose grandmother used to tease her about her dark skin and her weight, both of which her grandmother saw as hindrances to upward mobility in a society that valued whiteness and thinness. According to Thompson, Joselyn "began to think that although she could not change her skin color, she could at least try to be thin."[44] In this way, the development of an eating disorder became a reaction to white privilege and almost utilitarian in nature rather than something related to being beautiful for beauty's sake.

Although Thompson doesn't address the ways that living with a disabled body in a society that values able-bodiedness may give rise to eating disorders, she and Wendell seem to share a similar understanding of how what are seen as physical imperfections may more profoundly affect women's status. Of visible physical disabilities among women, Wendell observes: "'Physical imperfection' is more likely to be thought to 'spoil' a woman than a man by rendering her unattractive in a culture where her physical appearance is a large component of a woman's value."[45] In her memoir, *Poster Child,* Emily Rapp writes about her life as a person with proximal focal femoral deficiency, a congenital condition that led her parents to decide to have her left leg amputated at the age of four. The condition also led Rapp to become a poster child for the March of Dimes at the age of six. She seems well aware of how her missing leg "spoils" her and writes at length about developing an eating disorder because she believed she needed to compensate for being spoiled via her disability. In one of many moments in her memoir when she openly discusses her struggles with her embodiment and eating and exercise, she reveals, "I promised myself that I would make the one leg I had perfect. I would contain my body and control it. I would punish it for not being the way I desperately wanted it to be. I felt strangely empowered."[46] Rapp's experience is strikingly similar to Joselyn's, as they both have embodiments that fall outside mainstream definitions of beauty.

Given the Western beauty ideal of white skin, blue eyes, and blond hair, it seems possible that a young woman of color such as Maya may also feel the pressure to control her body size because the cultural narrative holds that weight can be controlled, whereas another "imperfection," such as race or disability, cannot. Like Rapp and Joselyn, Maya may try to control the one thing she feels she can—her weight—by feeling terrible about eating a piece of graham cracker and then working hard to exercise it away. I worry about Maya being at risk, and I also worry about other young women of color who are targeted by campaigns such as Strong4Life—young women who are considered at risk for obesity but who may not be understood to also be at risk for eating disorders because of the prevailing notion that such disorders affect only white women. For instance, in his book *Fat Land*, Greg Critser claims that "a few more Black Kate Mosses wouldn't be a bad thing" because he believes African American women are missing out on the stigma that keeps white women's weights lower.[47] What Critser fails to understand, however, is that young African American women may already be at risk of developing eating disorders because of the stress of living in a society that privileges whiteness.

MAKING MONEY FROM SHAME

Nike's recent commercial featuring Nathan Sorrell, a boy from London, Ohio, and the company's slogan "Just Do It" constitute another example of a campaign that centers on personal responsibility. In this particular case, the company actually stands to further its brand and make money from the shame of a child. Nike sought applicants from many different US towns named London before choosing Nathan, who is reported to be 5'3" tall and 200 pounds.[48] Nike's ad, which ran during the 2012 London Summer Olympics, featured Nathan, whom many would consider a fat boy, running in a pair of Nike athletic shoes and a sweat-drenched shirt (Figure 3.3). Nathan never spoke, but Nike spoke for him: "Greatness. It's just something we made up. Somehow we've come to believe that greatness is a gift reserved for a chosen few, for prodigies,

Figure 3.3: Still taken from Nike's advertisement featuring Nathan Sorrell

for superstars, and the rest of us can only stand by watching. You can forget that. Greatness is not some rare DNA strand, not some precious thing. Greatness is no more unique to us than breathing. We're all capable of it. All of us."[49]

Though many people found the ad inspirational (it was an instant web hit and reposted liberally),[50] the story behind it and behind Nathan was anything but inspirational. The boy talked openly about vomiting during the filming of the commercial, characterizing the director as "lenient" for giving him time to recover after being sick.[51] The expectation that any child can put on a pair of shoes and start running and continue to run—to the point of vomiting—and that doing so is a sign of "greatness" indicates an investment in children taking individual responsibility for their weight. Of course, youngsters should learn responsibility and understand that having goals and commitments is admirable, but those goals and commitments need to be reasonable and healthy.

Nathan's compensation hasn't been disclosed, but Nike has said that if he and his mother are successful in losing weight (not getting healthy but losing weight), they'll return for a follow-up ad.[52] Given that the median income in London, Ohio, is a bit over $39,000 and the per capita income is just under $21,000,[53] the appeal of Nike returning might be as driven by finances as by anything else. As with Maya Joi and her mother, Stormy, I don't mean to vilify Nathan or his mother, Monica; rather, I want to point out that financial and cultural pressures may be a part of the decision to participate in such ads and to lose weight. At the very least, the fact that a local newspaper reported during the filming of the commercial that Nathan was running behind a Porsche outfitted with a camera suggests who had the financial power in the scenario.[54] Yet, many people commenting about the ad seem focused only on its ability to inspire. When Nathan and his mother appeared on the *Today Show* the day after the London Olympics ended, they were accompanied by Donny Deutsch, the advertising guru and regular *Today Show* commentator, who literally applauded both Nike and Nathan. Clapping vigorously, Deutsch said he was thrilled with the possibility that the ad would inspire even one child to get up off the couch and go out and "get healthy."[55]

Lindy West, whose *Jezebel* blog raised vital questions about the ad and its use of Nathan, was criticized and accused of holding children like him back, as were others who took issue with the commercial. But as West points out, the commercial plays on the conventional story that being thin always means working hard and that being fat necessarily means being lazy. Why else would it be remarkable or "great" that Nathan is running? The assumption that fat people don't run is what drives the commercial. In other words, Nike is selling shoes by also selling a particularly popular and convenient story about fat people. Additionally, West notes that it may be physically impossible for some fat people to run, and—like it or not—this is true. It's also true for thin people with knee problems. Yet, acknowledging that some people just may not be able to run doesn't fit conveniently with the moralized story that willpower overcomes everything, nor does it fit with the stereotype that all fat people lack willpower. West also argues that the ad makes it clear that for a fat person to be great, he or she must become thinner, adding that she "can't imagine seeing a commercial with some big fat dude, like, doing some awesome science with the caption 'Find Your Greatness.' Fat people are just fat people, and the implication is that 'greatness' for this kid would be to become a thinner kid."[56]

Even after taking into account the fact that Nike's investment is in selling shoes and promoting its products as ones that lead to athleticism rather than great scientific discoveries, it is clear that the narrative the ad delivers carefully constructs greatness as something achieved through punishing physical work that should result in one becoming thinner. There are implications both for children who see the ad and for Nathan as an individual. Speaking specifically of Nathan, West asks her readers to consider that he is a middle schooler who may now be feeling pressure—from a nation—to lose weight. A staff writer at BuzzFeed.com dared to point out that the Nike ad was making money off a child who may have needed to take exercise more slowly, and then that writer was lambasted for suggesting the ad wasn't, in fact, so great. That writer went on to say that portraying Nathan in this way might also risk inducing other fat people to engage in unhealthy behaviors by implying that to be great, everyone who starts an exercise program should go from zero to sixty in one day and land in a ditch vomiting.[57] The comments on the story quickly devolved into claims that the article was "bullshit" and that the staff writer didn't understand that people had to "get up off their ass" to be great. Several especially misguided individuals accused the staff writer of "limiting" Nathan,[58] apparently believing that the writer thought no fat person could run rather than understanding that the issue was the commercial's implication that the *only* way a fat child could be great was to run.

The idea that thinness is equated with or necessary for greatness echoes Rapp's experience with believing that beauty is a necessary quality for possessing other admirable traits. She writes of her quest for beauty: "I had just turned sixteen, and what I wanted more than anything else in life was to be beautiful. I didn't care about being smart, successful, or good. In fact, I believed that beauty was the prerequisite for achieving any of these other qualities."[59] Rapp's belief that being smart, successful, or good requires being beautiful mirrors American culture's belief that thinness is also required for being smart, successful, or good, which is not surprising given how closely tied beauty and thinness are in this culture. What is surprising, however, is that some people seem unable to see how positing thinness as a prerequisite to or stand-in for greatness can be problematic. For example, during his *Today Show* appearance, Donny Deutsch also had some unkind words for critics of the Nike ad, saying they should be ashamed and that to dislike the ad was "discriminatory." In defense of Nike, Deutsch said that the company had represented all sorts of different people in its ads as a step toward inclusivity. I'm sure many people, including myself, would be pleased to see the diversity of fat people better represented. But *how* people are included matters; mere inclusion doesn't guarantee that people are justly presented or presented in ways that don't reify stereotypes.

Besides, Nathan is a child, a child who has now said that because people have criticized the ad, he wants to "do even more."[60] His pledge to do even more makes me worry for Nathan and for others who see him as a role model. I'm not sure what doing more means, but this child already worked himself into vomiting in a ditch. How much more must he do in order to satisfy himself and meet what he considers to be the challenge from people who have questioned the ethics of the ad, people he refers to as "haters."[61] There's no doubt that getting thin, regardless of how a person accomplishes it, almost always elicits a showering of praise, which is often unintended encouragement of what may be very unhealthy behaviors. In a quest to perfect what she saw as her damaged body, Rapp developed an eating and exercise disorder, and she reflects on how people responded to her body when she became ultrathin:

"I have never received as many compliments about my appearance as when I stopped menstruating and became monstrously thin. 'You look great!' 'Look at your cheekbones!' 'How did your ass get so small?' And this was the best one: 'You have the perfect body.'"[62]

There's also the question of how other children and parents will respond to Nathan's running and his pledge to do more. Wendell argues that the public often holds up a few disabled people as examples of what all disabled people ought to do or be able to do. She writes, "The public adoration of a few disabled heroes who are believed to have 'overcome their handicaps' against great odds both demonstrates and contributes to this expectation."[63] Given that being fat is a stigmatized identity, those who are weight-loss heroes are also held up as exceptional (think Jared Fogle and the Subway chain)—regardless of their ability status. People who have lost weight are constructed as individuals who have managed something exceptional—yet something others should also be able to accomplish—and they are used as litmus tests for everyone else. In this case, the standard of greatness for fat children becomes whether they're willing or able to run, and they may put this pressure on themselves or be under this pressure from other people in their lives. Nathan's mother, Monica, also commented during the *Today Show* interview that it was "something else to see your son on tv" and that she was "excited and wowed that Nike picked Nathan."[64] It seems reasonable that Nathan would also feel some pressure to continue to make his mom proud by running and/or losing weight. Facing the possibility of both public and family pressure, children such as Maya and Nathan, who are used in very visible campaigns, may be shouldering a heavy burden in terms of proving to themselves and others that they're doing something about their weight. Moreover, they are likely to become standard-bearers for other fat children.

If providing parents with an aha moment so they'll also take action about their child's weight (or their own weight) is one of the primary aims of such ads—whether they're part of a public health campaign or a commercial endeavor—then the campaigns appear to have worked for Maya Joi's mother, Stormy Bradley. Stormy maintains several blogs and a Facebook page that seem to be devoted to tracking her weight-loss and fitness goals, under the name "Big Butt Theory." The Facebook page is filled with statements in which Stormy confesses her shortcomings and continues to set new goals. On June 1, 2012, she posted, "Ate good today. Should've drank [*sic*] more water. Gonna hit [*sic*] get exercise in 2morrow" and "June 1st weigh 235. Not surprised but more importantly not giving up on my goal to be healthy."[65] She also allows the public to comment on and even help determine her goals and exercise routine, posting a meme on July 1, 2012, saying that for every new "like" she received on that particular meme, she would do two minutes of cardio the following Saturday.[66]

In many ways, the posts she makes on Facebook and those that her daughter, Maya, made on her blog are nearly interchangeable; at the very least, they share strikingly similar themes. In a piece on the website FierceFreethinkingFatties .com, a writer known as atchka posts thoughtfully about the "like mother like daughter" relationship that can so clearly be seen through a comparison of Maya's and Stormy's public writings. According to atchka, Maya and Stormy are caught up in a culture that conflates thinness with healthiness, a culture atchka calls WBHC (weight-based health culture). As atchka sympathetically writes, "I imagine that Stormy thought she was doing her daughter a favor by involving her in Strong4Life, and indeed, she sees their participation as being part of the 'solution' for childhood obesity."[67] I have no doubt that atchka is right.

There's good reason to worry over what it means for children and parents to consent to appearing in such campaigns or for parents to consent on behalf of their children, even with the best of intentions. When I initially contacted Children's Healthcare of Atlanta to ask about including the Stong4Life ads in this book, I was told that the only one that could be offered to me, due to parental consent issues, was the ad featuring Maya. Later, I was told that Children's Healthcare of Atlanta was no longer considering any requests to reprint the ads that year.[68] To be honest, I'm not sure if the parents simply didn't want to grant rights and permission to the ads featuring their children for the purposes of my work (perhaps because in follow-up e-mails, I'd told the representative from Children's Healthcare that I was a Fat Studies scholar and planned to be critical of the ads) or if the parents of the other children featured asked that—after the ads were pulled—their children's images no longer be used in *any* way. Regardless, parents consented to have their children featured in these ads, and they seem to be the ones who continue to provide or withhold consent. When asked if he'd ever thought about the negative attention that might come from participating in the Nike ad, Nathan said that he applied to be in the ad because he thought it would be "cool" and that he didn't anticipate the criticisms. His mother said they had both learned a lot through the process.[69]

It may also be that many of the parents felt sheepish after there was so much fallout from the Strong4Life billboards in particular. According to Emma Gray, several national associations that work with children and adults who suffer from eating disorders voiced opposition to the Strong4Life campaign; the National Association of Anorexia Nervosa, the Binge Eating Disorder Association, and the National Eating Disorder Association all issued statements condemning the billboards.[70] Concerns about the campaign actually ran so deep that an organization with alternative ads was created. Ragen Chastain's Support All Kids campaign launched a counterinitiative in Georgia by creating billboards that featured the message that all kids can benefit from nutritious food and movement—regardless of body size—and lines such as "WARNING: Shame Is Bad for Your Health"[71] that reworked the Strong4Life slogans. The Support All Kids founders and supporters saw the Strong4Life campaign as a kind of weight bullying, something they were deeply concerned about and addressed directly with a billboard that read "Please Stop Weight Bullies . . . Health Is for *Every* Body."

Those working with Strong4Life would surely make the argument that the billboards targeted obesity and not obese people, making the campaign distinctly different from weight-based bullying. But lawyer and journalist Paul Campos provides a poignant response to such claims. Campos contends that claiming such ads target obesity but not people who are obese is like saying that conversion therapy targets homosexuality but not people who are homosexual.[72] Most people recognize that it's impossible to make such a claim stick; it's *people* who identify as homosexual who are subjected to conversion therapy to make them straight, and it's fat *people,* including children, who are the subjects of antiobesity campaigns to make them thin.

TEASING IT OUT

Teasing is such a part of the discussion about childhood obesity that it's virtually impossible to find a source that doesn't address this topic. We've certainly learned that teasing hurts children. If nothing else, the tragic school shootings in recent history have shown that bullying is often cited as one of the reasons why shooters seek revenge.[73] Many schools have now adopted antibullying policies and practices meant to make the schools more welcoming environments for all students. In light of such concerns and the omnipresent discussion of teasing in conversations about childhood obesity, it seems not only fair but also important to question how ad campaigns that feature fat children as "problems" may influence what is already a culture of teasing that involves both parents and other children.

Teasing, of course, results from an obesity bias—that is, "the tendency to negatively judge an overweight or obese individual based on assumed and/ or false character traits."[74] This obesity bias can take various forms, including overt comments directed at a specific individual, but it can also involve hurtful comments about obese people in general or even comments that are meant to be helpful.[75] In other words, it's not just about being called fat, for a spectrum of behaviors and situations indicate obesity bias. Studies find that because of society's obesity bias, fat children tend to be seen as less likable than thinner children: "Obese youth are often attributed with negative characteristics such as being mean, lazy, unattractive, less intelligent, and less socially skilled."[76] According to researcher P. Warschburger, children begin to express this bias much earlier in life than many people would think, with children between three and five years old already showing a bias against chubbier silhouettes.[77] In explaining why some youngsters express this bias so early, researchers posit this is, in part, "because children are heavily reliant on physical cues in their social interactions" and "are likely influenced by stereotypes associated with physical cues."[78]

Weight-based teasing in school environments—where children are apt to spend the majority of their day and have more access to other children—appears to be a regular occurrence. In one school study that examined weight-based teasing in 4,746 participants, 43.2 percent of girls reported being teased by peers about their weight and 42.9 percent of boys reported weight-based teasing.[79] One reason researchers have been so interested in studying teasing is that being targeted appears to be much more than momentarily hurtful. That old adage about sticks and stones may not prove true: names also seem to hurt. Children who are teased by peers about their weight are five times as likely to engage in at least one "unhealthy weight control behavior," which may include bingeing and purging, overexercising, or extreme dieting.[80] Furthermore, "teasing in pre-adolescence and early adolescence is associated with weight gain in late adolescence and adulthood."[81] In their study of the efficacy of school-based weight interventions, P. B. Rukavina and W. Li argue that the weight gain may occur because teasing sets children on a path of unhealthy eating behaviors that are associated with weight gain, and they cite one five-year study of teasing's influence on eating that suggests boys who are frequently teased about their weight become binge eaters and that girls become frequent dieters.[82]

In spite of the perception that childhood obesity is now the statistical norm in American society, scholars point out that the prevalence of obesity hasn't decreased the stigma associated with it.[83] Researcher Nicole Taylor believes that at least among children, the need to distance oneself from "everyday fatness," the sort of fatness associated with negative stereotypes such as laziness, may be at play when children use teasing to distance themselves from their fat(ter) peers.[84] Taylor discusses what researchers often call "direct teasing" as a particular means of children putting distance between themselves and fat classmates—regardless of the body size of the child doing the teasing. Direct teasing is just what its name implies: a concentrated effort to target a specific child about his or her weight.[85] And it seems to sometimes reflect children's internalization of fatphobic or fat-shaming attitudes.

As Taylor contends, all children may feel the need to distance themselves from "everyday fatness" because they understand the stigma associated with being heavy and being a person who isn't trying to lose weight. She asserts that fatness creates a special kind of need for distancing because all bodies contain fat, which can make the need for the boundaries between those who are okay and those who are not okay more intense and make the establishment of those boundaries especially difficult. In current American society, *fat* can mean anything from someone who is so large that he or she is no longer ambulatory to a thigh that jiggles. *Fat* is a slippery term. Taylor asserts that "because the boundary between thin and fat is so insecure, the adolescents in [my] study had to continually negotiate body fat norms, which they largely did through direct and indirect teasing." Further, she says, the negotiation of these norms represents a kind of "borderwork."[86]

The concept of borderwork originated in Fredrik Barth's work with racial groups and was then borrowed by sociologist Barrie Thorne for her germinal book *Gender Play: Girls and Boys in School*. Thorne describes borderwork related to gender as functioning in this way among children:

> When gender boundaries are activated, the loose aggregation of "boys and girls" consolidates into "the boys" and "the girls" as separate and reified groups. In the process, categories of identity that on other occasions have minimal relevance for interaction become the basis of separate collectivities. Other social definitions get squeezed out by heightened awareness of gender as a dichotomy and of "the girls" and "the boys" as opposite and even antagonistic sides.[87]

Thorne observes the establishment of these borders, as did Taylor, as needing to be continually reestablished or replayed by the children because they are fluid and contextual rather than fixed.

It's fair to argue that in contemporary American society, "the fat" and "the thin" are also important social categories that organize the culture in significant ways and may often do so alongside categories such as gender. Campaigns that heighten youth's awareness of "the fat" and "the thin" categories as social organizing tools likely increase the amount of borderwork that occurs. I would also argue that the fact that the children featured in these ads are, as I've already noted, quite average looking (that is, they're not supersize but rather just fat children[88]) further intensifies the need to reinforce those borders between fat and thin via teasing. Taylor's idea about children trying to distance themselves from everyday fatness, or *ordinary* fatness, also proves useful for understanding both Maya's and Nathan's desire to make themselves appear *extraordinary* by their feats of dieting, exercise, and even confession. In these ways, they may gain a higher social status or at least feel better about themselves because the assumption is that they, unlike others, are actually doing something about their weight. In the same way that Wendell describes the public admiring disabled people who seem "superhumanly heroic"[89] because they appear to overcome all odds, as Rapp does when she becomes a ski and diving champion with only one leg, Maya and Nathan seem to be striving for the sort of acceptance Rapp's memoir suggests she was given because of her efforts. Much of the response to Nathan, at least, indicates he's gaining similar acceptance.

For Rapp, being a poster child for a campaign that sought both to prevent "defects" like hers and to present poster children as wonderful and exceptional left her with mixed feelings about her embodiment and her role in the world. It's easy to imagine that the Strong4Life campaign that features Maya or the Nike commercial featuring Nathan might produce the same confusion for these young people. Writing on how she felt about what it might mean to be an ordinary person with a disability, Rapp says, "I did not want to be abnormal or *less than* because of my grievous, irrevocable physical flaw, so I had to be abnormally fantastic in order to compensate. The paradox: Being extraordinary was the only way to be ordinary."[90] Only by her ability to stand out as a worthwhile person with a disability, a person so extraordinary she could inspire others, did Rapp find herself able to feel "normal." At one point, she says that she needed to prove that she wasn't a "cripple,"[91] in the sense that she wasn't a poor, pitiable disabled person who was unable to participate in activities such as diving or skiing. Similarly, Nathan and Maya seem to feel that they must convince others they are not "fat" in the sense that they aren't lazy or pitiable but rather are actively trying to be thin.

Rapp describes her attempts to be inspiring as ultimately being attempts to "compensate" for her embodiment.[92] I believe the same can be argued for Maya and Nathan. What seemed to inspire so many people about Nathan's story was that he was doing something extraordinary by running. Similarly, Maya's weigh-ins and her efforts to control her weight may be seen as extraordinary. Of course, there's nothing inherently special about running or monitoring one's food, but because the children who are engaging in those activities have a physical difference from what is considered the norm or ideal, they may be seen as extraordinary. In the case of fatness, it's a physical difference that comes with a plethora of representations that imply fat people neither run nor monitor their food. Discussing how children come to develop their sense of self, Nicole Martins and Kristen Harrison argue that "efforts to maintain or bolster one's self-concept are dependent on the types of comparisons that are made available."[93] Ironically enough, performances of extraordinary feats are performances that mediate physical difference in ways that shift those performing them closer to the category of normal or ordinary. In other words, children stand a better chance of fitting in by making it clear that their physical differences don't make them *different* in terms of their values and behaviors. They really want to be thin like the rest of us.

One reason why children take up narratives about weight that foreground personal responsibility is that other available accounts, such as medicalized accounts, may inspire pity or suggest that they're damaged. Perhaps because of the importance of borderwork in fat children's lives, it appears that medicalized accounts can actually further stigmatize them. Rukavina and Li argue that medical explanations for obesity, which seem more palatable to some people, may actually make children see obese individuals as "non normal."[94] In another study focused on weight-based teasing among children, the authors found that medical explanations for obesity tended to highlight differences, especially when such explanations were provided to older children.[95] Because these researchers ultimately concluded that educating children about the medical causes of obesity is potentially more harmful, they suggest alternative strategies. Rukavina and Li propose that providing more comprehensive education that emphasizes the humanity of fat people might be more effective, such as depictions of heavy people with successful careers. In other words, they suggest the same kinds of representations that West suggests when she advocates for images of fat guys doing science. In sum, Rukavina and Li believe that children ought to be taught size acceptance rather than being taught that their peers are different from them due to a medical condition.[96] This approach might help youngsters acquire a very different understanding of the physical cues they use to help organize their world.

WHERE ARE THE ADULTS?

Some teasing, of course, is explicit and intended to be hurtful, but other teasing, especially what might be called "playful" teasing from adults, is often more implicit and actually meant to be helpful. Given that one study of schoolteachers found 50 percent of those surveyed believe obesity is caused by overeating and not exercising,[97] many adults need to be educated along with children. Doing so may be especially important because data show that both the frequency of weight-based teasing and the number of sources of weight-based teasing are positively correlated to depression among the children being teased.[98] In other words, to reduce the effects of teasing, campaigns can't only be directed at children. Many scholars contend that educating parents is especially key to improving the lives of overweight and obese children and teens,[99] with some researchers arguing that the most serious work to be done is that geared to "reducing the child's exposure to teasing in the home and at school."[100] Antibullying and antiteasing programs are so often aimed only at children that many people forget about how adults—and above all parents—may affect children's lives.

Teasing from parents may be especially harmful because children are likely more sensitive to their parents' criticism. Recently, Rebecca M. Puhl, Jamie Lee Peterson, and Joerg Luedicke published a study in *Pediatrics* noting that 64 percent of the teens they surveyed reported having faced "weight-based victimization" (WBV). Though the teens said that most of the WBV came from peers and friends, 42 percent of those surveyed reported that they were also regularly teased by adults.[101] From their findings, Puhl and her colleagues conclude that "even well-intentioned parents may inadvertently criticize or tease their overweight children in ways that are extremely damaging."[102] These scholars concede that one limitation of their study was that children were asked to self-report teasing, but I would argue that the children's perceptions of teasing are as important as the actual teasing because it's their perceptions and feelings that will most likely govern their behavior.

In a recent article from *Journal of Advanced Nursing,* the authors note that in their study of 455 participants, obese children regularly perceived parental comments as teasing, indicating that youngsters are more apt to view parental comments about their weight negatively.[103] Some researchers assert that fat children may interpret comments from parents negatively because they suffer from an "interpretation bias," which "reflects a tendency to interpret situations in a personally relevant and negative way."[104] In part because fat children live in a culture where they're told that being fat is a bad thing, they come to view ambiguous comments through that lens. The more children are encouraged to see their weight as a problem, the more they may see it as the cause of *all* of their problems.

Interestingly, frequently failing at losing weight via dieting further increases the likelihood that heavy youth will interpret situations and comments as related to their weight: "The data indicate that more frequent but unsuccessful diet attempts increase the number of negative interpretations to ambiguous situations in terms of self-esteem. Being unsuccessful in dieting may lower self-esteem in young overweight children."[105] It seems that failed attempts to control their weight also lead children to believe that their weight is their biggest problem. And there's a good chance their dieting attempts will be unsuccessful. As Campos reasons in a piece about the Strong4Life campaign, fat children have already been given information about food and activity—and with few results. He points to a recent metareview of antiobesity programs and their efficacy as proof that such campaigns have poor results. Out of 30,000 children who were included in the fifty-five studies examined, the average weight loss of each child was around 1 pound.[106]

Looking at how children feel about their bodies, researchers have found that youngsters, especially girls, may develop a negative self-concept when their parents focus on their weight. In their article entitled "Weight Status, Parent Reaction, and Self-Concept in Five-Year-Old Girls," Kirsten Krahnstoever Davison and Leanne Lipps Birch discuss their study of "197 5-year-old girls and their parents," a study meant to assess the girls' self-image and what, if any, correlation there was to the "parents' concern about their child's weight status and restriction of their child's access to food."[107] Davison and Birch found that "parents' concern about their child's weight status and restriction of access to food [were] associated with negative self-evaluations among girls."[108] For young girls, the need to feel thin is urgent; indeed, Janet D. Latner and Marlene B. Schwartz report that "among girls [seven to nine] the preference for thinness is so strong that even average weight is unacceptable."[109] The more concern parents express, then, the more likely children, especially girls, may be to develop negative self-images and unrealistic body ideals.

Keenly aware of the potential for problems when parents feel pressured to have a thin child, Davison and Birch conclude that "public health programs that raise parental awareness of childhood overweight without also providing constructive and blame-free alternatives for addressing child weight problems may be detrimental to children's mental health."[110] Although campaigns such as those from Strong4Life and Blue Cross and Blue Shield of Minnesota raise awareness of childhood obesity as a problem, parents would have to visit the website, at the very least, in order to find any sort of constructive help. If the need to be thin feels urgent, there is also a good chance that the restriction of food may not necessarily be undertaken with particularly deep knowledge; we know people restrict their food in all sorts of problematic ways when weight loss is the goal. We also know that even when parents try to restrict food in ways that feel subtle, doing so can have profound effects on children. Speaking of some of the tactics parents adopt that are hurtful to children, Puhl notes that even asking a kid if he or she *really* needs an extra helping of something can make the child feel bullied.[111] Given such complexities, it seems wise to carefully consider what it means for parents to put children on diets, restrict their food, or express constant concern over their weight; it also seems wise to take a step back from the notion that the only way to be a good parent is to put one's child on a diet, with weight loss as the goal.

In stark contrast to portrayals of children as ticking time bombs or warning signs, the representations of fat people created by Marilyn Wann's I STAND against Weight Bullying campaign feature vibrant, active, loved, and loving fat children and adults (Figures 3.4 and 3.5). Some of the children are shown running and engaging in physical activities; others are shown smiling and hugging family members. Some adults merely stand in front of the camera and smile; others strike a dance pose.

All the images stand in stark contrast to those offered by Strong4Life billboards, whose black-and-white photographs of mournful-looking children imply that fatness is always a cause for sadness and shame. Neither the Support All Kids campaign nor Wann's campaign, which shared strategies and images as they worked to combat what they saw as the weight bullying being promoted by the Strong4Life campaign, appear to suggest there is a particular way that fat children or adults are expected to be, emphasizing a slogan shared by both these campaigns: "We Stand for Living Well and Embracing Our Differences." Speaking about campaigns that promote body shame, the Support All Kids mission statement asserts that "there is a better way. Focusing on kids' weight and making them feel ashamed of their bodies is not the answer. If we are truly interested in healthy kids, then it's time to start having real conversations about health for kids of all sizes."[112] As Rapp tells her readers, she became so obsessed with beauty that she believed attaining it was necessary in order to achieve anything else in her life. If we replace *beauty* with *thinness,* for the terms are nearly interchangeable in American culture, Rapp's reflection feels strikingly similar to how children such as Maya and Nathan feel about themselves and their futures. Neither of these children ought to feel that they have to be thin in order to have a good life. Surely, everyone can agree that we should support all children and work toward making a world where they needn't feel guilty for eating a piece of a graham cracker or feel compelled to run until they vomit in order to prove themselves great.

Figure 3.4: Sara Silverstein in an ad from the I STAND campaign. This and several other ads were posted on Fat activist websites and were also posted in Cincinnati, Ohio, bus stops from March to May 2012 as part of I STAND's mission to provide alternative representations of fat children and their families. The bus stop campaign was initiated by Fat activist Ragen Chastain and helped along by fellow Fat activist Marilyn Wann. Photo credit, Laura Chenault; graphic design credit, Nicole Peirce.

Figure 3.5: Louisa Fletcher-Pacheco, Candice Fletcher-Pacheco, and Oliver, featured in the I STAND campaign. This ad also ran as part of the bus stop campaign in Cincinnati, Ohio. This photo was provided by the participants.

CHAPTER FOUR

What If the Cure Is Worse Than the Disease?

How We Treat Children in the Age of Obesity

The value systems of any society have been lived out
in its treatment of children.
> —Lisette Burrows and Jan Wright, "The Discursive Production
> of Childhood, Identity, and Health"[1]

As I argued in the introduction, in the midst of a war the most innocent of activities, what might even be considered the quintessential moments of childhood, may be coded and understood as moments of risk. Something as simple as eating an ice-cream cone can become a symbol of the downfall of a nation. Even more disturbing, a child may be seen as a nuisance—or even an enemy—for eating that ice-cream cone. The imagery of ice cream and children has become iconic in media accounts of the childhood obesity epidemic, as evidenced by covers from *Time* and *Newsweek,* as well as the cover of Greg Critser's monograph *Fat Land: How Americans Became the Fattest People on Earth* (see Figures 0.1, 0.2, and 0.3). Although these works were published over the course of some eight years, they work in concert to establish children and ice cream as symbolic of a kind of gluttonous demise of our youngest citizens, their faces and bodies literally taken over by the ice cream and toppings.

As with concepts such as health and fitness as well as good and bad parenting, "what being a child means is repeatedly negotiated in relation to a range of other people in their lives (for example, parents, teachers, peers) and in relation to institutional and cultural discourses."[2] In other words, the child and childhood are shaped and defined by the surrounding culture as much as anything else is sculpted by context. Given the sharp focus on obesity, especially on childhood obesity, the contours of what it means to be a child and what is appropriate for childhood are under cultural construction. Put another way, children aren't just children any more than ice cream is just ice cream. The child also becomes a symbol for whether one has succeeded as a teacher or as a parent by producing a thin child. Children's bodies serve as rulers for measuring the supposed demise of American culture. They become litmus tests for whether efforts to stem the tide of obesity are working. In the war on obesity, children exist as symbols, tools, and even weapons.

This is not the vision of childhood that most of us hold, for in this construction, childhood can hardly be a carefree time when one has no worries or strife. Most Americans would assert that they want children to be happy and carefree. But as Lisette Burrows argues in her scholarship about fatness, "an annexing of health and fitness and non-fatness to just about everything—and particularly to ordinary practices like eating, moving and playing is not necessarily generative of the kind of happy young person . . . policies are hopeful of producing."[3] Recalling the *Time* and *Newsweek* covers, we should keep in mind that when an ice-cream cone becomes an icon of danger, nearly anything can become frightening rather than pleasurable. It is all the more sad and concerning, then, that children are proving to be some of the most useful shills in the war on obesity. According to Abigail Saguy, "If you can play the child card or the youth card, you are more effective. People are worried about their children, and if you play up those fears, you will get more mileage."[4]

Ice cream may literally be frightening for children who have undergone bariatric surgeries as a "cure" for their obesity. After some bariatric procedures, foods such as ice cream and other sweets are likely to cause "dumping," a horrible process that can involve sweating, vomiting, dizziness, and diarrhea but is nonetheless actually touted as being helpful for controlling a patient's eating. Perhaps even more disturbing, bariatric surgeries on children are often justified by recounting horror stories of bullying, suggesting that American society has become a culture that believes those who are victimized ought to change themselves to avoid abuse. In order not to be dumped on, children and teens are expected to take on dumping syndrome.

A great deal of the discussion in the mainstream media and in medical literature features the central claim that bariatric surgeries are about the health of children and adolescents. But a careful reading of these conversations, their evidence, and their rhetoric leaves little doubt that such surgeries are also about weight-based discrimination—against fat children and their parents. At the very least, the specter of weight-based discrimination in children's imagined futures helps to drive the endorsement of these surgeries as a way of changing their bodies and ending discrimination. Cultural values position obesity as a serious social problem, which children are increasingly expected to help solve by surgically altering their bodies. One must wonder if an alleged cure such as bariatric surgery may indeed be worse than the supposed disease of obesity.

WHAT IS BARIATRIC SURGERY?

Bariatric surgery is an umbrella term used to describe several different kinds of operations that aim to cause weight loss by restricting the amount of food a person can eat, by causing malabsorption of food that is consumed, or by employing a combination of restriction and malabsorption. For example, gastric banding, which involves placing a band around the stomach to restrict food intake, is a restrictive surgery. Roux-en-Y, one of the most popular bariatric surgeries, entails sectioning off a portion of the stomach so that the pouch that can accept food is significantly smaller, holding only a few tablespoons of content at once. Additionally, the Roux-en-Y procedure prompts malabsorption of calories and nutrients from food because the pouch is connected to the intestines in a way that circumvents a large portion of the intestinal tract. Because food spends less time in the intestinal tract, fewer calories and nutrients are taken into the body from anything that is consumed.[5] Gastric banding and Roux-en-Y are the most commonly performed procedures, and even though they work a bit differently in terms of their mechanics, many of the procedures' risks and side effects are similar. Within the medical literature, for instance, a large number of studies simply refer to the risks, benefits, and follow-up needs for bariatric surgeries writ large. For that reason, I use *bariatric surgery* or *bariatric surgeries* as umbrella terms within this chapter and only differentiate between types of procedures when necessary for context or clarity.

Many Fat activists and Fat Studies scholars who oppose bariatric surgeries refer to these procedures by different names, following Marilyn Wann's lead in calling them "stomach amputations," "gut lobotomies," and "digestive bonsais."[6] The terms are meant, of course, to be shocking and provocative, but they're also fairly accurate. Many of the procedures, including Roux-en-Y, do arguably amputate a part of the patient's stomach. Likewise, the language of lobotomy is appropriate because the aim of making the stomach smaller is to work on the brain by tricking neural sensors into feeling fullness. And to speak of digestive bonsais is no less accurate, especially considering that the art of bonsai involves not only trimming the diminutive plant into a new shape but also implementing a kind of ongoing training so that the tree then behaves in a particular way. In the case of a bonsai, this may mean adapting to growing on a rock or having weight applied to a particular branch so that it cascades down a container over time. In the case of a bariatric surgery, the ongoing training applies to the patient who learns to eat in ways that facilitate weight loss. For Roux-en-Y, the reference to bonsai is especially appropriate, for that procedure is often used because it supposedly "trains" a patient to eat in a prescribed way by reconstructing the gastrointestinal tract. As a result, eating too many simple carbs at once usually causes dumping syndrome, which occurs when food leaves the stomach and enters the intestine too rapidly for the body to adjust. In addition to the side effects I've already mentioned, such as vomiting and dizziness, dumping syndrome is sometimes accompanied by dangerous drops in blood sugar levels.[7]

No one set of guidelines exists for performing bariatric surgeries on teens, but certain generally agreed upon protocols are endorsed by organizations such as the American Society for Metabolic and Bariatric Surgery,[8] as well as clinics such as the Cincinnati Children's Hospital.[9] These guidelines specify that to be considered for bariatric surgery, an adolescent should have tried and failed at traditional methods of losing weight via diet and exercise for at least six months and have a BMI of 40 or higher. Some practitioners suggest the adolescent should have a BMI of 40 with other health concerns, and some will consider an adolescent a candidate if he or she has a BMI of 35 or greater with at least one other health problem that experts consider to be obesity re-lated, such as type 2 diabetes or sleep apnea. All agree that adolescents need to have already tried to lose weight, have a supportive family environment, and be mature enough to understand the process of the surgery and the required follow-up care. The guidelines suggest that females be at least thirteen and males at least fifteen so that they are close to their adult heights, which prac-titioners see as important because it's widely acknowledged that the surgeries may affect children's growth due to the malnutrition they prompt.

In spite of general agreement, some bariatric surgeons work outside these guidelines, operating on younger children. Even gastric bands, devices that are not approved by the Food and Drug Administration (FDA) for use in adoles-cents, are regularly employed by bariatric surgeons in so-called off-label uses, and nothing prohibits surgeons doing that. The same is true for procedures such as Roux-en-Y. In their article "How Young for Bariatric Surgery in Chil-dren?," Allen F. Browne and Thomas Inge explain that "the procedures that do not involve the implantation of a device [such as Roux-en-Y] do not come under the regulational jurisdiction of the FDA. Practitioners use their best clinical judgment and adapt the procedures to children as they seem clinically indicated."[10] In other words, because there's no band or other device implanted and only a restructuring of the patient's own organs, these procedures are not subject to FDA approval. Noting that children from two to eighteen with BMIs above the ninety-fifth percentile for their gender and age are "obese and need to have their weight gain stopped or reversed,"[11] Browne and Inge state that in these circumstances, "the question is not how young to treat [children], but *which* aggressive, effective treatments can be most safely used to effect a healthy weight."[12] With such an attitude, it's not surprising that, though rare, reports indicate children are having bariatric surgeries as young as twelve in the United States and as young as five in Saudi Arabia.[13] The guidelines and much of the bariatric literature employ the term *adolescents* rather than *children*, and therefore, I most often adopt that language within this chapter, with the understanding that younger children may undergo these surgeries and that *adolescent* may connote an age category but not necessarily a level of maturity that indicates they're no longer children.

From 2000 to 2003, there was a threefold increase in bariatric surgeries for what doctors call "pediatric extreme obesity,"[14] that is, obesity in the under eighteen population. Some bariatric specialists admit that it's unclear how many surgeries are being performed on adolescents or how many are tracked in ways that yield meaningful long-term data. In a 2011 article entitled "Developing Criteria for Pediatric/Adolescent Bariatric Surgery Programs," the authors claim that only 662 adolescent records have been captured in the Bariatric Longitudinal Outcomes Database, which was designed to "track all patients cared for in American Society for Metabolic and Bariatric Surgery–designated center-of-excellence programs."[15] During the same period, those programs captured records for nearly 260,000 adult patients.[16] Although the authors admit that they don't know exactly how many surgeries were performed on adolescents during that period, they speculate that many of those records are not being meaningfully tracked, for hospital discharge records indicate that in 2003 alone, 770 adolescents were discharged from hospitals after having bariatric surgery.[17]

Even those who are publishing in the field are often at a loss in terms of having clear data. Julie Ingelfinger's 2011 article, "Bariatric Surgery in Adolescents," notes that though no one data source is tracking the number of procedures, "it appears that somewhere between just under 1,000 and several thousand adolescents undergo bariatric surgeries each year."[18] Many currently consider that the best ongoing source of data collection is the Teen-Longitudinal Assessment of Bariatric Surgery (Teen LABS), which began in 2006 and represents a partnership among several major centers for adolescent bariatric surgery.[19] Yet, data collection of this type doesn't represent the kind of rigorous clinical trials one might expect to see for a medical treatment. Writing specifically about the risks of performing bariatric surgeries on children and adolescents, C. Hearn-shaw and K. Matyka are quick to point out that "there do not appear to be any randomized control trials of surgical interventions in children and young people with problems of overweight and obesity" and that the number of patients attending follow-up sessions decreases with time.[20]

COMPLICATIONS

Momentarily setting aside ethical issues regarding what it means to be performing these surgeries on such young patients, there are vital medical reasons why such surgeries demand careful follow up and tracking over the short and long term. First, there are the potential complications of the procedures themselves. The most current statistics suggest that 1 in 2,000 gastric-banding patients will die, as will 1 in 900 gastric-bypass patients.[21] With gastric banding, which many people would consider much less drastic than a gastric bypass such as Roux-en-Y, 30 percent of patients still need follow-up surgeries within fourteen years; among teenagers in particular, a third of them will need follow-up surgeries within one to two years because of "pouch dilation" that occurs when patients "eat too much."[22] One study in the United Kingdom determined that "66% of patients had at least one complication" during their first year after a gastric-banding procedure, with problems ranging from nutritional deficiencies to the inability to eat.[23] Roux-en-Y also carries serious risks, with increased chances of bleeding and infections immediately following surgery due to the multiple incisions involved, including incisions to the stomach and intestines. Over the longer term, some patients also develop scar tissue where the newly created stomach joins to the intestines, making the opening shrink to the point that food can't pass, a condition called stenosis that also requires a follow-up surgery.[24]

Some doctors, however, point out that current figures about bariatric surgeries and complications represent significant decreases in risks to all patients. But they also admit that risks have decreased—at least in part—due to the fact that they are beginning to operate on what they describe as "skinnier, healthier patients."[25] In other words, experts in the field of bariatric surgery are able to claim better physical outcomes because they're now operating on healthier (or healthy?) patients. In fact, in a recent *New York Times* piece about weight-loss procedures among adolescents, one doctor, talking specifically about Shari Goffman, an adolescent who was about to undergo gastric banding, described his patient as "relatively skinny" and seemed pleased that this would mean her surgery would be easier.[26] In fact, the BMI threshold for performing gastric-band surgeries on patients was recently lowered to 30, which is also the medically defined threshold for obesity.[27] That means that a patient who is 5'7" and about 191 pounds would qualify; such a patient, if she were female, might wear size 10/12 pants.

In spite of being described as relatively skinny and despite her surgeon's bravado about the operation being easy, Shari Goffman experienced postsurgery side effects such as violent vomiting after eating and pain while waiting for meals to pass through the gastric band. She also gained back quite a bit of weight after her initial weight loss, which is very common with nearly all bariatric procedures; added to that, her weight gain triggered shame that in turn caused her to avoid follow-up care.[28] The avoidance of follow-up care sometimes happens because patients feel as if *they* have failed rather than that the procedure has failed. In what appears to be the only existing monograph by someone who underwent a bariatric surgery and then had it reversed, Dani Hart provides insight into why many people experience such shame. When Hart went into online chat rooms for post-op bariatric patients, looking for support and information about the problems that eventually led her to choose to have her procedure reversed,[29] she was called "crazy, weak willed, neurotic, a failure" and virtually run out of the forum. She was also told by members of an online support group, a group specifically for post-op bariatric patients, that anyone who regained weight was a failure.[30] The medical literature characterizes failures in ways that suggest they occur because of individual shortcomings rather than because of problems inherent to the procedure. Discussing patients who regain some or all of their weight over the long term, David B. Sarwer and Rebecca J. Dilks say that "these suboptimal results typically are attributed to poor adherence to the post-operative diet or a return of maladaptive eating behaviors."[31]

It is no wonder, then, that people might feel ashamed and blame themselves, especially given the mainstream narrative indicating that any failed weight-loss attempt results from user error. When young Goffman finally returned to see her physician after regaining weight, he tightened her band so that it took her "1.5 hours to force down two scrambled eggs."[32] This is because such a surgery can reduce a patient's stomach to the point that it holds a meager 4 ounces, which is one-tenth of normal stomach capacity.[33] At the time the *New York Times* article was published, Goffman opted not to disclose her weight, but she admitted that she was "fighting constant hunger."[34] In spite of her struggles, she later returned to her doctor's office to have her band tightened even more in hopes of losing weight again.

One might conclude from her unwillingness to share her weight that Goffman still feels ashamed—even though she's now altered her body to the point that it takes her over an hour to eat a meal, which is quite a sacrifice and not uncommon for postsurgery life among bariatric patients.[35] The commonplace nature of complications and the need for revisions to these surgeries ought to indicate that user error may not be the main problem, yet the story of willpower overcoming all obstacles so powerfully structures understandings of weight loss that even those who have tried—in every way possible—seem to still end up blaming themselves and/or being blamed by others when they don't succeed at losing weight.

Like Goffman, many adults don't seem to understand what their reconstructed digestive tracts require of them after surgery or how much their daily lives will change. In her blog about life after weight-loss surgery, a woman known only as Lisa writes that she wishes someone had told her that after her operation, she'd still have to be obsessed with food because she'd be forced to count grams of protein religiously in order to get enough nutrition.[36] Likewise, another individual, Lisa Sargese, who calls herself a "survivor" of bariatric surgery, writes in her blog *Lisa Loves Life Lessons* about her struggles to avoid dumping syndrome because dumping means she loses her appetite entirely, guaranteeing malnourishment. As a result of ongoing malnourishment, Sargese had to take iron treatments intravenously. She writes specifically about dumping: "Dumping syndrome is a hellish experience that includes . . . a general wish to be bashed over the head with a mallet to end one's misery. It's awful. I dump at least twice a day. Yep. Welcome to post-op life."[37]

Some adults who have had the surgeries and experienced the side effects of dumping seem to believe the painful effects are acceptable or even that they deserve the pain and punishment that dumping inflicts. In March 2002, *Today Show* weatherman Al Roker underwent gastric-bypass surgery, knowing that at the time of his surgery, the procedure "after more than two decades in use, still carried a frightening one in two hundred fatality rate."[38] Once he was over 100 pounds lighter, Roker spoke openly about the surgery he initially hid from the public and his *Today Show* colleagues. In addition to singing the praises of bariatric surgery and his newfound health, he also spoke about one of the downsides of the surgery: dumping syndrome. He recounted his first experience with dumping in his November 2002 cover story for *People*: "'I took a couple of bites of these ribs, and while it was going down, I thought, "That was a bad move,"' he says. 'We got off the air, and I just kind of sidled off to the bathroom.'"[39] Roker didn't follow up on his comment with any sort of analysis or statement that indicated this was particularly concerning to him. In early 2013, he published his memoir about his surgery and weight loss, called *Never Goin' Back,* and he displayed this same nonchalance when he began speaking publicly about his surgery again as part of promoting his book. Recently, he spoke about soiling himself at the White House only a few months after his surgery. "I pooped my pants," he said. "Not horribly, but enough that I knew." Afterwards, Roker reported that he took his underwear off, threw it away, and went "commando" for the remainder of the event he was attending.[40] He writes about both the barbecue segment for the *Today Show* and the White House accident in the book, but the only real commentary he offers is that he was "petrified" for the rest of the afternoon while at the White House.[41]

Roker's experiences and his seemingly blasé attitude about them mirror Carnie Wilson's descriptions of her numerous struggles with dumping after her first bariatric surgery, which was broadcast online.[42] Interestingly enough, Roker's wife, Deborah Roberts, who is also a television personality and journalist, covered Wilson's 1999 surgery and was the first person to mention the procedure to Roker.[43] Though Roker's descriptions of dumping are more general, Wilson's first experience is described in vivid detail. After serving her dinner guests Jell-O and Cool Whip for dessert, she was forced to apologize to her friends and then go upstairs until her dumping episode passed: "Let me just tell you that dumping is the most horrible feeling in the world. Your heart beats really fast, you're sweating, your nose gets totally stuffy, and you feel really dizzy. It's like a panic attack combined with a terrible stomachache and a horrible cold. Basically there isn't a part of your body that doesn't feel like total shit."[44]

She goes on to say that she had other "world class dumping experiences," such as the one that occurred when eating yogurt and carob chips made her so ill that one of her friends had to care for her until it passed. Yet, most disturbing about Wilson's treatment of dumping is the joy she expresses when she writes about what is, according to her own representation, a very punishing physical and mental process. In a section at the end of her memoir, *I'm Still Hungry,* called "How to Be a Good Weight Loss Surgery (WLS) Patient (If You Care),"[45] Wilson writes:

Dumping isn't fun—however, it's my lifesaver now because I feel a certain reaction after I eat specific foods. If those foods are high in sugar or fat and I eat too much of them (which might only be two or three bites), I'll have a nasty reaction. . . . This could go on from 15–45 minutes, as the degree of dumping varies. Sometimes I don't even know what caused it. You've got to be ready for the possibility of this happening. . . . That's why I'm happy that I dump. Why would I want to be able to eat a lot of the foods that made me fat in the first place? I love being able to write that![46]

Wilson believes dumping syndrome and the pain and panic that accompany her "failures" are apt punishment for eating forbidden foods. In fact, she never says anything critical about the surgery and its horrendous side effects, further emphasizing that she thinks any problems encountered are because she alone has misbehaved and thus deserves the sort of misery the surgery inflicts. Extrapolating from the literature on adults in this case would mean acknowledging that a certain amount of self-blame exists among bariatric patients even after the great efforts they've taken to lose weight. It's regrettable that an adult would feel this way, but it's especially worrisome that an adolescent might take on this kind of attitude about him- or herself.

Post-op patients who don't adopt this sort of attitude about dumping, however, may find it difficult, if not impossible, to locate support as they struggle to adjust. Writing about her experience with trying to find support online after her surgery and echoing Wilson's description of dumping as the result of eating even a small amount of food, Sargese states, "It takes only one forkful or one sip over the limit (a ping pong ball's size of food is the limit) to push me over the edge into dumpville. Mind you, the WLS 'community' regards dumping syndrome as one of the positive tools that can prevent one from overeating thereby causing weight loss which is the Holy Grail which leads to Cinderella getting her glass slipper to fit."[47] Sargese goes on to claim that as a post-op patient, "if you complain about dumping you'll be reminded by post-op cheerleaders that you knew what you were getting into when you had the surgery and isn't it great that dumping syndrome will stop you from overeating!"[48] It's easy to imagine other patients, like Wilson, having that reaction, perhaps because they don't want to believe that they made the wrong decision by having the surgery or that they weren't fully informed. People are usually hesitant to admit, after all, that they bought a pig in a poke. I also think it's likely that such a reaction would be even more pronounced among adolescents, for they are already struggling to be seen as adults and might not want their parents, who also consented to the surgery, to feel responsible for something as horrible as dumping.

Beyond the immediate risks of surgery, more long-range problems are associated with these procedures, including side effects and outcomes that may be more difficult to manage than constant hunger or even dumping—problems that may be especially difficult for young bodies that are still growing. For instance, many articles that view bariatric procedures favorably still openly acknowledge that beriberi, caused by vitamin B deficiency, is not uncommon in patients. Beriberi can cause fatigue, problems with balance that may lead to falling, hearing loss, and lack of menstruation in women.[49] Because of the restrictive nature of a surgery such as Roux-en-Y and its imposed malnutrition, anyone undergoing the procedure must take a host of supplements for a lifetime, but this is especially important for still-growing bodies. The nutritional deficiencies resulting from the surgery can cause immediate effects that range from anemia to learning difficulties, yet follow-up studies on adolescent patients suggest that only 14 percent actually take the recommended supplements.[50] Further, bariatric experts note that they're not really sure which supplements may be necessary yet.[51] Perhaps because of this uncertainty, many physicians and clinics advise patients that any bariatric weight-loss surgery demands "lifelong supervision" due to the potential for nutritional deficiencies.[52] The experts performing these procedures continue to do so without always understanding what ongoing supervision should look like—at least in terms of nutritional supplements—and with the knowledge that many adolescent patients will not follow any regimen.

In fact, Inge and his coauthors, who are quite bold in their assertions that bariatric surgeries are often necessary and the best course of action for adolescents who have been unsuccessful with dieting and exercise, also acknowledge that vitamin D deficiency and osteoporosis are developing areas of concern for adolescents who have undergone bariatric procedures.[53] Although many people think of something such as osteoporosis as a nuisance rather than a serious problem, the disease can lead to weakened bones, which can cause serious problems later in life, especially for women. As a result of osteoporosis, "up to 30% of patients suffering a hip fracture will require long-term nursing home care. Elderly patients can further develop pneumonia and blood clots in the leg veins that can travel to the lungs (pulmonary embolism) due to prolonged bed rest after a hip fracture. Some 20% of women with a hip fracture will die in the subsequent year as an indirect result of the fracture."[54] John Hopkins reports that in one of the few studies on teens and gastric banding, those "who underwent weight loss surgery experienced an average loss of 7.4 percent of their bone mass."[55] Given that banding only restricts the intake of food, it's reasonable to assume that this kind of deficiency would be worse after a surgery such as Roux-en-Y, which promotes both limited food consumption and malabsorbtion. Still, in the bariatric field, Roux-en-Y is considered "the gold standard"—even for teens.[56]

GENDER MATTERS

For females, who comprise the majority of patients undergoing weight-loss surgeries,[57] the complications from nutritional imbalances may be especially serious. Women who menstruate or who become pregnant—regardless of what kind of procedure they have—may face the most significant nutritional deficiencies. The anemia from resulting iron deficiencies can be so serious that women, especially menstruating women, may require blood transfusions and other treatments to raise their hemoglobin levels. The issue of iron deficiency alone is serious enough to warrant attention, especially given that all menstruating women who have bariatric surgery—again, regardless of the kind of procedure performed—are at risk for developing serious iron deficiencies: "A study comparing bypass [such as Roux-en-Y] and banding techniques found that menstruating women, no matter the surgical procedure that they received, had significantly lower postsurgical hemoglobin and serum iron levels than nonmenstruating women."[58] Researchers are not certain why this happens, but they speculate that because 50 percent of patients have an intolerance of meat after procedures, their diets may not include sufficient iron—even in the case of banding-only procedures. Furthermore, restricting the stomach also means there are fewer secretions to metabolize any available iron in foods. Add together a meat intolerance and a diminished ability to absorb iron, as is the case with Roux-en-Y, which both restricts the stomach and prompts malabsorption, and it's easier to understand why such nutritional deficiencies can develop, especially among menstruating women. According to Aileen Love and Henry Billett, because so many menstruating women who have bypasses such as Roux-en-Y develop anemia, 10 percent end up having a hysterectomy.[59] As a result of the lack of clarity and the risks involved, many practitioners suggest that regular blood tests to check vitamin levels should be part of lifelong follow up after bariatric surgeries.[60]

Pregnant women, who are trying to nourish their body and a fetus as well, sometimes also require blood transfusions due to severe anemia. Although it's recommended that patients not become pregnant within at least twelve to eighteen months following surgery (with some guidelines suggesting pregnancy should be avoided for as long as it takes for the individual to reach a weight plateau), many patients do become pregnant, especially adolescents. In fact, female adolescents who have bariatric surgery have a higher rate of pregnancy than female adolescents nationwide.[61] Although researchers don't fully understand why this is the case, some speculate that it may be because these young, female patients have the surgery out of a desire to get married and have a family.[62] Other experts posit that losing weight means sex is simply more available than it was before surgery.[63] In one clinic where adolescent females who become pregnant are being tracked, the clinicians report that "these adolescent pregnancies occurred despite published guidelines to postpone pregnancy for at least 24 months after surgery and [our] own program recommendations, which stipulate postponing sexual activity and using contraception."[64]

In the 2005 "Best Practice Guidelines in Pediatric Adolescent Weight Loss Surgery," the authors were so concerned about the risks of pregnancy in the postbariatric population that they even suggested that clinics should exclude women who hoped to become pregnant within two years after a bariatric surgery.[65] The vitamin deficiencies that are common after bariatric procedures can put both a woman and her developing fetus at risk, for some deficiencies may cause birth defects.[66] Of course, it's not surprising that guidelines about contraception aren't followed, given that doctors know "the compliance rate with nutritional treatment is dramatically low,"[67] indicating what would likely be a low compliance rate in general. Even women who comply, however, still risk becoming pregnant, especially since oral birth control pills may also be poorly absorbed with a Roux-en-Y procedure. Consequently, female patients engaging in sex with men must be especially vigilant about using barrier methods of contraception.[68]

IS THERE A SURGERY FOR THAT?

For many people, an adolescent's immediate health may prompt the greatest concern, and bariatric surgeries promise nearly instant relief from some conditions, including diabetes, a condition so conflated with obesity that the shorthand moniker *diabesity* is regularly used within medical literature.[69] Type 2 diabetes, the sort most often attributed to obesity, is, however, a complex condition that often involves a host of factors, including family history and eating habits. There is a strong correlation with obesity, but it's unclear—despite a term such as *diabesity*—whether obesity actually causes diabetes.[70] Many thin people develop type 2 diabetes, and many fat people never get the disease. Still, diabetes is serious and affects virtually every bodily organ. It is no wonder, then, that a child and parents hearing that the child has an increased risk for developing diabetes may be desperate to find a cure.

In March 2011, the International Diabetes Federation "endorsed bariatric surgery as a type 2 diabetes treatment for obese patients, citing studies indicating that it triggers remission in about 85% of patients."[71] Discussing how the procedure treats diabetes, one bariatric surgeon, Julio Teixiera, goes so far as to call gastric bypass "magic."[72] Although exactly how it works is still poorly understood, studies support claims that patients do have normal blood glucose readings immediately following bariatric surgeries. The medical community believes the remission of type 2 diabetes could be due to several different metabolic and hormonal processes that are altered when the stomach is made smaller and the intestines are shortened.[73]

Many people have come to believe that bariatric surgeries cure diabetes, but not all doctors are convinced this is the case. In the same article in which Teixiera refers to bariatric surgery as a diabetes cure, endocrinologist and researcher Blandine Laferrere refuses to go so far.[74] Similarly, Eleanor Mackey, a psychologist who screens adolescents prior to bariatric surgery, says, "We worry a lot if we have a child who thinks the surgery is going to be a magic fix."[75] Despite Teixiera's zeal, recent and more long-term studies have suggested that it's not wise to refer to bariatric surgeries as magical, at least not where diabetes is concerned. Despite the fact that 68 percent of the patients followed went into remission after surgery, 35 percent of those patients experienced a resurgence of their diabetes five years after surgery. Most people would be tempted to attribute the return of diabetes to the return of weight, but the study actually concluded that—regardless of regaining weight—patients whose diabetes was severe and/or those who had had the condition for longer periods prior to surgery were likely to experience a relapse.[76] Those who advocate for bariatric surgeries on adolescents may want to use these data to argue that such operations should be done as early as possible, hopefully catching diabetes in its earliest stages and avoiding the problems the adults in this study experienced with relapse. I think, however, that the relapses should be considered a cautionary tale regarding the assertion that bariatric surgeries can "cure" anyone's diabetes.

Likewise, it appears that depression, which is often said to dissipate after bariatric surgery, may also reappear over the long term. Psychosocial stress is constantly described in ways that indicate it's a reason to have a bariatric surgery; indeed, it's difficult to find an article about bariatric surgery for adolescents that doesn't comment on them being depressed and/or socially isolated. Yet, many studies have pointed out that very little is known about how undergoing bariatric procedures affects people's long-term "psychosocial functioning,"[77] and some scholars have documented that, among those who already have some form of psychosocial challenge such as depression, there are actually higher rates of suicide in the postbariatric population.[78] Given that depression is so often discussed in the bariatric literature, physicians obviously understand that psychosocial issues are very real for teens, and it's likely that many adolescents undergoing the procedure already have problems, which may put them at even greater risk after the procedures. As Valerie Taylor, Brian Stonehocker, Margot Steele, and Arya M. Sharmer succinctly write, "Bariatric surgery is not a treatment for depression and is not a panacea to improve dysfunctional interpersonal relationships or psychosocial stress."[79] In addition to the rate of suicide rising in the postbariatric population, there is also a higher chance of alcohol abuse, indicating that patients may still be struggling with underlying issues.[80]

Nonetheless, the alleviation of psychosocial problems is often used as a justification for performing the surgeries. For instance, in an article about creating a bariatric surgery program for adolescents at a teaching hospital, Beverly Haynes notes that via the surgeries, "self image is enhanced."[81] Similarly, the authors of one systematic review on whether bariatric surgeries improve psychosocial functioning claim that the surgeries are "particularly good" for dealing with anxiety issues.[82] Essentially, these authors grant that the surgeries are being performed, at least in part, as a means of addressing body image and anxiety disorders that are likely psychosocial in nature. Clearly, teasing and self-image issues are quite real, with some studies finding that obese children have "[quality-of-life] scores similar to those of children with cancer."[83] Equally as important, however, is considering what may cause obese children to report such low quality of life: "One could speculate that the severity of the [quality-of-life] impairments in the extremely obese adolescent is because of the visible nature of extreme obesity, the social stigma attached to it, and the cumulative impact of medical comorbidities."[84] Even if there are medical comorbidities, the hypervisibility of one's body size and the stigma that visibility provokes seem to be just as salient to heavy children's quality of life.

Social issues apparently lead many adults to seek out bariatric surgeries. From tracking adults who have had bariatric procedures, scholars have discovered that among "gastric restriction" patients "59% . . . requested the surgery for social reasons, such as embarrassment, and only 10% emphasized medical reasons."[85] Further, before the surgery, "87% [of bariatric surgery patients] reported . . . that their weight prevented them from being hired for a job, 90% reported stigma from coworkers, and 84% avoided being in public places due to their weight. Following surgery, all patients reported reduced discrimination."[86] The problems adult patients describe here are social problems, and it is disturbing that the main means used to reduce discrimination seems to be having surgery. In the case of fat children, ameliorating social discrimination by changing their bodies is often one of the rationales for offering bariatric surgeries to more children. For example, Browne and Inge discuss discrimination of obese people at length in their article about bariatric surgeries in young people, arguing that "obese people are the last legally discriminated against group in the USA."[87] They detail the kinds of discrimination fat people face, bemoaning the fact that "discrimination from health care workers has been documented."[88] But they do so with the underlying assumption that the way to end that discrimination is to perform surgeries on obese people, including children. If someone proposed that racial discrimination be "treated" by turning a person white, most people would be appalled. Unless weight-based discrimination is constructed as being somehow vastly different from racially based discrimination, performing surgeries on children's bodies as a treatment for discrimination warrants a similar response.

One area of concern mentioned in the literature but not always properly addressed is that bariatric surgeries may actually cause other psychosocial issues via their severe restriction of food intake. Although dieting has become a very normalized part of American culture, we know it doesn't always have the desired effect of making children (or adults, for that matter) thin. Bariatric surgeries are a kind of forced dieting through the physical restriction they impose on how much food as well as what type of food one may be able to consume (or want to consume), considering the possibility of horrible side effects. Researchers in the field of nutrition and child psychology have pointed out that dieting may have negative long-term effects on children's eating habits and their relationships with their bodies and food. In particular, it appears that food restriction is associated with weight gain.[89] Researchers such as Esther Jansen, Sandra Mulkens, and Anita Jansen have proposed that one reason for this association is that making some foods off-limits actually makes children want them more. In their study of five- and six-year-old children who were prohibited from eating a snack in the first phase of an experiment but then allowed to eat that snack (and several others) in the second phase, the results showed "that the desire to eat forbidden food indeed increased after a prohibition."[90] Thus, these researchers conclude that "forbidden 'fruit' becomes more attractive."[91] If the aim, then, is to help children have good, healthy relationships with food, restrictive dieting, including that caused by bariatric surgeries, wouldn't seem to be the best strategy.

Although the literature is even more sparse in this respect, a developing area of concern is that these procedures may actually lead to a new kind of eating disorder. In one metareview of existing scholarship about bariatric surgeries and eating disorders, the authors reviewed 171 available articles and found that a significant number of patients reported vomiting at least occasionally or even weekly.[92] The patients "attributed this to eating certain foods or quantity of food that they knew they should not eat."[93] The authors state that "vomiting does not seem to represent the purging behavior associated with bulimia nervosa, but is rather the result of overeating or eating intolerable foods" and that experts studying this phenomenon have come "to the conclusion that because gastric restrictive procedures make it physiologically very difficult to binge eat, vomiting might be a new eating pathology after operation and represents failed attempts to binge."[94] In other words, the urge to binge is still there.

In general, scholars have found that restricting food for adolescents and children can cause disordered eating. Janet Polivy's work on this subject is perhaps best known. Polivy has produced numerous studies indicating that food restriction—whether for weight loss or other reasons—often leads to an inability to follow internal cues of satiety, as well as a tendency toward bingeing and other behaviors considered to be on the spectrum of disordered eating.[95] Therefore, although bariatric surgeries are often talked about as tools for helping patients learn better eating habits, a good deal of evidence indicates that many bariatric patients may actually be malnourished, and there's emerging evidence that patients may develop eating disorders in cases where none existed before. Developing eating disorders makes perfect sense, given that the available data about labeling some foods taboo and/or restricting certain foods lead many children and adolescents toward disordered eating. Thinking of preexisting or newly developed eating disorders as psychosocial issues, it's not surprising, then, that patients leave these surgeries with the same impulses and behaviors intact or that they develop new issues—because surgeries can't cure psychosocial issues.

If, say, a person's excessive weight is caused by an addiction to food, which is certainly possible in some cases, at least one study suggests that the addiction is likely to be transferred rather than eliminated after surgery. The rationale behind what experts in the bariatric field refer to as "'transference' or addiction transfer" is that "since food is no longer an option for people who elect [bariatric surgeries], new compulsions may replace eating, such as gambling, sex, and excessive drinking."[96] The study followed over 12,000 bariatric surgery patients for twenty-five years, and the findings suggest that gastric-bypass patients are especially at risk for "moving on to another substance addiction," with "patients who undergo gastric-bypass surgery" being "four times more likely to require in-patient care for alcohol abuse than the general population."[97] It makes perfect sense that in cases where a patient has a problem with addiction, stopping the ability to eat food doesn't stop the compulsive drive that is the underlying problem.

Because bariatric surgeries only target weight, as Jeremy Garrett and Leslie Ann McNalty note, "it is critical that the social sources of the obesity epidemic be taken seriously in order to prevent a skewed analysis of bariatric surgery that vastly overestimates its potential as a solution."[98] Although many people acknowledge that issues with the American food system are leading to higher weights, these and any other potential social or psychosocial causes are largely ignored in discussions of bariatric surgeries. In their meta-analysis of available articles regarding the treatment of obesity in children, V. A. Shrewsbury, K. S. Steinbeck, S. Torvaldsen, and L. A. Baur claim that they only found two articles that suggested "engaging professional help" for any existing or developing psychosocial problems in adolescents undergoing weight-loss surgeries.[99] Bariatric surgery can't be a solution for the causes of obesity, which may sometimes be social or psychosocial, nor can it necessarily be a solution for psychosocial issues that may result from how one is treated due to one's obesity or how one feels about one's self, regardless of weight.

WHOSE CONSENT?

Many people who advocate for surgeries on adolescents argue that girls as young as thirteen and boys as young as fifteen can understand the issues surrounding bariatric surgeries and provide consent. But it seems fair and warranted to question adolescents' abilities to make truly informed choices, not to mention the even younger children who may undergo surgeries, especially given that the available literature suggests that many *adults* don't understand the full implications of these procedures. After all, adults—including Carnie Wilson and Al Roker—seem not to have fully comprehended that their bodies would be drastically altered, that the initial surgery might present them with complications that required other surgeries, that eating what some in dieting culture call "red light" foods would bring on a special kind of sickness,[100] or that losing so much weight would leave them with layers of excess skin.[101] To be fair, these adults also indicate that—even knowing all this—they would have still undergone the surgeries. Nonetheless, there is reason to be concerned about adolescents and their understanding of these procedures if adults can't comprehend what it will mean to live with a restructured stomach and/or intestinal tract and the new body that will result from so much weight loss.

The literature on adolescents and bariatric surgeries acknowledges these problems pertaining to a lack of understanding, yet it also seems to suggest that surgeons should take advantage of the fact that younger patients may not fully understand but are generally more compliant. For example, one surgeon grants that even older adolescents and adults have a low rate of compliance with vitamin regimens and other required maintenance but then suggests that it's best to do the surgeries on twelve-, thirteen-, and fourteen-year-olds who "*may* have better adherence . . . [because] they *tend* to do what they're told and are even better than adults in many cases."[102] In short, it seems it's not a fully informed consent that's being sought but rather compliance, and I would contend that these are two different issues—each warranting its own kind of ethical consideration. Certainly, higher rates of compliance allow those recommending and performing the surgeries to talk at far greater length about their "successes." But this may also mean that more adolescents will change their bodies in drastic ways without fully understanding what lies ahead.

With adolescents, not only their consent but also the consent of their parents or guardians must be acquired. Many may wonder why parents would consent to these procedures. In today's climate, it's possible that desperate parents see this as the only way to treat their child, or they may even worry about losing custody of the child. In "Moral Aspects of Bariatric Surgery for Obese Children and Adolescents: The Urgent Need for Empirical-Ethical Research," the authors claim that the "biggest benefits to patients' parents is a 'normal' looking child and the diminishment of fear of losing custody."[103] These are not unfounded fears on the part of the parents, nor should the pressures on them be minimized or their bowing to those pressures be understood as solely their own fault. In addition to the court cases I discussed in the previous chapters, there have recently been several high-profile cases in which charges have been filed against parents and/or children have been removed from homes because the children's weight was construed as a sign of neglect, most notably in California, Illinois, and South Carolina.[104] Parents who feel that they must make a choice between facing legal charges (and perhaps losing custody of their children) and consenting to bariatric surgery may not be able to make the best-informed decisions. They're hindered not because they don't care for their children but because of the environment in which those decisions must be made, an environment in which a visibly fat child draws attention to both the child and the parent.

It's also possible that parents consent to surgeries because they hear about their children being teased about their weight. It's understandable that these parents would want to protect their children from hardship and pain, and the medical literature represents bariatric surgeries as a way to protect such youngsters. Yet, this narrow understanding of how a parent might offer protection or comfort fails to take into account some of the most important aspects of parenting. What seems most salient here, for instance, is for children to understand that they are not responsible for being teased. Adrienne Asch, a

Disability Studies scholar and activist who supports the rights of children to make decisions about their bodies and their health care, notes that "if children hear from their parents and doctors that they are not what needs to change, that the world's response to them needs to change, they have a better chance at having a confident and competent self with which to make whatever decisions they make about the battles they take on in their lives."[105] Put another way, protecting a child from teasing or from the depression that may follow doesn't necessarily mean helping that child lose weight but rather supporting the child and helping him or her develop a strong sense of self and an understanding of social issues—regardless of body size.

But this is undoubtedly hard to keep in mind given the nearly constant discussion of teasing and how much it hurts, especially since teasing is sometimes cited as being more serious than what one might immediately consider a "medical" issue. One researcher notes that although the medical issues some fat adolescents face may be serious, "these medical issues [such as diabetes] may be less painful than the stigma of obesity and the frequent experience of isolation, bullying and discrimination."[106] On a recent *Today Show* segment about teens and bariatric surgeries, the report opened with a young woman about to undergo a gastric-sleeve procedure saying that the hardship of being teased about her weight was why she decided to "do something" about it. She also said her goal for the surgery was to fit into her prom dress.[107] Researchers note that when obese teens present for bariatric surgery, they often report a low health-related quality of life (HRQoL) but that it's likely their low quality of life is deeply influenced by the social stigma surrounding obesity and not just health problems.[108]

Given Western standards of beauty, young women are apt to face more discrimination as a result of being fat. Writing explicitly about females, Sarwer and Dilks argue that the stigma of obesity is even worse for young women: "The social impact of obesity, especially on females, is staggering. As obese female adolescents age, they are likely to suffer extreme social consequences from obesity, including achieving less educational status, earning less money, being more likely to live in poverty, and being less likely to marry."[109] Sarwer and Dilks are correct about the consequences an obese woman is likely to face in modern US society, but I would posit that they've attributed those consequences to the wrong source. They've said these problems stem "from obesity," but it's not obesity itself that causes these problems. These are social problems caused by fatphobia, and they can't be fixed by operating on an adolescent's body.

According to Thomas Inge and his coauthors, however, these are precisely the reasons why adolescents *should* undergo bariatric surgeries. In fact, in their 2006 article, Inge et al. claim that "opportunities for socialization missed in adolescence [due to obesity] may represent losses that cannot be replaced. These 'co-morbidities' are hard to quantify and judge but are real and must be considered."[110] Similarly, Michael G. Sarr asserts that the key question for parents to consider is how a child's obesity is likely to affect his or her hypothetical future: "In my opinion, [how obesity will affect their future] is really the most pertinent and immediate question for these children and although the long-term consequences of bariatric surgery are unknown, the psychosocial consequences, if left untreated (i.e. the child being/remaining clinically morbidly obese), can be devastating; no parent wishes this burden on their child."[111] Sarr goes so far as to say that "the very real problem that is present at their current time in life is the *psychosocial retardation* that so many of these kids suffer—their interaction (or lack thereof) with their peers and society leaves 'emotional scars' and lifelong social retardation."[112] Here again, the child is expected to curtail poor treatment by changing him- or herself, and it's easy to imagine that parents would see ending a child's pain as paramount. Certainly, no parent wants to place a burden on a child, but bariatric surgery and the lifelong supervision it requires is—like it or not—its own kind of burden.

Where the blame is attributed is critical, especially when we're talking about a population that, by physicians' accounts, is at increased risk of mortality due to surgery—both because of the patients' young age and their body size. As a thought experiment, consider the difference between saying someone's sexuality caused him or her to get less of an education or earn less money versus saying that homophobia results in women who identify as lesbian earning less money. Or think of the stark contrast between saying that someone's blackness caused him or her to live in poverty and saying that institutionalized racism makes it more likely that he or she will live in poverty. Before the appropriate route for change can be plotted, the problem has to be accurately named. If doctors find that adolescents are suffering due to social stigma as much as anything else, then the route for change seems to be ending fatphobia rather than operating on individual bodies. Even for those who see the physiological consequences of obesity as the bigger issue, there seems to be agreement that serious social issues must be considered. Given how many fat adolescents may never have bariatric surgery—because they can't afford it, because they have health problems that prohibit it, or because they simply don't want it—addressing the social problems becomes even more pressing and is arguably the best way to improve children's lives.

Taking that route may be especially important for an obese adolescent's long-term happiness, especially considering how many of even those who undergo surgeries will be made, as physician David Ludwig puts it, "less obese," rather than thin. To put it another way, even after surgery, many of these adolescents will still face the same social stigma that they're trying to escape—because they don't become thin as an immediate result of the surgery, because they may become smaller than they were but may never be read as thin, or because they may regain enough weight to be considered obese again.[113] There's also some reason to believe that even children who become conventionally thin and stay that way often still face what researchers call "residual stigma."[114] After presenting research subjects with different accounts of people who had lost weight and those who had been "weight stable," researchers found that their subjects still stigmatized those who had once been fat: "These results suggest that residual stigma remains against people who have previously been obese, even when they have lost substantial amounts of weight and regardless of their weight loss method."[115] Al Roker alludes to this type of residual stigma when he says that people still watch what he eats very closely because "he used to be fat," with some going so far as to ask him if he's "supposed to be eating that."[116] In other words, the pressure and the stigma are still very much in his life. Medical literature acknowledges that social stigma affects people's health, and fat people, according to Peter Muennig, face enough stigma to negatively impact their health. In his article "The Body Politic: The Relationship between Stigma and Obesity," Muennig asserts that some of the diseases seen in heavy people may be the result of living with social stigma rather than being *only* a result of the pathology of fatness.[117] Muennig suggests that a combination of both physiological changes from obesity and stress may combine to cause disease, but even so, stigma may be playing a role in people's health and longevity,[118] which means there are good reasons to focus on the social environment and not just on children's bodies.

IS IT A COSMETIC SURGERY?

Since there's so much emphasis on social stigma in the medical literature, it is hard to deny that bariatric surgery is, at least at some level, a cosmetic surgery. Yet, many practitioners in the field explicitly deny that there's any cosmetic element to these procedures. Dr. Marc Michalsky, who is the surgical director of the Center for Healthy Weight and Nutrition at Nationwide Hospital in Cincinnati, Ohio, states plainly, "[Bariatric surgery] is not a cosmetic procedure."[119] Likewise, Bill Hyman, Kari Kooi, and David Ficklen echo those words in their article "Bariatric Surgery in Adolescents," affirming that "bariatric surgery is not cosmetic surgery."[120] But with so much discussion in the bariatric surgery literature about the visibility of weight and the stigma against fat people, it seems undeniable that part of what is being diagnosed and treated is a problem of aesthetics. It's not, after all, sleep apnea that's causing a child to be teased. Nor are children usually teased for having diabetes or a fatty liver or any of the other conditions attributed to obesity that would most likely be invisible to their peers. Obese children are teased because of how they look and also, perhaps, because of what are assumed to be their personal characteristics, namely, that they, like all fat people, are stupid, lazy, and generally unworthy.

Even allowing for the fact that most insurance companies don't pay for cosmetic procedures and that this might be why doctors would be hesitant to name the surgery as only cosmetic surgery, these repeated denials of any cosmetic element in bariatric surgery are still curious. Perhaps denials arise from a fear that bariatric surgeries will no longer be seen as legitimate procedures. At the very least, it is important to acknowledge that there is *some* cosmetic element. Surgeries on children with cleft lips or palates, for instance, often correct a physiological problem, such as difficulty eating or drinking, but organizations such as Operation Smile also own, by their very name, the cultural and cosmetic norms that such surgeries involve. Having the ability to smile, after all, doesn't necessarily improve a child's health, and the value and meaning of a smile surely changes from culture to culture. In its mission statement, however, Operation Smile apparently acknowledges that giving children what they think of as a more socially acceptable face via the ability to smile is, indeed, part of what they aim to do: "Operation Smile is an international children's medical charity that heals children's *smiles,* forever changing their lives."[121] The donation page for the organization also tells donors that they're providing children with "smiles."[122] Without debating the politics of an organization such as Operation Smile, it is fair to say that this group does not openly deny that the procedures it performs have a cosmetic element, which is not the case with bariatric surgery for adolescents.

In some ways, it appears society has become overly enamored with the very idea of intervention—the idea that *something* must be done—even if it is largely cosmetic. This certainly seemed to be part of what drove early interventions into the lives of children with intersex conditions. Of course, neither parents nor surgeons are purposefully trying to hurt children via bariatric surgeries or genital surgeries—or any surgeries. Instead, these people genuinely care about children, but they might not always be fully aware of the range of implications involved or give those implications thorough consideration. In her article titled "What to Do When You Have the Child You Weren't Expecting," Alice Dreger notes that many surgeons see surgeries as "evidence of pure devotion to children. Surgeons understand the world to be cruel to people who look funny. Moreover, they believe it is not in their power to change society, and so they do what they can to help; they do surgery."[123] In the end, parents and surgeons are as susceptible as anyone else to the pressures of American society, a society that values a thin body at nearly any cost, and they likely see these procedures as helpful remedies.

Much like surgeons, parents must also have a difficult time thinking about bariatric surgeries as being invested in cosmetic results and must sometimes feel compelled to have surgeries performed. Writing directly to parents (but also noting that mothers may feel particularly pressured), Dreger states that they are under tremendous pressure to have surgeries performed on children embodied in atypical ways—even when those atypical embodiments don't cause health issues. She notes, "People may also treat you, the parent, as if you are shameful also because people tend to think that if a child has a congenital 'problem,' it is the parents' 'fault.' You must have done something wrong, especially if you're the mother. If you're getting the message that it's all your fault, then surgery might seem like something you have to do to prove you're a responsible parent."[124] Regardless of whether obesity is a congenital or an environmental problem (or both), Dreger's point is still salient. Parents with children who look different are often under a great deal of pressure to make them "normal"—even if doing so requires surgical intervention.

Recently, even professional organizations have acknowledged the pressure parents may face when they have a fat child and how parental feelings about a child's size may affect decision making. Well aware of the kinds of pressures parents confront, the American Society for Metabolic and Bariatric Surgery (ASMBS) cautions that parents may steer an adolescent toward bariatric surgery because they may perceive the child's obesity as being more problematic than the child does him- or herself.[125] Roker writes poignantly in his memoir about how his father's deathbed wish that he lose weight influenced his decision to go ahead with his bariatric surgery. Roker went to see a surgeon for a consultation and recounts the details of the visit in this way:

> He explained how he would crack me open from the top of my rib cage to just above my belly button, do the bypass, sew me back up and wait for the result. Oh, and by the way, I would be in the hospital for a week or more and then recuperate for another six to eight weeks. So, I would have an excruci-

atingly painful procedure. Then I would be out of work and off the air for two months, assuming no complications. Ooooooh. Sign me up . . . NOT![126]

Yet, only a few sentences later in the memoir, Roker writes, "But then I started thinking about my dad and the promise I had made to him on his deathbed just a few weeks earlier. I could hear his voice saying, 'Promise me you are going to lose the weight, Al.'"[127] Roker's story is a powerful and moving reminder of the significance of parental influence on children—even adult children. And though surgeons and surgical centers work hard to make sure that adolescents understand the procedures and provide informed consent, parents may still be incredibly influential in the decision-making process. I'm sure Roker's father only wanted the best for his son, but he saw achieving that goal as necessarily involving weight loss. After hearing about shortened life spans, diseases, social retardation, and lack of opportunities, most parents would want to protect a child from such hardships. But how to protect that child is still in question, especially given all the complications with bariatric surgeries and how little is known about their long-term outcomes for adolescents.

OUTCOMES

In the same ways that Fat Studies has been critical of the diet industry and its profit motives, we need to scrutinize the sociomedical complex behind bariatric surgeries and its motives. Careers, reputations, salaries, and funding sources are on the line for many of the health care providers who are pushing bariatric surgeries as a cure for nearly everything. There are good reasons to be critical of the differences between informed consent and compliance, the pressures fat children and their parents face, and the solving of social problems via the cutting of children's bodies. Even those who practice the surgeries lack meaningful outcome studies about the long-term consequences of restricting eating and nutrient absorption in children and adolescents. But even if outcome studies suggested that bariatric surgeries were safe and effective, I firmly believe that many of the ethical questions they raise would remain. The one thing I think we know for certain, especially from a thoughtful examination of the history of surgeries on other marginalized children (such as children with intersex conditions who have atypical genitalia) is that one doesn't "cure" social problems or psychosocial problems through surgery. Consensus statements about the treatment of intersex conditions now acknowledge this.[128]

Significantly, many health care professionals oppose bariatric surgeries on adolescents. In many cases, those who have said they would not suggest bariatric surgeries for their patients are general practitioners. Bariatric surgeons often attribute the unwillingness of general practitioners to suggest or recommend bariatric surgery to misunderstandings about the consequences of obesity. Another way to read their misgivings, however, would indicate that general practitioners understand more about the *whole* patient. These physicians may be less inclined to see every problem as a surgical problem. I should also point out that general practitioners don't stand to profit from the bariatric surgeries the way that those in the bariatric field do, with current figures suggesting that nearly $6 billion a year are being spent on bariatric surgeries at present.[129]

Furthermore, in many cases, the doctors who perform the bariatric surgeries are the same doctors who are publishing the research that claims these surgeries are the best option for ending obesity. For example, Thomas Inge, whose name pops up everywhere in data searches for articles about adolescent bariatric surgery, is employed by Cincinnati Children's Hospital, whose bariatric treatment center for adolescents is nationally known. Recently, when the media began reporting that an article in the *New England Journal of Medicine* was presenting bariatric surgeries as a cure for diabetes, journalist Kate Scannell pointed out that the mainstream reports failed to mention the surgeon in charge of the study was on the payroll of the company that produced the equipment used in the surgeries. According to Scannell, the whole study, in fact, was funded by Ethicon Endoscopic Surgery,[130] a company that produces equipment used in laparoscopic bariatric surgeries.

Despite all the money being made and the cloudy outcomes, some practitioners want to see more children undergo these procedures, suggesting it's discriminatory to deny them treatment. Bemoaning statistics that suggest more children ought to be given bariatric surgeries, some health care providers find it perplexing that a larger number of children aren't allowed insurance coverage for such operations. Claiming that one in four children between the ages of eight and twelve are obese, the authors of "Revisiting Childhood Obesity: Persistent Underutilization of Surgical Intervention?" write, "Despite these disturbing statistics, less than one percent of the entire study population [over 250,000 children] was admitted for a bariatric procedure, which indicates a very low penetration of the procedure even after years of documented efficacy."[131] They also claim that the *real* discrimination may lie in criteria that exclude some children from coverage for such surgeries.[132]

I think, though, that the discrimination actually may lie in the very notion that children can and should change their bodies in order to appear "normal" or "healthy," to ease people's anxieties about the childhood obesity epidemic, or to curb discrimination against them. The forerunners of today's bariatric surgeries were procedures originally performed on cancer patients who'd had stomach or intestinal cancer that necessitated removing portions of and/or reconstructing their gastrointestinal tracts. As a result of the surgeries, many patients lost weight and showed some initial improvements in blood glucose readings.[133] Today, if most people were told that sectioning off part of a fully functioning and healthy organ and bypassing part of another would improve their well-being, they would guffaw, much like Roker did when he first went to see a surgeon. If they were told this was the route to ending discrimination against them and any poor treatment they received, they'd probably run away. Yet, this is exactly what's being done to adolescents, and increasingly younger children, who undergo bariatric surgeries.

A Cramped Room

To abstain from doing harm.
The Hippocratic Oath[1]

To do nothing is not the answer.
Dr. David Ludwig, speaking about the controversy surrounding his call to remove obese children from their homes on *Good Morning America*[2]

The first time I heard of Marlene Corrigan's daughter Christina dying was on an episode of the *Oprah Winfrey Show*. I still remember seeing Marlene sitting in a lonely chair on a stark stage. I was more shocked by how angry the audience was with her and how she was repeatedly blamed for her daughter's death than I was by the details of Christina's death, including that she weighed 680 pounds at the time. She died in the house where she and her mother lived, and the coroner listed her cause of death as heart failure. The court records reflected that Christina had been seen more than ninety times at local health facilities in the years before her death and that Marlene had repeatedly contacted school officials and health care providers for help. However, at the age of fifteen, Christina said that she no longer wanted to attend school or go to medical appointments; she also no longer wanted her mother's help with bathing and dressing. Marlene followed her wishes. After her daughter's death at the age of sixteen, she was charged with felony child neglect because local authorities maintained that at the time of death, Christina had both bedsores and feces on her body.[3] Her case is still regularly referenced in discussions of childhood obesity.

The *Oprah* audience was not at all sympathetic to the fact that Marlene had lost her daughter or that she was a single working mother who had been forced to make difficult choices about how to spend her time and how to feed her daughter. No one seemed to consider that in addition to caring for her daughter, she was working outside the home and also caring for her elderly parents; nor did anyone seem to notice that she had asked for help with her daughter so many times. The only thing that apparently mattered to the audience was that Marlene's daughter had been very fat. For me, the most poignant moment of the show was when a woman in the audience stood up and boldly defended Marlene by saying that if the daughter had died of anorexia, she would be offered sympathy rather than scorn. That woman was right, and she pointed out the difference in reactions that few advocates of the war against obesity have ever considered.

The truth is that most of the audience members had shown up that day not even knowing what the program was about, much less the details of Marlene's life that would come out years later after Fat Studies scholars began to study and write about the case. Yet, in spite of a lack of understanding or evidence, the audience was ready, willing, and able to pass judgment on Marlene. Although the US surgeon general wouldn't declare the war on obesity until nearly thirteen years after Christina's death,[4] the 1996 case became both a flashpoint and a lasting icon for the late twentieth-century and early twenty-first-century fight against fat. Marlene's appearance on *Oprah,* as well as the public reaction to her, was one of the reasons I became interested in Fat Studies. It is also, in part, why the case became a touchstone for me as I began understanding the war on obesity as a war being waged with the strategy of firing first and asking questions later and as a war with particularly harmful effects for women and children.

Without a doubt, part of what drives the popular assertion that something must be done about childhood obesity—even if the path isn't entirely clear—is the fear that a child such as Christina will die. Yet, looking back at the case against Marlene Corrigan, it certainly seems the panic and judgment was about far more than Christina's death or even Marlene's supposed neglect. As I've argued in the preceding chapters, the discussions surrounding children's bodies and parents' roles in their children's lives and embodiments, especially mothers' roles, are deeply influenced by cultural values and norms regarding gender, bodies, and parenting as much as the concern for children's health. In many ways, the case of Christina Corrigan *was* a worst-case scenario—not necessarily for the reasons many people might argue but because mainstream tropes about obesity and its causes meant that both Christina and Marlene were blamed for the tragedy, as are many parents and children today. As a result, the youngsters' bodies have become the primary targets of intervention.

Because health advocates and policy makers are trying to understand the rise in children's weights, they are seeking and constructing explanatory frameworks; in doing so, they are making incredibly vital choices concerning the stories that are told about children's bodies and mothers' roles. After all, in trying to understand and discuss children's weight, any number of explanatory frameworks can be adopted. A child's weight may be understood medically, if he or she has a metabolic disorder or underlying problem that causes weight gain. A child's weight may also be viewed through the lens of cultural influences, such as ubiquitous fast food or a lack of safe spaces in which to exercise. Many of these frameworks feature prominently in conversations about the obesity epidemic. Yet, in the case of childhood obesity, the overwhelmingly popular framework involves parental blame. In a society where mothers are still more often assumed to be the primary parents, mother blame has become the most popular means of understanding childhood obesity. As legal scholar Jo Bridgeman argues, in American society even when other factors are acknowledged, the "responsibility for personal health" is "on the individual" and "responsibility for children's health rests with their mother."[5] This is especially true for obesity, which is always assumed to be volitional at some level—even in light of mounting medical and cultural evidence that suggests otherwise. The framework of choice, then, is to blame mothers and aim interventions there.

One might assume that learning more about the effects of environment on body weight would have shifted blame away from mothers, but today's dominant legal opinions are actually strikingly similar to the rationale used to convict Marlene Corrigan in 1996, suggesting that any other factors contributing to childhood obesity remain irrelevant. Legal scholars point out that "thus far, judicial intervention in childhood obesity matters has explicitly rejected any arguments relating to external factors beyond the family unit, such as school or social environment, socioeconomic status, and genetics."[6] In her 2012 article entitled "The Family That Eats Together, Stays Together: Setting Table Standards for Childhood Obesity, Neglect, and the Family Unit," J.D. candidate Alaina Anderson, who ultimately contends that there are good reasons for removing obese children from homes, bluntly writes, "Placing blame on external environmental factors further perpetuates the obesity crisis by ignoring the true root of the problem—childhood obesity is the result of poor parenting in the home."[7] The most popular explanatory framework, then, appears to still be that of parental blame, which in the end is both antiwoman and antichild, for both women and children are punished under such ideological frameworks and policies.

FOOD FOR THOUGHT

The conviction that parents are ultimately responsible for their children's weight is so strong, in fact, that courts have roundly rejected charges that companies such as McDonald's are to blame for childhood obesity despite the ubiquitous nature of fast food in Americans' lives as well as the fast-food industry's widely acknowledged targeting of populations such as the poor and the young.[8] Time and time again in my research, I've discovered the most regularly cited legal opinions hold that, even though McDonald's spends a great deal of money to market its less expensive items specifically to children, neither a parent's need for quick and easy food nor a child's desire for it is a defense.[9] In other words, even those who firmly believe that a reliance on and taste for McDonald's and other fast food is causing the obesity epidemic also believe that mothers are responsible for ending that epidemic. Within such frameworks, mothers are expected to cook meals for their families, overcoming any obstacles that stand in the way of doing so. As I've shown, a nostalgia for homecooked meals is often inherent in arguments about obesity among children, with the suggestion being that if more women were in the home, more children would eat nutritious food and therefore be thinner. Yet, as scholars such as Michael Gard and Jan Wright assert, we have little or no real evidence that homecooked meals would necessarily produce thinner children.[10] In today's society, many parents, especially mothers, are forced to make choices about how to spend their time, and saving time is supposed to be one of the conveniences of modern-day food. After all, as Food Studies scholar Amy Bentley posits, "modern food allows people more choices, not just of food but of what they do with their lives."[11] In this way, the idea that a mother should stay at home and cook is, at some level, not only about childhood obesity but also about controlling women's choices,[12] and it is another example of women's needs coming second, all of which suggests a deep-seated urge to keep women in traditional roles rooted in the domestic sphere.

FAILING MOTHERS

Although we often don't name such an antimother sentiment as one of the "isms" about which we ought to be concerned, mothers who are judged inadequate, neglectful, or abusive by virtue of having fat children are the victims of what scholar Paula Caplan refers to as momism. Caplan writes, "Perhaps it is time to use the word *momism* to label mother-blame and mother-hate explicitly and succinctly as a form of prejudice as virulent as the other 'isms' are acknowledged to be."[13] As I've argued, the war on obesity produces a kind of momism that begins when children are in utero and seems to have no end, with the mother being consistently blamed for any undesirable trait or behavior in her child even though the focus on the mother's role "is to the exclusion of debate about the relevance of other factors which are beyond [her] control and which may endanger health."[14] Even women who aren't currently pregnant are subjected to momism, as they are warned that their own body weight may affect their future children through the uterine and/ or household environment, creating a whole other set of reasons for women in America to become weight obsessed. And whereas the obsession around weight created by advertising and weight-loss products has been widely criticized and named as a kind of misogyny, the obsession apt to be created by the emphasis on childhood obesity has a veil of scientific authority and is unlikely to be questioned in the same ways—even though it's apt to produce similar effects in women's lives.

The notion that fatness in women has a negative influence on children's weight has become well accepted and has gained a great deal of scientific and cultural authority. And that is a deeply troubling development because as a consequence, parents' bodies and especially women's bodies may also be read as evidence of an inability to parent. Currently, legal scholars discuss "secondhand obesity" in the same way one might discuss secondhand smoke as an influence on a child's health, suggesting that a fat parent pollutes the home environment simply by virtue of his or her own fatness. Some legal scholars are now going even further by comparing fat parents to parents who are incarcerated,[15] arguing that both are physically limited in how they can interact with their children (and calling to mind the familiar trope of the fat body as a kind of prison). In these cases, however, the fat body of the parent is also depicted as confining to the child, as the fat body's presence is thought to be so strong an environmental factor that a child simply cannot avoid its contaminating and suffocating influence. I cannot help but think of the ways disabled parents have struggled to assure courts that they are capable of raising happy and healthy children and of the similarities the war on obesity continues to share with other historical struggles of marginalized people who have simply wanted the right to raise a family.

VICTIM BLAMING

In the case of fatness, part of what drives the rationalization of the interventions now so popular in the war against obesity is a kind of victim blaming. Though many people now see obesity as a disease, a large number of those same people still choose to blame obese people for their situations, as I've argued is often the case with HIV or other embodiments or diseases associated with stigmatized groups. We are living in a time when discrimination against fat people is well documented and widely acknowledged. Legal journals, medical journals, and the popular press regularly report on discrimination that occurs in employment, education, and even health care environments. It's even sadder, then, that children and their families are often blamed for their own victimization in a society that is known to so despise fatness. The discrimination that children are apt to face is used by many professionals in the medical field as a justification for performing bariatric surgeries on these same youngsters. Similarly, evolving legal frameworks also suggest that discrimination against fat children in social environments, such as schools, is sufficient reason to remove children from the home environments that are believed to be causing their obesity, rather than working to change those environments. Further, discrimination is also used as a reason to intervene in women's reproductive lives, as the goal of keeping women slim is to limit not only the physical fatness of their children but also the social stigma that will be visited on their future children if they are fat. The strategy employed in such interventions is to ease the social stigma by changing women's and children's bodies or preventing them from becoming fat in the first place. In other words, those who are discriminated against are expected to also be the ones who will "fix" the problem by changing their bodies, leaving the discriminatory environment largely untouched.

These strategies bring to mind a sort of victim blaming that is inherent in mainstream ideas about women's roles in preventing sexual assault, an attitude I often encounter when I teach about sexual assault in undergraduate classes. In a short but insightful piece in the *Independent,* Natasha Devon compares conversations about school dress codes meant to stop young women from enticing young men to make sexual advances to conversations about fat children being asked to lose weight in order to thwart bullies; in the process, Devon showcases the very direct way that the blame to which victims of sexual assault have been subjected for years can be mapped onto fat children and their parents. She writes that in an e-mail conversation she was having with school officials about the way young women at a particular school were dressing, one person had this to say about the female students: "They need to understand the effect that what they are wearing is having and the trouble they could get themselves into."[16] Not long after that exchange, Devon participated in a radio interview about childhood obesity, during which a commentator stated, "If parents allow their children to become overweight they're going to get bullied at school and that is entirely the parents' fault."[17] As Devon goes on to note and as I have argued throughout the preceding chapters, the real problem of discrimination lies with fatphobic bullies and those who choose to commit sexual assaults, not with children who are fat or young women wearing a particular kind of clothing. In these ways, the cultural narrative that suggests women are primarily—or even solely—responsible for protecting themselves from sexual assault shares territory with the narrative that fat children and the parents of heavy children who are bullied must also be responsible for protecting themselves. Whether it's the expectation that women remain thin during pregnancy, that they keep themselves and their children svelte after birth, or that children lose weight through dieting or surgery, the war on obesity places the onus for change on the victims in ways that remind us of the notion that a woman is "asking for it" by wearing a short skirt or a revealing blouse—or, in this case, being fat.

WHOSE FAMILY VALUES?

The very things that are now considered some of the most useful weapons in the war on obesity, then, are proving to be harmful to women and children, especially those who are marginalized via race or class. Historically, many marginalized groups have been targeted for interventions when their parenting styles seemed to go against white, middle-class norms of parenting. For example, indigenous children in both the United States and Australia were formerly removed from homes due to a rationale now largely considered to be based more on racial bias and a privileging of a certain kind of parenting rather than any actual harm that was going to come to the children.[18] African American children faced a much higher likelihood of being removed from homes for similar reasons.[19] In other words, the privileging of particular standards of child care and the pathologizing of certain populations have previously resulted in children being removed from families without good cause, a fact now widely acknowledged by historians. Similarly, women have been more easily and readily subjected to interventions on their bodies, their pregnancies, and their family lives. The war on poverty spawned policies around required birth control for women on public assistance; the war on drugs and on HIV led to the mandatory testing of women who were pregnant and sometimes to legal charges and incarcerations. The war on obesity appears to be following a similar path. Given that more women are likely to be obese than men, that more women are apt to be raising children alone, and that it's more often people of color and working-class people who are obese in contemporary America, women and those marginalized by class or racial status are constructed as the most problematic and the most logical points of intervention. I find myself wondering if historians will one day look back on the removal of fat children from homes, the medical literature and burgeoning policies about women's pregnancies and weight, US public health campaigns, and bariatric surgeries done on children and also read these interventions as steeped in bias and part of America's larger cultural history of harmful interventions into the lives of marginalized people.

THE FINAL WORD

Although Christina Corrigan's case became a touchstone for many people, a tragic example of what might happen if a child's weight wasn't controlled, the assumption that her mother could have saved her was called into question during the trial when the coroner who had signed Christina's death certificate was cross-examined by Marlene's attorneys. He admitted that he had lied on his initial report. According to Bridgeman, he confessed that no autopsy had ever been performed on Christina; he had simply assumed—most likely because of her fatness—that she had died of heart failure.[20] This fact, however, has been largely lost in the reporting on Christina's case as so many rush to judge, to blame, and to act in the war against obesity. Even today, the case is often cited without any attention being paid to the details surrounding Christina's death or Marlene's prior struggles to get help. Christina is remembered only as a fat girl who died because of a neglectful mother, and Marlene is mostly remembered as an uncaring mother who didn't fulfill her responsibilities. The truth of the situation and the humanity of a very complicated case are glossed over in favor of a quick and easy assessment, which is a kind of microcosm of what is happening in the war on obesity itself.

I've shown how the war on obesity has become a war on mothers and children, as they have become not just collateral damage but also the intended targets of an army of doctors, public health officials, and a judicial system that all claim to want to save them. We can see how they have become the intended targets if we look at how harmful the interventions being used on them are—including bariatric surgeries, limits on access to reproductive technologies, court decisions designed to separate them from their loved ones, and socially sanctioned bullying via health campaigns that position fat people only as problems. Obesity is incredibly complicated and, in most cases, multifactorial. Yet, American society has developed a dangerous habit of boiling obesity down to blame. News reports expressed sadness over Christina Corrigan being found dead in what was supposedly "a cramped room," and I'm sure many people reading about Marlene Corrigan wondered how she could have allowed her daughter to get to the point of weighing 680 pounds. When I think about the society that's been created out of the hysteria around childhood obesity, I wonder how we could have let things get to this point with the interventions that now appear so normal and warranted to so many, creating an ideological cramped room of sorts for women and children.

The epigraph I used to open this book is from Australian scholars Michael Gard and Jan Wright, who argue that "the reason why the 'obesity epidemic' has come about could not be less important. The future will be decided along moral and ideological—that is, political—grounds."[21] If we are in the midst of an obesity epidemic, we may not be able to unweave those threads to take us back to a time when children were thinner, but we certainly have choices to make about how to go forward. I hope that the moral, ideological, and political decisions we all make about how we understand childhood obesity can get us to a better future, a future where women and children needn't be afraid of being subjected to beliefs and policies that are dangerous and harmful—all in the name of trying to save them.

Notes

PREFACE

The term *diabesity* is now used as a shorthand conflation of *obesity* and *diabetes*, with the implication being that the two are so closely associated that the conflation is warranted. For a concise explanation of the use of *diabesity*, see http://www.eufic.org /article/en/diet-related-diseases/diabetes/artid/diabetes-diabesity/.

INTRODUCTION: THE MOTHER OF ALL WARS

1   Michael Gard and Jan Wright, *The Obesity Epidemic: Science, Morality and Ideology* (New York: Routledge, 2005), 151.
2   Although the Regino case took place before the official announcement of the war on obesity, an argument can certainly be made that the culture was already headed in that direction in 2000. Regardless, the Regino case remains an important touchstone.
3   Kristen E. Brierly, "Family Law—Childhood Morbid Obesity: How Excess Pounds Can Tip the Scales of Justice in Favor of Removing a Child from the Home and/or Termination of Parental Rights," *Western New England Law Review* 35, no. 1 (2013): 129.
4   Alyssa Newcomb, "Obese Third Grader Taken from Mom, Placed in Foster Care," ABC News.com, November 27, 2011, http://abcnews.go.com/blogs/health/2011/11/27 /obese-third-grader-taken-from-family-placed-in-foster-care/.
5   Quoted in Dan Harris and Mikaela Conley, "Childhood Obesity: A Call for Parents to Lose Custody," ABC News, July 14, 2011, http://abcnews.go.com/Health/child hood-obesity-call-parents-lose-custody/story?id=14068280#.UKpFeYWvy2Q.
6   Ibid.
7   John Evans and Brian Davies, "Sociology, the Body, and Health in a Risk Society," in *Body Knowledge and Control: Studies in the Sociology of Physical Education and Health,* ed. John Evans, Brian Davies, and Jan Wright (New York: Routledge, 2004), 39.
8   See Gard and Wright, *Obesity Epidemic*; Michael Gard, *The End of the Obesity Epidemic* (New York: Routledge, 2011); Paul Campos, *The Obesity Myth: Why America's Obsession with Weight Is Hazardous to Your Health* (New York: Gotham Books, 2004); Julie Guthman, *Weighing In: Obesity, Food Justice, and the Limits of Capitalism* (Berke-

ley: University of California Press, 2011); Eric J. Oliver, *Fat Politics: The Real Story behind America's Obesity Epidemic* (New York: Oxford University Press, 2006).

9 For examples, see Tara Parker-Pope, "Better to Be Fat and Fit Than Skinny and Unfit," *New York Times*, August 18, 2008, http://www.nytimes.com/2008/08/19/health/19well.html?_r=0; Gretchen Reynolds, "Getting Fat but Staying Fit," *New York Times Wellblog*, March 7, 2012, http://well.blogs.nytimes.com/2012/03/07/getting-fat-but-staying-fit/?_r=0; and Reynolds, "Phys Ed: Can You Be Overweight and Still Be Healthy?" *New York Times Wellblog*, January 6, 2010, http://well.blogs.nytimes.com/2010/01/06/phys-ed-can-you-be-overweight-and-still-be-healthy/.

10 Trevor Butterworth, "Top Science Journal Rebukes Harvard's Top Nutritionist," Forbes.com, May 27, 2013, http://www.forbes.com/sites/trevorbutterworth/2013/05/27/top-science-journal-rebukes-harvards-top-nutritionist/.

11 Ibid.

12 Gard, *End of the Obesity Epidemic*, 5–7.

13 Ibid.

14 Ibid.

15 Ibid., 7.

16 Karen Zivi, *Making Rights Claims: A Practice of Democratic Citizenship* (New York: Oxford University Press, 2012), 102.

17 The war on obesity was officially declared at a press conference held by C. Everett Koop and David Satcher on December 13, 2001.

18 Brian Doherty, "Fatwa on Fat: The Surgeon General Snoops into Private Health, Again," December 19, 2001, http://reason.com/archives/2001/12/19/fatwa-on-fat.

19 Greg Critser, *Fatland: How Americans Became the Fattest People on Earth* (New York: Houghton Mifflin, 2003), 82.

20 Peter Stearns, *Fat History: Bodies and Beauty in the Modern West* (New York: New York University Press, 1997), 23.

21 Hillel Schwartz, *Never Satisfied: A Cultural History of Diets, Fantasies, and Fat* (New York: Free Press, 1986), 143.

22 Ibid., 140–141.

23 Ibid.

24 Ibid., 143.

25 Campos, *Obesity Myth*, 3.

26 *The Weight of the Nation*, directed by Kevin Kindle, 2012, HBO Documentary Films and Institute of Medicine, http://theweightofthenation.hbo.com/.

27 Susan Sontag, *Illness as Metaphor and AIDS and Its Metaphors* (New York: Picador, 1989), 104.

28 Ibid., 173.

29 Anna Mollow, "Sized Up: Why Fat Is a Queer and Feminist Issue," bitch.com, http://bitchmagazine.org/article/sized-up-fat-feminist-queer-disability.

30 Ibid.

31 Greg Critser, "Let Them Eat Fat," *Harper's Magazine*, March 2000, 41–49.

32 I've previously written about Critser's work in an article entitled "Collateral Damage from Friendly Fire? Race, Nation, Class, and the 'War on Obesity,'" *Social Semiotics* 15, no. 2 (2005): 127–141. Some material from that article is included here.

33 Natalie Boero, *Killer Fat: Media, Medicine, and Morals in the American "Obesity Epidemic"* (New Brunswick, N.J.: Rutgers University Press, 2012), 44.

34 Ibid., 75–76.

35 Quoted in Sontag, *Illness as Metaphor*, 113. For the original citation, see Erving Goffman's *Stigma: Notes on the Management of Spoiled Identities* (New York: Simon and Schuster, 1963), especially the chapter called "Stigma and Social Identity."

36 James F. Childress, "The War Metaphor in Public Policy: Some Moral Reflections," in *The Leader's Imperative: Ethics, Integrity, and Responsibility*, ed. J. Carl Ficarrotta (West Lafayette, Ind.: Purdue University Press, 2001), 191.

37 Mollow, "Sized Up."

38 Ibid.; see the "Comments" section specifically.

39 Meredith Bennett-Smith, "Geoffrey Miller, Visiting NYU Professor, Slammed for Fat-Shaming Obese PhD Applicants," HuffingtonPost.com, June 4, 2013, http://www.huffingtonpost.com/2013/06/04/geoffrey-miller-fat-shaming-nyu-phd_n_3385641.html.

40 Sontag, *Illness as Metaphor*, 135.

41 George Lipsitz, *American Studies in a Moment of Danger* (Minneapolis: University of Minnesota Press, 2001), 12.

42 Boero, *Killer Fat*, 1.

43 Quoted in Charlotte Biltekoff, "The Terror Within: Obesity in Post 9/11 U.S. Life," *American Studies* 48, no. 3 (2007): 40.

44 Stearns, *Fat History*, 259.

45 Oliver, *Fat Politics*, 74–75.

46 Mollow, "Sized Up."

47 Amy Erdman Farrell, *Fat Shame: Stigma and the Fat Body in American Culture* (New York: New York University Press, 2011), 176.

48 Critser, "Let Them Eat Fat," 3.

49 Michael Pollan, "You Want Fries with That?" NYTimes.com, January 12, 2003, http://www.nytimes.com/2003/01/12/books/you-want-fries-with-that.html?pagewanted=all&src=pm.

50 Michael Sherry, "The Language of War in AIDS Discourse," in *Writing AIDS: Gay Literature, Language and Analysis*, ed. T. Murphy and S. Poirer (New York: Columbia University Press, 1993), 41.

51 Boero, *Killer Fat*, 101.

52 Sontag, *Illness as Metaphor*, 99.

53 This commercial was sponsored by the Partnership for a Drug Free America and can be viewed at http://www.youtube.com/watch?v=nl5gBJGnaXs.

54 William N. Elwood, *Rhetoric in the War on Drugs: The Triumphs and Tragedies of Public Relations* (Santa Barbara, Calif.: Praeger Press, 1994), 84.

55 Biltekoff, "Terror Within," 33.

56 Elwood, *Rhetoric in the War on Drugs*, 70.

57 Campos, *Obesity Myth*, xxiii.

58 "Childhood Obesity Facts," Centers for Disease Control and Prevention, February 19, 2013, http://www.cdc.gov/healthyyouth/obesity/facts.htm.

59 "Childhood Obesity," US Department of Health and Human Services, December 20, 2012, http://aspe.hhs.gov/health/reports/child_obesity/.

60 "Childhood Obesity," American Heart Association, December 20, 2012, http://www .heart.org/HEARTORG/GettingHealthy/WeightManagement/Obesity/Childhood -Obesity_UCM_304347_Article.jsp.

61 S. Jay Olshanky, Douglas J. Passaro, Ronald C. Hershaw, Jennifer Layden, Bruce A. Carnes, Jacob Brody, Leonard Hayflick, Robert N. Butler, David B. Allison, and David S. Ludwig, "A Potential Decline in Life Expectancy in the United States in the 21st Century," *New England Journal of Medicine* 352, no. 11 (2005): 1138–1145.

62 *Fat talk* is an umbrella term used by Fat Studies scholars to name the constant chatter about weight, diet, and body fat that goes on in the United States. Examples include everything from women complaining about their thighs being fat to people justifying why it's okay to eat a piece of cake at a birthday party.

63 "About Let's Move!" Let's Move! January 12, 2013, http://www.letsmove.gov/about.

64 Portions of this section were previously published on my *Psychology Today* blog in a piece entitled "My Beef with Michelle Obama's *Let's Move!* Campaign," April 25, 2012, http://www.psychologytoday.com/blog/dry-land-fish/201204/my-beef-michelle -obamas-lets-move-campaign.

65 "Public Health Grand Rounds," Centers for Disease Control, accessed June 17, 2010, http://www.cdc.gov/about/grand-rounds/archives/2010/06-June.htm.

66 "Paying the Price for Those Extra Pounds," Harvard School of Public Health, January 21, 2013, http://www.hsph.harvard.edu/obesity-prevention-source/obesity-consequences /economic/#costs-rising.

67 Ibid.

68 "Childhood Obesity Facts," Centers for Disease Control, accessed December 13, 2012, http://www.cdc.gov/healthyyouth/obesity/facts.htm.

69 Critser, *Fatland,* 121.

70 Lindsey Abrams, "A Case for Stigmatizing Obesity," *Atlantic,* accessed January 23, 2013, http://www.theatlantic.com/health/archive/2013/01/a-case-for-shaming-obese- people-tastefully/267446/.

71 Lisette Burrows, "'This Is How "We" Do It': Pedagogising Families in Obesity Dis- course," *Childrenz Issues* 13, no. 1 (2009): 10.

72 Biltekoff, "Terror Within," 41.

73 "Suing McDonald's over Happy Meals Won't Keep Kids from Getting Fat," *Crain's Chi- cago Business,* December 20, 2010, http://www.chicagobusiness.com/article/20101218/ ISSUE07/312189992/editorial-suing-mcdonald-s-over-happy-meals-won-t-keep -kids-from-getting-fat.

74 Dr. Klein's ad ran in the *Washington National Times Weekly* from May 30 to June 5, 2006.

75 J. Clinton Smith, *Understanding Childhood Obesity* (Jackson: University Press of Mis- sissippi, 1999), 84.

76 Ibid.

77 Paula Ford-Martin, *The Everything Parents Guide to the Overweight Child* (Avon, Mass.: Adams Media Corporation, 2005), 48.

78 Quoted in Gard and Wright, *Obesity Epidemic*, 132.

79 Ibid., 133.

80 Natalie Boero, "Fat Kids, Working Moms and the 'Epidemic of Obesity': Race, Class

and Mother Blame," in *The Fat Studies Reader,* ed. Esther Rothblum and Sondra Solovay (New York: New York University Press, 2009), 115.

81   Paula Caplan, *Don't Blame Mother: Mending the Mother-Daughter Relationship* (New York: Harper & Row, 1989), 135.

82   The fetal overnutrition hypothesis seems to first appear in medical literature around 2002.

83   Lauren Neergaard, "Mom's Obesity Surgery May Help Break Cycle in Kids," Yahoo News.com, May 27, 2013, http://news.yahoo.com/moms-obesity-surgery-may-help -break-cycle-kids-192322482.html.

84   Rebecca Kukla, *Mass Hysteria: Medicine, Culture, and Mothers' Bodies* (New York: Rowman & Littlefield, 2005), 118.

85   Neergaard, "Mom's Obesity Surgery."

86   Karen Zivi, "Contesting Motherhood in the Age of AIDS: Maternal Ideology in the Debate over Mandatory HIV Testing," *Feminist Studies* 31, no. 2 (2005): 349.

87   "Weight-Loss Surgery and Children," US Library of Medicine and the National Institutes of Health, July 11, 2011, http://www.nlm.nih.gov/medlineplus/ency/patient instructions/000356.htm.

88   Kathleen LeBesco, *Revolting Bodies? The Struggle to Redefine Identity* (Amherst: University of Massachusetts Press, 2004), 115.

CHAPTER 1: CHILDREN FIRST

1   Zivi, "Contesting Motherhood," 350.

2   Ford-Martin, *Everything Parent's Guide,* 107.

3   S. Y. Huh, S. L. Rifas-Shiman, C. A. Zera, J. W. Edwards, E. Oken, S. T. Weiss, and M. W. Gillman, "Delivery by Caesarean Section and Risk of Obesity in Preschool Age Children: A Prospective Cohort Study," *Journal of Archives of Disease in Childhood* 97, no. 7 (2010): 610–616.

4   Smith, *Understanding Childhood Obesity,* 92.

5   "Fetal overnutrition hypothesis" is often referenced in literature about childhood obesity and pregnancy. For one key example, see Debbie A. Lawlor, George Davey Smith, Michael O'Callaghan, Rosa Alati, Abdullah Mahmun, Gail M. Williams, and Jake M. Najiman, "Epidemiologic Evidence for the Fetal Overnutrition Hypothesis: Findings from the Mater-University Study of Pregnancy and Its Outcomes," *American Journal of Epidemiology* 165, no. 4 (2006): 418–424.

6   Zivi, "Contesting Motherhood," 349.

7   Ibid., 347–348.

8   Ibid., 352–353.

9   Ibid., 353.

10   Although both Shape Up America! and Let's Move! attempt to position themselves as health campaigns, the focus is clearly on weight loss. The home page of the Let's Move! website is littered with references to weight loss and preventing childhood obesity rather than fostering a certain set of eating and exercise habits for all children.

11 John G. Kral, Ruth A. Kava, Patrick M. Catalano, and Barbara J. Moore, "Severe Obesity: The Neglected Epidemic," *European Journal of Obesity* 5, no. 2 (2012): 255.

12 This trend of proposing to talk about "parents" while actually talking about mothers is also very common in parenting manuals. For a longer discussion of my work on that subject, please see my article "Mommy Made Me Do It: Mothering Fat Children in the Age of the Obesity Epidemic," *Food, Culture and Society* 13, no. 3 (2010): 331–349.

13 Kimberly M. Mutcherson, "No Way to Treat a Woman: Creating an Appropriate Standard for Resolving Medical Treatment Disputes Involving HIV-Positive Children," *Harvard Women's Law Journal* 25, no. 221 (2002), August 14, 2012, http://papers.ssrn .com/sol3/papers.cfm?abstract_id=2125988.

14 Ibid.

15 Kral et al., "Severe Obesity," 257.

16 Ibid.

17 Ibid., 260.

18 Megan Warin, Tanya Zivkovic, Vivienne Moore, and Michael Davies, "Mothers as Smoking Guns," *Feminism and Psychology*, published online May 16, 2012, 10, http:// fap.sagepub.com/content/early/2012/05/16/0959353512445359.

19 Samantha Murray, "Normative Imperatives vs. Pathological Bodies: Constructing the 'Fat' Woman," *Australian Feminist Studies* 23, no. 56 (2008): 214.

20 Ibid. (emphases in the original).

21 Quoted in Warin et al., "Mothers as Smoking Guns," 11, and originally published in John G. Kral, "Preventing and Treating Obesity in Girls and Young Women to Curb the Epidemic," *Obesity Research* 12, no. 10 (2004): 1539–1546.

22 Quoted in Mutcherson, "No Way to Treat a Woman."

23 Zivi, "Contesting Motherhood," 352.

24 Susan Bordo, *Unbearable Weight: Feminism, Western Culture, and the Body* (Berkeley: University of California Press, 1993), 201.

25 *Flashdance,* directed by Adriene Lyne, 1983, DVD, Los Angeles: Paramount Pictures, 2002.

26 Bordo, *Unbearable Weight*, 110.

27 Fat women are also sometimes seen as asexual, which seems to suggest that the fat body falls outside the norms of sexuality and femininity in many different—and sometimes even contradictory—ways. For a discussion of the asexuality of fat women, see Angela Stukator's essay "It's Not Over until the Fat Lady Sings: Comedy, the Carnivalesque, and Body Politics," in *Bodies Out of Bounds: Fatness and Transgression,* ed. Jana Evans Braziel and Kathleen LeBesco (Berkeley: University of California Press, 2001), 197–213.

28 Marcia Millman, *Such a Pretty Face: Being Fat in America* (New York: W. W. Norton, 1989): 20.

29 Warin et al., "Mothers as Smoking Guns," 2.

30 Ibid., 8–9.

31 Zivi, "Contested Motherhood," 352–353.

32 David Kassirer and Marcia Angell, "Losing Weight: An Ill-Fated New Year's Resolution," *New England Journal of Medicine* 338, no. 1 (1998): 52–54; Linda Bacon and Lucy

Aphramor, "Weight Science: Evaluating the Evidence for a Paradigm Shift," *Nutrition Journal* 10, no. 19 (2011), http://www.nutritionj.com/content/10/1/9; Traci Mann, A. Janet Tomiyama, Erika Westling, Ann-Marie Lew, Barbara Samuels, and Jason Chatman, "Medicare's Search for Effective Obesity Treatments: Diets Are Not the Answer," *American Psychologist* 62, no. 3 (2007): 220–233.

33 Zivi, "Contested Motherhood," 353.

34 Fiona Macrae, "Obesity Legacy of Mums-to-Be: Carrying Too Many Pounds during Pregnancy Can Give Your Baby a Life of Weight Problems," *Daily Mail*, May 14, 2012, http://www.dailymail.co.uk/health/article-2144243/Obesity-pregnancy-Carrying -pounds-baby-life-weight-problems.html.

35 C. Y. W. Lee and G. Koren, "Maternal Obesity: Effects on Pregnancy and the Role of Pre-conception Counseling," *Journal of Obstetrics and Gynaecology* 30, no. 2 (2010): 103.

36 Christine M. Olson, Myla St. Strawderman, and Barbara A. Dennison, "Maternal Weight Gain during Pregnancy and Child Weight at Age 3 Years," *Maternal and Child Health Journal* 13 (2009): 840.

37 J. Laitinen, A. Jaaskalainen, A. L. Hartikainen, U. Sovio, M. Vaarasmaki, A. Pouto, M. Kaakanen, and M. R. Jarvelin, "Maternal Weight Gain during the First Half of Pregnancy and Offspring Obesity at 16 Years: A Prospective Cohort Study," *British Journal of Obstetrics and Gynaecology: An International Journal of Obstetrics and Gynaecology* 119, no. 6 (2012): 722 (my emphasis).

38 "Obesity and Extreme Slimness Cause Risks in Pregnancy," *Science Daily,* April 19, 2012, http://www.sciencedaily.com/releases/2012/04/120419090719.htm.

39 Caplan, *Don't Blame Mother,* 39.

40 Ibid., 47.

41 Boero, "Fat Kids, Working Moms," 114.

42 Bordo, *Unbearable Weight*, 81.

43 Warin et al., "Mothers as Smoking Guns," 2.

44 Judith Shulevitz, "Why Fathers Really Matter," *New York Times Sunday Review,* September 8, 2012, http://www.nytimes.com/2012/09/09/opinion/sunday/why-fathers -really-matter.html?pagewanted=all.

45 Ibid.

46 Ibid.

47 John Cloud, "Why Your DNA Isn't Your Destiny," *Time Magazine,* January 6, 2010, http://www.time.com/time/magazine/article/0,9171,1952313,00.html.

48 Shulevitz, "Why Fathers Really Matter."

49 JaneMaree Maher, Suzanne Fraser, and Jan Wright, "Framing the Mother: Childhood Obesity, Maternal Responsibility and Care," *Journal of Gender Studies* 19, no. 3 (2010): 241.

50 Ibid., 241.

51 Warin et al., "Mothers as Smoking Guns," 11.

52 This photo is strikingly similar to photos on the covers of *Newsweek* and *Time* that also use ice-cream cones and obscured faces as props. For a discussion of the culture of fear around ice cream and these two magazine covers, please see the introduction to this book.

53 Nancy Kubasek, "The Case against Prosecutions for Prenatal Drug Use," *Texas Journal of Women and the Law* 8 (1999): 177.

54 Ibid., 176.

55 Quoted in Ada Calhoun, "The Criminalization of Bad Mothers," *New York Times,* April 25, 2012, http://www.nytimes.com/2012/04/29/magazine/the-criminalization-of -bad-mothers.html?pagewanted=all.

56 W. Charisse Goodman, *The Invisible Woman: Confronting Weight Prejudice in America* (Carlsbad, Calif.: Gurze Books, 1995), 2.

57 Terry Poulton, *No Fat Chicks: How Big Business Profits by Making Women Hate Their Bodies—and How to Fight Back* (Seacaucus, N.J.: Birch Lane Press, 1997), 87.

58 Kral et al., "Severe Obesity," 255.

59 Dorothy E. Roberts, "Punishing Drug Addicts Who Have Babies: Women of Color, Equality, and the Right of Privacy," *Harvard Law Review* 104, no. 7 (1991): 1419–1482.

60 Ibid., 1420.

61 Ibid.

62 Kristen Scharmberg, "Prosecutors Targeting Pregnant Drug Users: Some Fear Women Will Shun Treatment," *Chicago Tribune News,* November 23, 2003, http://articles .chicagotribune.com/2003–11-23/news/0311230450_1_prosecutions-pregnant-women -pregnant-drug-users.

63 Mutcherson, "No Way to Treat a Woman"; Roberts, "Punishing Drug Addicts"; Scharmberg, "Prosecutors Targeting Pregnant Drug Users."

64 Mutcherson, "No Way to Treat a Woman."

65 Bordo, *Unbearable Weight,* 78.

66 Krista Stone-Manista, "Protecting Pregnant Women: A Guide to Successfully Challenging Criminal Abuse Prosecutions of Pregnant Drug Addicts," *Journal of Criminal Law and Criminology* 99, no. 3 (2009): 836.

67 Susan Okie, "The Epidemic That Wasn't," *New York Times,* January 26, 2009, http:// www.nytimes.com/2009/01/27/health/27coca.html?_r=1&pagewanted=all&, accessed September 15, 2012.

68 Ibid.

69 Quoted in ibid.

70 Amanda Gardner, "Many Obese Americans Struggle with Stigma, Discrimination, Poll Finds," *U.S. News and World Report,* August 23, 2012, http://health.usnews.com/ health-news/news/articles/2012/08/23/many-obese-americans-struggle-with-stigma -discrimination-poll-finds; Mark V. Roehling, Patricia V. Roehling, and L. Maureen Odland, "Investigating the V=Validity of Stereotypes about Overweight Employees," *Group and Organization Management* 23, no. 4 (2008): 392–424; R. M. Puhl, T. Andreyeva, and K. D. Brownell, "Perceptions of Weight Discrimination: Prevalence and Comparison to Race and Gender Discrimination in America," *International Journal of Obesity* 32 (2008): 992–1000.

71 US Department of Health and Human Services, "Childhood Obesity," October 12, 2012, http://aspe.hhs.gov/health/reports/child_obesity/.

72 Centers for Disease Control, "Adult Obesity Facts," October 24, 2012, http://www.cdc .gov/obesity/data/adult.html.

73 Roberts, "Punishing Drug Addicts," 1434.

74 Ibid.

75 Ibid., 1435.

76 Bordo, *Unbearable Weight*, 79.

77 Zivi, "Contesting Motherhood," 364.

78 Jennifer Weiner, "The F Word," *Allure: The Beauty Expert,* October 2010, http://www.allure.com/allure-magazine/2012/10/fat-the-f-word.

79 Roberts, "Punishing Drug Addicts," 1472.

80 Julie Anne Barnes and Fiona Macrae, "Babies Treated in the Womb for Obesity: Overweight Mothers-to-Be Get Diabetes Pill to Cut the Risk of Having a Fat Child," *Mail Online,* April 1, 2012.

81 Ibid.

82 Zivi, "Contested Motherhood," 349–350.

83 Ibid.

84 Critser, *Fatland,* 150.

85 Ibid.,151.

86 Ibid.

87 Ibid.

88 *Weight of the Nation.*

89 Quoted in Kathleen LeBesco, "Quest for a Cause: The Fat Gene, the Gay Gene, and the New Eugenics," in *The Fat Studies Reader,* ed. Esther Rothblum and Sondra Solovay (New York: New York University Press, 2009), 67.

90 Macrae, "Obesity Legacy."

91 LeBesco, "Quest for a Cause," 73.

92 Zivi, "Contesting Motherhood," 353.

93 Quoted in Adrienne Asch, "Why I Haven't Changed My Mind about Prenatal Diagnosis: Reflections and Refinements," in *Prenatal Testing and Disability Rights,* ed. Adrienne Asch and Erik Parens (Washington, D.C.: Georgetown University Press, 2000), 244.

94 "Costs and Paying for Treatment," Fertility Associates, November 30, 2012, http://www.fertilityassociates.co.nz/paying-for-treatment.aspx.

95 C. M. Farquhar and W. R. Gillett, "Prioritising for Fertility Treatments—Should a High BMI Exclude Treatment?" *British Journal of Obstetrics and Gynaecology: An International Journal of Obstetrics and Gynaecology* 113, no. 10 (2006): 1108.

96 S. Pandey, A. Maheshwari, and S. Battacharya, "Should Access to Fertility Treatment Be Determined by Female Body Mass Index?" *Human Reproduction* 25, no. 4 (2010): 817; M. M. Peterson, "Assisted Reproductive Technologies and Equity of Access Issues," *Journal of Medical Ethics* 31 (2005), 281.

97 Pandey, Maheshwari, and Battacharya, "Should Access to Fertility Treatment," 816–817.

98 Ibid., 815.

99 Peterson, "Assisted Reproductive Technologies," 281.

100 Christine Leary, "Should Obese Women Be Denied Access to Fertility Treatment on the NHS?" *Biologist* 58, no. 2 (2011), 24.

101 Rebecca Puhl and Kelly D. Brownell, "Bias, Discrimination and Obesity," *Obesity Research* 9, no. 12 (2001): 788–805.

102 Peterson, "Assisted Reproductive Technologies," 282.

103 Human Fertilization and Embryology Authority, "NHS Fertility Treatment," May 9, 2012, http://www.hfea.gov.uk/fertility-treatment-cost-nhs.html.

104 Anjel Vahratian and Yolanda R. Smith, "Should Access to Fertility-Related Services Be Conditional on Body Mass Index?" *Human Reproduction* 24, no. 7 (2009): 1536.

105 Peterson, "Assisted Reproductive Technologies," 284.

106 Vahratian and Smith, "Should Access to Fertility-Related Services," 1532.

107 Pandey, Maheshwari, and Battacharya, "Should Access to Fertility Treatment," 817.

108 Vicky Allan, "The War on Fat People: Time for a Truce," *Sunday Herald,* September 11, 2011, 29.

109 Leary, "Should Obese Women," 26.

110 Annemarie Jutel, "Weighing Health: The Moral Burden of Obesity," *Social Semiotics* 15, no. 2 (2005): 117.

111 Farquhar and Gillett, "Prioritising for Fertility Treatments," 1108.

112 Ibid.

113 Vahratian and Smith, "Should Access to Fertility-Related Services," 1536.

114 Puhl and Brownell, "Bias, Discrimination and Obesity," 788.

115 Ibid., 792.

116 Natasha Schvey, "Weight Bias in Healthcare," *American Medical Association Journal of Ethics* 12, no. 4 (2010): 288.

117 Puhl, Andreyva, and Brownell, "Perceptions of Weight Discrimination," 32.

118 N. K. Amy, A. Aalborg, P. Lyons, and L. Keranen, "Barriers to Routine Gynecological Cancer Screening for White and African American Obese Women," *International Journal of Obesity* 30 (2006): 150.

119 Ibid., 147.

120 Ibid., 151–152.

CHAPTER 2: THERE'S NO PLACE LIKE HOME

1 Harris and Conley, "Childhood Obesity." During this interview, Dr. Orentlicher made it clear that he disagrees with removing children from homes due to obesity. Here, he's making the argument that those who suggest removing children are essentially taking the "easy" way out by pointing to parents as the problem, since fixing food systems or school lunch programs is too difficult, expensive, or time consuming.

2 Lindsey Murtagh and David S. Ludwig, "State Intervention in Life-Threatening Childhood Obesity," *Journal of the American Medical Association* 306, no. 2 (2011): 206.

3 Ibid.

4 Todd Varness, David. B. Allen, Aaron L. Carrel, and Norman Fost, "Childhood Obesity and Medical Neglect," *Pediatrics* 123, no. 1 (2009): 399.

5 Ibid., 404.

6 Gaia Bernstein and Zvi Triger, "Over-Parenting," *University of California Davis Law Review* 44, no. 4 (2011): 1221–1279.

7 Adrian Lowe, "Is This Child Abuse? Courts Think So," July 12, 2012, http://www.theage.com.au/victoria/is-this-child-abuse-the-courts-think-so-20120711-21wdb.html.

8 Rogan Kersh, "The Politics of Obesity: A Current Assessment and Look Ahead," *Millbank Quarterly* 87, no. 1 (2009): 298; see also Abigail Saguy's book *What's Wrong with Fat?* (New York: Oxford University Press, 2012), which takes up the issue of how obesity is framed at length.

9 *The Morning Show with Mike and Juliet*, June 2007, http://www.youtube.com/watch?v=gBdLKNKqeAY.

10 Maher, Fraser, and Wright, "Framing the Mother," 233.

11 Bernstein and Triger, "Over-Parenting," 1272.

12 Ibid.

13 Boero, "Fat Kids, Working Moms," 116.

14 Ron Barnett, "S. C. Case Looks on Child Obesity as Abuse. But Is It?" *USA Today*, July 17, 2009, http://usatoday30.usatoday.com/news/health/weightloss/2009-07-20-obesity boy_N.htm?csp=34.

15 Bernstein and Triger, "Over-Parenting," 1230.

16 Ibid., 1279.

17 Gard and Wright, *Obesity Epidemic*, 23.

18 Legal scholar Melissa Mitgang points out that many of the relevant opinions are, in fact, sealed; see Mitgang, "Childhood Obesity and State Intervention: An Examination of the Health Risks of Pediatric Obesity and When They Justify State Involvement," *Columbia Journal of Law and Social Problems* 44, no. 553 (2011): 553–587.

19 Caplan, *Don't Blame Mother*, 43.

20 *In the Interest of L. T., a Minor Child*, 494 N.W.2d 450 (Court of Appeals of Iowa, 1992).

21 Ibid.

22 Ibid.

23 *In re D. K.*, 202 WL 31968992 (Pa.com.PI.), 58 pa. (D. & C. 4th 353, 2002).

24 *In the Matter of Brittany T.*, N-0142–03/06 G (Family Court of New York, Chemung County, 2007).

25 *In the Interest of L. T.*

26 Ibid.

27 *In re D. K.*

28 *In the Matter of Brittany T.*

29 Gail Landsman, "Real Motherhood: Class and Children with Disabilities," in *Ideologies and Technologies of Motherhood: Race, Class, Sexuality and Nationalism*, ed. Helene Ragone and France Winddance Twine (New York: Routledge, 2000), 173.

30 Jane Taylor McDonnell, "On Being the 'Bad' Mother of an Autistic Child," in *"Bad" Mothers: The Politics of Blame in Twentieth-Century America*, ed. Molly Ladd-Taylor and Lauri Umansky (New York: New York University Press, 1998), 221.

31 Landsman, "Real Motherhood," 173.

32 A search on Amazon.com using key terms *childhood obesity* and *parenting* turns up more than 100 advice manuals.

33 Deena Patel, "Super-Sized Kids: Using the Law to Combat Morbid Obesity in Children," *Family Court Review: An Interdisciplinary Journal* 43, no. 1 (2005): 166. It is important to note that Patel's article is widely cited. In fact, it's cited in the piece by Murtagh and Ludwig.

34 Ibid.

35 Murtagh and Ludwig, "State Intervention," 206.

36 *In the Interest of L. T.*

37 Sondra Solovay, *Tipping the Scales of Justice: Fighting Weight-Based Discrimination* (Amherst, N.Y.: Prometheus Books, 2000), 74.

38 See Strong4Life's website at http://www.strong4life.com/.

39 See chapter 4 for a more detailed discussion of this campaign and the controversy.

40 Iris Marion Young, *Throwing Like a Girl and Other Essays in Feminist Philosophy and Social Theory* (Bloomington: Indiana University Press, 1990), 145.

41 Stukator, "It's Not Over," 199.

42 Farrell, *Fat Shame,* 129.

43 Sylvia Rimm, *Rescuing the Emotional Lives of Overweight Children: What Our Kids Go through and How We Can Help* (Emmaus, Pa.: Rodale Press, 2004), 39.

44 Barnett, "S. C. Case."

45 In 2012, a boy in Sandusky, Ohio, was starved to death by his parents and grandmother, all of whom were eventually charged. There have also been recent cases in North Mankato, Minnesota, and Madison, Wisconsin, of parents being prosecuted for starving their children to death.

46 Quoted in Peg Tyre, "Fighting Anorexia: No One Is to Blame," National Association of Anorexia and Associated Disorders, December 5, 2005, http://www.anad.org/news/fighting-anorexia-no-one-is-to-blame-newsweek/.

47 Ibid.

48 Ibid.

49 I discuss this case in more detail in the conclusion.

50 Solovay, *Tipping the Scales,* 75.

51 Tyre, "Fighting Anorexia."

52 Ibid.

53 Cecilia Hartley, "Letting Ourselves Go: Making Room for the Fat Body in Feminist Scholarship," in *Bodies Out of Bounds: Fatness and Transgression,* ed. Kathleen LeBesco and Jana Evans Braziel (Berkeley: University of California Press, 2001), 68.

54 Sondra Solovay, "Remedies for Weight-Based Discrimination," in *Weight Bias: Nature, Consequences and Remedies,* ed. Kelly D. Brownell, Rebecca M. Puhl, Marlene B. Schwartz, and Leslie Rudd (New York: Guilford Press, 2005), 220 (my emphases).

55 *In the Matter of Brittany T.*

56 Ibid.

57 Ibid.

58 Interestingly enough, Dr. Cochran also testified in the case involving L. T.

59 *In the Matter of Brittany T.*

60 Ibid.

61 Murray, "Normative Imperatives," 221.

62 Anna Kirkland, *Fat Rights: Dilemmas of Difference and Personhood* (New York: New York University Press, 2008), 110.

63 Bordo, *Unbearable Weight,* 203.

64 *In re D. K.*

65 Ibid.

66 Ibid.

67 Ibid.

68 Ibid.

69 Ibid.

70 Ibid. (my emphases.)

71 A Google search of this and similar phrases brings up a host of greeting cards, blogs, and tributes where this and like ideas are expressed.

72 *In re D. K.*

73 April Herndon, "Disparate but Disabled: Fat Embodiment and Disability Studies," *National Women's Studies Association Journal* 14, no. 3 (2002): 120–137. In this article, I make the case that large people are very often perceived as disabled because of the stigma and stereotypes attached to fatness in American culture. I also posit that ADA legislation could be used to protect large people from discrimination based on perceived disability and physical disability.

74 Ibid.; "Americans with Disabilities Act of 1990, as Amended," March 25, 2009, http://www.ada.gov/pubs/ada.htm.

75 Kathleen LeBesco and Jana Evans Braziel, "Introduction," in *Bodies Out of Bounds: Fatness and Transgression,* ed. Kathleen LeBesco and Jana Braziel (Berkeley: University of California Press, 2001), 2.

76 Susan Wendell, *The Rejected Body: Feminist Philosophical Reflections on Disability* (New York: Routledge, 1996); Simi Linton, *Claiming Disability: Knowledge and Identity* (New York: New York University Press, 1998); Adrienne Asch, "Critical Race Theory, Feminism and Disability: Reflections on Social Justice and Personal Identity," *Ohio State Law Journal* 62 (2001), accessed January 5, 2013, http://moritzlaw.osu.edu/students/groups/oslj/files/2012/03/62.1asch_.pdf.

77 I discuss people's concern about fat people and the "choice" to be fat and disabled at length in my article "Disparate but Disabled."

78 David Skuse, Assunta Albanese, Richard Stanhope, Jane Gilmore, and Linda Voss, "A New Stress-Related Syndrome of Growth Failure and Hyperphagia in Children, Associated with Reversibility of Growth Hormone Insufficiency," *Lancet* 348, no. 9024 (1996): 353–358.

79 G. F. Powell, J. A. Brasel, and R. M. Blizzard, "Emotional Deprivation and Growth Retardation Simulating Idiopathic Hypopituitarism—Clinical Evaluation of the Syndrome," *New England Journal of Medicine* 276, no. 23 (1967): 1271–1278.

80 I'm indebted to a conversation with Dr. David Sandberg regarding these sources on psychosocial dwarfism and for my understanding of the condition.

81 Murtagh and Ludwig, "State Intervention," 207. Osteogenesis imperfecta is a condition that causes children to have incredibly fragile bones, which often break with very little force.

82 LeBesco and Braziel, "Introduction," 3.

83 See the Strong4Life campaign's Facebook page, https://www.facebook.com/S4LGA.

84 Wendell, *Rejected Body,* 43–44.

85 *In re D. K.*

86 Ibid.

87 Murray, "Normative Imperatives," 214.

88 Burrows, "'This Is How "We" Do It,'" 10.

89 For more information on the show, see http://tlc.discovery.com/fansites/honey/honey.html.

90 To watch a sample of the show, see http://www.youtube.com/watch?v=qMmqc8mMjKU.

91 Mitgang, "Childhood Obesity and State Intervention," 561.

92 Ibid., 562.

93 Ibid., 563.

94 See nearly any of the studies about bariatric surgery on children that are cited in chapter 4.

95 Harris and Conley, "Childhood Obesity."

96 Murtagh and Ludwig, "State Intervention," 207.

97 Solovay, *Tipping the Scales*, 65.

98 Cheryl George, "Parents Supersizing Their Children: Criminalizing and Prosecuting the Rising Incidence of Childhood Obesity as Child Abuse," *DePaul Journal of Healthcare* 13, no. 1 (2010): 70.

99 Susan L. Brooks, "A Family Systems Paradigm for Legal Decision Making Affecting Child Custody," *Cornell Journal of Law and Public Policy* 6, no. 1 (1996): 12–13.

100 Stone-Manista, "Protecting Pregnant Women," 836.

101 Newcomb, "Obese Third Grader."

102 *In the Matter of Brittany T.*

103 Thomas J. Sheeran, "Ohio Officials Take 200-Pound Boy from Mother," *Huffington-Post,* November 29, 2011, http://www.huffingtonpost.com/2011/11/29/ohio-officials-take-200-p_n_1118186.html.

104 Nara Schoenberg, "Obese Children, Government Intervention: High-Profile Case Generates Fears among Families and Their Advocates," *Chicago Tribune,* December 20, 2011, http://articles.chicagotribune.com/2011-12-20/features/sc-fam-1220-obese-kids-20111220_1_obese-kids-obese-children-pediatrics.

105 Murtagh and Ludwig, "State Intervention," 207.

106 Ibid., 207.

107 Ibid., 206–207. Also, for a more detailed discussion of bariatric surgery and children, see chapter 4.

108 Murtagh and Ludwig, "State Intervention," 207.

109 Ibid.

110 Harris and Conley, "Childhood Obesity."

CHAPTER 3: PUBLIC AND PRIVATE SHAME

1 Emanuella Grinberg, "Georgia's Child Obesity Ads Aim to Create Movement out of Controversy," CNN, February 7, 2012, http://www.cnn.com/2012/02/07/health/atlanta-child-obesity-ads/index.html.

2 Since the billboards were taken down, the Strong4Life campaign no longer has the images on its website. They can be found on other websites, such as the Mamavation site, http://www.mamavation.com/2012/02/victory-strong-4-life-billboards-coming-down.html, and through Google searches.

3   S. Creighton, J. Alderson, S. Brown, and C. L. Minto, "Medical Photography: Ethics, Consent, and the Intersex Patient," *British Journal of Urology International* 89 (2002): 67–72; Charlotte Cooper, "Headless Fatties," accessed February 25, 2013, http://www .charlottecooper.net/docs/fat/headless_fatties.htm.

4   Rosemarie Garland-Thomson, *Staring: How We Look* (New York: Oxford University Press, 2009), 185.

5   Ibid., 81.

6   Ibid., 3.

7   Of course, there are many representations within Fat culture and Fat Studies that posit the fat body as free from shame and even beautiful. In particular, photographers have excelled with such representations. Collections such as Laurie Toby Edison's photography collection *Women en Large* and Leonard Nimoy's *The Full Body Project* feature diversely embodied large women in very positive ways.

8   Garland-Thomson, *Staring*, 9.

9   Quoted in Grinberg, "Georgia's Child Obesity."

10   James Elkins, *The Object Stares Back: On the Nature of Seeing* (New York: Harcourt, 1996), 21, 27.

11   Garland-Thomson, *Staring*, 185 (emphases in the original).

12   Quoted in Grinberg, "Georgia's Child Obesity."

13   To view the campaign materials, visit http://mktg.bluecrossmn.com/campaigns /obesity/.

14   The commercial was removed from several sites. For example, it's no longer available on YouTube or in Lindy West's article where it was originally embedded. It has also been removed from the Blue Cross and Blue Shield of Minnesota website.

15   To view the commercial, go to http://www.youtube.com/watch?v=1gCTX2EfUUs& feature=youtu.be.

16   Selena Simmons-Duffin, "New Anti-obesity Ads Blaming Overweight Parents Spark Controversy," NPR, September 27, 2012, http://www.npr.org/blogs/the salt/2012/09/27/161831449/new-anti-obesity-ads-blaming-overweight-parents-spark -criticism.

17   Nicole Martins and Kristen Harrison, "Racial and Gender Differences in the Relation-ship between Children's Television Use and Children's Self Esteem: A Longitudinal Panel Study," *Communication Research* 39, no. 3 (2012): 352.

18   Abrams, "Case for Stigmatizing Obesity."

19   Lindy West, "It's Hard Enough to Be a Fat Kid without the Government Telling You You're an Epidemic," *Jezebel*, March 3, 2013, http://jezebel.com/5945955/its-hard -enough-to-be-a-fat-kid-without-the-government-telling-you-youre-an-epidemic (emphasis in the original).

20   Simmons-Duffin, "New Anti-obesity Ads."

21   Lucy Wang, "Weight Discrimination: One Size Fits All Remedy?" *Yale Law Journal* 117, no. 8 (2008): 1914.

22   The commercial and campaign materials can be viewed at http://www.stillaproblem .com/.

23   Quoted in *Weight of the Nation*.

24 Using the search terms *children, advertising,* and *food,* I turned up thousands of articles in LexisNexis, Academic Search Premier, and PubMed.

25 American Psychological Association, "The Impact of Food Advertising on Childhood Obesity," February 13, 2013, http://www.apa.org/topics/kids-media/food.aspx?item=6.

26 Mary Story and Simone French, "Food Advertising and Marketing Directed at Children and Adolescents in the US," *International Journal of Behavioral Nutrition and Physical Activity* 1, no. 3 (2004), http://www.ncbi.nlm.nih.gov/pmc/articles/PMC416565/.

27 Ibid.

28 Ibid.

29 Berkeley Media Studies Group, *Fighting Junk Food Marketing to Kids: A Toolkit for Advocates,* 2006, www.bmsg.org/pdfs/BMSG_Junk_Food_toolkit.pdf11.

30 American Heart Association and American Stroke Association, "Facts: Unhealthy and Unregulated Food Advertising and Marketing to Children," American Heart Association, December 20, 2012, www.heart.org/idc/groups/heart-public/@wcm/ . . . /ucm_301781.pdf, 1.

31 West, "It's Hard Enough."

32 Ibid.

33 Saguy, *What's Wrong with Fat?* 170–171.

34 There was enough controversy that the billboards were pulled. See "Victory: Strong4Life Billboards Coming Down," Mamavation, February 26, 2012, http://www.mamavation.com/2012/02/victory-strong-4-life-billboards-coming-down.html.

35 Grinberg, "Georgia's Child Obesity Ads."

36 For example, see her appearance on the *Today Show,* Seamus McGraw, "Teen Actress: Anti-obesity Ads Made Me More Confident," TodayShow.com, May 6, 2011, http://www.today.com/id/42929825/site/todayshow/ns/today-today_health/t/teen-actress-anti-obesity-ads-made-me-more-confident/#.UTOMmoWvxrd.

37 The ad featured as the background of Maya's website includes a different caption than the ad pictured here. The caption on the second advertisement reads "My Fat May Be Funny, but It's Killing Me."

38 *Maya Joi's Journey to Being Strong4Life,* January 2, 2013, http://mayajoi4life.blogspot.com/.

39 Ibid. (my emphasis.)

40 *Fat, Sick, and Nearly Dead,* directed by Joe Cross and Kurt Engfehr, 2010, http://www.fatsickandnearlydead.com/.

41 *Maya Joi's Journey to Being Strong4Life.*

42 Wendell, *Rejected Body,* 52.

43 Becky W. Thompson, *A Hunger So Wide and So Deep: American Women Speak Out on Eating Problems* (Minneapolis: University of Minnesota Press, 1994), 1–2.

44 Ibid., 32.

45 Wendell, *Rejected Body,* 43.

46 Emily Rapp, *Poster Child: A Memoir* (New York: Bloomsbury, 2007), 146.

47 Critser, "Let Them Eat Fat," 4.

48 "Nathan Sorrell, Nike Olympic Commercial: *Today Show* Interviews Overweight Boy Running," News Channel 5, August 13, 2012, http://www.wptv.com/dpp/news/

local_news/water_cooler/nathan-sorrell-nike-olympic-commercial-youtube-video
-today-show-interviews-overweight-boy-running.

49 See "Nike's 'Great' Fat Kid Commercial Is Not Great," BuzzFeed.com, August 7, 2012,
http://www.buzzfeed.com/copyranter/nikes-great-fat-kid-commercial-is-notgreat
?fb_comment_id=fbc_10152050583855145_34412435_10152051863405145#fbee8c1d
5c4df4 to view the embedded video.

50 The ad is on YouTube with many different titles, some of which have received up to
60,000 views. Additionally, because the ad was the source of controversy, it was also
embedded in online publications from the likes of *Time*, *Salon*, and the *Washington
Post*.

51 Dean Shipley, "London Student Featured in Nike Ad," *Record Herald,* August 1, 2012,
http://www.recordherald.com/main.asp?SectionID=1&SubSectionID=1&Article
ID=144055.

52 Ibid.

53 "London, Ohio City Data," City-Data.com, November 3, 2012, http://www.city-data.
com/city/London-Ohio.html.

54 Shipley, "London Student Featured."

55 "Nathan Sorrell, Nike Olympic Commercial."

56 Lindy West, "Nike Uses Fat Kid to Sell Shoes, Nation Rejoices," *Jezebel,* August 6, 2012,
http://jezebel.com/5932248/nike-uses-fat-kid-to-sell-shoes-nation-rejoices.

57 "Nike's 'Great' Fat Kid Commercial."

58 Ibid.

59 Rapp, *Poster Child,* 128.

60 "Nathan Sorrell, Nike Olympic Commercial."

61 Ibid.

62 Rapp, *Poster Child,* 153.

63 Wendell, *Rejected Body,* 52.

64 "Nathan Sorrell, Nike Olympic Commercial."

65 Quiet Storm Bradley, "Big Butt Theory," *Facebook,* https://www.facebook.com/Big
ButtTheory/info.

66 Ibid.

67 atchka, "Stormy Weather," Fierce, Freethinking Fatties, March 1, 2012, http://fierce
fatties.com/2012/03/01/stormy-weather/.

68 Robin Applebaum, e-mail message to the author, November 2, 2012.

69 "Nathan Sorrell, Nike Olympic Commercial."

70 Emma Gray, "Ragen Chastain Launches 'Support All Kids' Campaign to Counter
Georgia Anti-obesity Ads," *Huffington Post,* February 23, 2012, http://www.huffing
tonpost.com/2012/02/23/support-all-kids-ragen-chastain-georgia-anti-obesity-
ads_n_1295047.html.

71 See http://supportallkids.virb.com/.

72 Paul Campos, "Anti-obesity Ads Won't Work by Telling Fat Kids to Stop Being Fat,"
Daily Beast, January 4, 2012, http://www.thedailybeast.com/articles/2012/01/04/anti
-obesity-ads-won-t-work-by-telling-fat-kids-to-stop-being-fat.html.

73 Although it's seldom acknowledged in mainstream discussions of school violence,
gender is a salient issue. For an excellent discussion of masculinity and young men as

the perpetrators of school-based violence, I recommend Jackson Katz's video *Tough Guise: Violence, Media, and the Crisis in Masculinity*, directed by Sut Jhally, produced by Susan Ericsson and Sanjay Talreja, Media Education Foundation, 1999.

74 P. B. Rukavina and W. Li, "School Physical Activity Interventions: Do Not Forget about Obesity Bias," *Obesity Reviews* 9 (2008): 67.

75 Ibid.

76 Wendyn Gray, Nicole A. Kahhan, and David M. Janicke, "Peer Victimization and Pediatric Obesity: A Review of the Literature," *Psychology in the Schools* 46, no. 8 (2009): 720.

77 P. Warschburger, "The Unhappy Obese Child," *International Journal of Obesity* 29 (2005): 127.

78 Ian Janssen, Wendy M. Craig, William F. Boyce, and William Pickett, "Associations between Overweight and Obesity with Bullying in School-Aged Children," *Pediatrics* 113, no. 5 (2004): 1192.

79 J. Madowitz, S. Knatz, T. Maginot, J. Crow, and K. N. Boutelle, "Teasing, Depression, and Unhealthy Weight Control Behavior in Obese Children," *Pediatric Obesity* 7 (2012): 447.

80 Ibid., 449.

81 Ibid.

82 Rukavina and Li, "School Physical Activity Interventions," 68–69.

83 Gray, Kahhan, and Janicke, "Peer Victimization and Pediatric Obesity," 721.

84 Nicole L. Taylor, "Guys, She's Humongous: Gender and Weight-Based Teasing in Adolescence," *Journal of Adolescent Research* 26, no. 2 (2011): 178.

85 Ibid., 184.

86 Ibid., 195.

87 Barrie Thorne, *Gender Play: Girls and Boys in School* (New Brunswick, N.J.: Rutgers University Press, 1995), 65.

88 The term *supersize* is sometimes used in the Fat community to denote the largest people in the community. There's no hard-and-fast definition of the term, but in online dating communities, for example, it is often used to describe women who are larger than a size 38/30, which is usually the largest clothing size mainstream outlets such as Lane Bryant carry. Sometimes, the term is also used to describe people who are over 300 pounds.

89 Wendell, *Rejected Body*, 43.

90 Rapp, *Poster Child*, 205.

91 Ibid., 81.

92 Ibid., 55.

93 Martins and Harrison, "Racial and Gender Differences," 343.

94 Rukavina and Li, "School Physical Activity Interventions," 70.

95 Gray, Kahhan, and Janicke, "Peer Victimization," 723.

96 Rukavina and Li, "School Physical Activity Interventions," 70.

97 Gray, Kahhan, and Janicke, "Peer Victimization," 724.

98 Madowitz et al., "Teasing, Depression, and Unhealthy Weight," 448.

99 Kyung-Sook Bang, Sun-Mi Chea, Myung-Sun Hyun, Hye Kyung Nam, Ji-Soo Kim, and Kwang-Hee Park, "The Mediating Effects of Perceived Parental Teasing on Rela-

tions of Body Mass Index to Depression and Self-Perception of Physical Appearance and Global Self-Perception in Children," *Journal of Advanced Nursing* 68, no. 12 (2012): 2646; Gray, Kahhan, and Janicke, "Peer Victimization," 724; Madowitz et al., "Teasing, Depression, and Unhealthy Weight," 450.

100 Ibid.

101 Rebecca M. Puhl, Jaimie Lee Peterson, and Joerg Luedicke, "Weight-Based Victimization: Bullying Experiences of Weight Loss Treatment–Seeking Youth," *Pediatrics* 31, no. 1 (2013): e1–e6, http://pediatrics.aappublications.org/content/early/2012/12/19/peds.2012–1106.

102 Ibid., e6.

103 Bang et al., "Mediating Effects," 2646.

104 Anita Jansen, Tom Smeets, Brigette Boon, Chantelle Nederkoorn, Anne Roefs, and Sandra Mulkens, "Vulnerability to Interpretation Bias in Overweight Children," *Psychology and Health* 22, no. 5 (2007): 562.

105 Ibid., 571.

106 Campos, "Anti-obesity Ads Won't Work."

107 Kirsten Krahnsoever Davison and Leanne Lipps Birch, "Weight Status, Parent Reaction, and Self-Concept in Five-Year-Old Girls," *Pediatrics* 107, no. 1 (2001): 225.

108 Ibid., 228.

109 Janet D. Latner and Marlene B. Schwartz, "Weight Bias in a Child's World," in *Weight Bias: Nature, Consequences and Remedies,* ed. Kelly D. Brownell, Rebecca M. Puhl, Marlene B. Schwartz, and Leslie Rudd (New York: Guilford Press, 2005), 56.

110 Davison and Burch, "Weight Status, Parent Reaction," 220.

111 Harriet Brown, "Feeling Bullied by Parents about Weight," *New York Times,* January 9, 2013, http://well.blogs.nytimes.com/2013/01/09/feeling-bullied-by-parents-about-weight/.

112 "What Is Support All Kids?," Support All Kids, accessed January 5, 2013, http://support allkids.virb.com/.

CHAPTER 4: WHAT IF THE CURE IS WORSE THAN THE DISEASE?

1 Lisette Burrows and Jan Wright, "The Discursive Production of Childhood, Identity and Health," in *Body Knowledge and Control: Sociology of Education and Physical Education and Health,* ed. John Evans, Brian Davies, and Jan Wright (New York: Routledge, 2003), 85. Although Burrows and Wright have paraphrased the work, they credit A. James and A. Prout's 1990 book *Constructing and Reconstructing Childhood: Issues in the Sociological Study of Childhood.*

2 Ibid., 83.

3 Burrows, "'This Is How "We" Do It,'" 11.

4 Quoted in Gina Kolata, *Rethinking Thin: The New Science of Weight Loss—and the Myths and Realities of Dieting* (New York: Picador, 2007), 196.

5 Michelle Kominiarek, "Pregnancy after Bariatric Surgery," *Obstetrics and Gynecology Clinics of North America* 37, no. 2 (2010): 306.

6   Marilyn Wann, "Foster Care for Fat Children? Gastric Bypass Surgery? Two Wrongs Call for a Fight," *San Francisco Weekly,* July 21, 2011, http://blogs.sfweekly.com/exhibitionist/2011/07/foster_care_fat_children_gastric_bypass.php.

7   Mayo Clinic Staff, "Dumping Syndrome," Mayo Clinic, January 12, 2013, http://www.mayoclinic.com/health/dumping-syndrome/DS00715.

8   Marc Michalsky, "Adolescent Bariatric Surgery Best Practice Guidelines," American Society for Metabolic and Bariatric Surgery, January 25, 2013, http://asmbs.org/2012/01/adolescent-bariatric-surgery-best-practice-guidelines/.

9   "Eligibility for Bariatric Surgery," Cincinnati Children's Hospital, January 20, 2013, http://www.cincinnatichildrens.org/service/s/weight-loss/bariatric/eligibility/.

10   Allen F. Browne and Thomas Inge, "How Young for Bariatric Surgery in Children?" *Seminars in Pediatric Surgery* 18 (2008): 183.

11   Ibid., 177.

12   Ibid., 183 (my emphasis).

13   Carrie Gann, "How Young Is Too Young for Bariatric Surgery?" ABC News, June 13, 2012, http://abcnews.go.com/Health/gastric-sleeve-helps-obese-12-year-shed-pounds/story?id=16552766#.UMziSIWvwm1.

14   T. H. Inge, S. A. Xanthakos, and M. H. Zeller, "Bariatric Surgery for Pediatric Extreme Obesity: Now or Later?" *International Journal of Obesity* 31 (2007): 1.

15   Marc Michalsky, Robert E. Kramer, Michelle A. Fullmer, Michele Polfus, Renee Porter, Wendy Ward-Begnoche, Elizabeth Getzoff, Meredith Dreyer, Stacy Stolzman, and Kirk W. Reichard, "Developing Criteria for Pediatric/Adolescent Bariatric Surgery Programs," *Pediatrics* 128, no. 2 (2011): 66.

16   Ibid.

17   Ibid.

18   Julie Ingelfinger, "Bariatric Surgery in Adolescents," *New England Journal of Medicine* 365, no. 15 (2011): 1366.

19   Cincinnati Children's Hospital, "Teen-Longitudinal Assessment of Bariatric Surgery," accessed February 6, 2013, http://www.cincinnatichildrens.org/research/divisions/t/teen-labs/default/?utm_source=TeenLongitudinal%2BAssessment%2Bof%2BBariatric%2BSurgery%2B%28Teen-LABS%29&utm_medium=shortcut&utm_campaign=teen-labs.

20   C. Hearnshaw and K. Matyka, "Managing Childhood Obesity: When Lifestyle Change Is Not Enough," *Diabetes, Obesity, and Metabolism* 12 (2010): 952.

21   Anemona Hartcollis, "Young, Obese and in Surgery," *New York Times,* January 7, 2012, http://www.nytimes.com/2012/01/08/health/young-obese-and-getting-weight-loss-surgery.html?pagewanted=all&_r=0.

22   Ibid.

23   J. P. H. Shield, E. Crowne, and J. Morgan, "Is There a Place for Bariatric Surgery in Treating Childhood Obesity?," *Archives of Disease in Childhood* 93, no. 5 (2008): 370.

24   "Roux-en-Y Bypass," Salt Lake Regional Medical Center, March 1, 2013, http://www.saltlakeregional.com/services/weight_loss_surgery/rouxeny/.

25   Hartcollis, "Young, Obese and in Surgery."

26   Ibid.

27   Ibid.

28 Ibid.

29 It's actually more dangerous to have the surgery reversed than having it done in the first place, which is why so many physicians consider the surgeries irreversible. See Hilary Busis, "Can Bariatric Surgery Be Reversed?" *Slate,* February 24, 2010, http://www.slate.com/articles/news_and_politics/explainer/2010/02/can_bariatric _surgery_be_reversed.html; Roker, *Never Goin' Back,* 56.

30 Dani Hart, *I Want to Live: Gastric Bypass Reversal* (Fort Collins, Colo.: Mountain Stars, 2003), 67–68.

31 David B. Sarwer and Rebecca J. Dilks, "Childhood and Adolescent Obesity: Psychological and Behavioral Issues in Weight Loss Treatment," *Journal of Youth and Adolescence* 41 (2012): 100–101.

32 Hartcollis, "Young, Obese and in Surgery."

33 Bijal P. Trivedi, "The Bypass Cure," *Discover Magazine,* December 2012, http://discover magazine.com/2012/dec/29-bypass#.UM44w4Wvwm1.

34 Hartcollis, "Young, Obese and in Surgery."

35 Lisa, "Before Gastric Bypass Surgery: What I Wish I Had Known," *Gastric Bypass Truth: The Skinny on Life after Weight Loss Surgery,* accessed December 12, 2013, http://gastricbypasstruth.com/before-gastric-bypass-surgery/before-gastric-bypass- surgery-what-i-wish-i-had-known/.

36 Ibid.

37 Lisa Sargese, "Gastric Bypass and the Pretzel Issue," *Lisa Loves Life Lessons,* accessed January 5, 2012, http://theskinnyonline.blogspot.com/2012/01/gastric-bypass-and-pretzel -issue.html.

38 Al Roker, with Laura Morton, *Never Goin' Back*: *Winning the Weight-Loss Battle for Good* (New York: New American Library, 2013), 55.

39 Michelle Tauber and Mark Dagostino, "100 and Counting," *People,* November 18, 2002, 104–110.

40 David Knowles, "Al Roker: 'I Pooped My Pants during 2002 White House Visit, Ditched Soiled Underwear in Bathroom and Went Commando," *New York Daily News,* January 2, 2013, http://www.nydailynews.com/entertainment/tv-movies/al- roker-pooped-pants-white-house-article-1.1235259.

41 Roker, *Never Goin' Back,* 62.

42 The original online broadcast of Wilson's surgery appears to no longer be available, but Wilson discusses the procedure and her decision to have it broadcast in the chapter titled "Going Public" in her first book, *Gut Feelings: From Fear and Despair to Health and Hope* (Carlsbad, Calif.: Hay House, 2002).

43 Roker, *Never Goin' Back,* 51.

44 Carnie Wilson, with Cindy Pearlman, *I'm Still Hungry: Finding Myself through Thick and Thin* (Carlsbad, Calif.: Hay House, 2003), 25.

45 The acronym WLS (weight-loss surgery) is sometimes used rather than *bariatric surgery.*

46 Wilson, *I'm Still Hungry,* 150.

47 Sargese, "Gastric Bypass and the Pretzel Issue."

48 Ibid.

49 Inge, Xanthakos, and Zeller, "Bariatric Surgery," 5.

50 Ibid.

51 Thomas Inge, Michael Helmrath, Mark Vierra, and Sayeed Ikramuddin, "Challenges of Adolescent Bariatric Surgery: Tips for Managing the Extremely Obese Teen," *Journal of Laparoendoscopic and Advanced Surgical Techniques* 18, no. 1 (2008): 158; Kominiarek, "Pregnancy after Bariatric Surgery," 312.

52 Bill Hyman, Kari Kooi, and David Ficklen, "Bariatric Surgery in Adolescents," *Journal of School Health* 78, no. 8 (2008): 454.

53 Inge, Xanthakos, and Zeller, "Bariatric Surgery," 5.

54 "When Bone Breaks: Osteoporosis Health Center," WebMD.com, October 15, 2011, http://www.webmd.com/osteoporosis/osteoporosis-complications.

55 "Gastric Banding for Teens," Johns Hopkins Medicine, accessed December 20, 2012, http://www.hopkinsmedicine.org/healthlibrary/test_procedures/gastroenterology/gastric_banding_surgery_for_teens_161,3/.

56 Hyman, Kooi, and Ficklen, "Bariatric Surgery in Adolescents," 454.

57 Gabriella G. Gosman, Wendy C. King, Beth Schrope, Kristene J. Steffen, Gladys W. Strain, Anita P. Courcoulas, David R. Flum, John R. Pender, and Hyagriv N. Simhan, "Reproductive Health of Women Electing Bariatric Surgery," *Fertility and Sterility* 94, no. 4 (2010): 1426.

58 Aileen Love and Henry Billett, "Obesity, Bariatric Surgery, and Iron Deficiency: True, True, True, and Related," *American Journal of Hematology* 83, no. 5 (2008): 406; O. Ziegler, M. A. Sirveaux, L. Brunaud, N. Reibel, and D. Quilliot, "Medical Follow Up after Bariatric Surgery: Nutritional and Drug Issues—General Recommendations for the Prevention and Treatment of Nutritional Deficiencies," *Diabetes and Nutrition* 35 (2009): 544.

59 Love and Billett, "Obesity, Bariatric Surgery, and Iron Deficiency," 405–406.

60 International Pediatric Endosurgery Group, "IPEG Guidelines for Surgical Treatment of Extremely Obese Adolescents," *Journal of Laparoendoscopic & Advanced Surgical Techniques* 19, no. 1 (2009): xv; Ziegler et al., "Medical Follow Up," 554; Kominiarek, "Pregnancy after Bariatric Surgery," 308; Love and Billett, "Obesity, Bariatric Surgery, and Iron Deficiency," 408.

61 Helmut R. Roehrig, Stavra A. Xanthakos, Jenny Sweeney, Meg H. Zeller, and Thomas H. Inge, "Pregnancy after Bypass Surgery in Adolescents," *Obesity Surgery* 17 (2007): 873.

62 Ibid., 876.

63 Inge, Xanthakos, and Zeller, "Bariatric Surgery," 6.

64 Roehrig et al., "Pregnancy after Bypass Surgery," 875.

65 Caroline Apovian, Christina Baker, David Ludwig, Alison Hoppin, George Hsu, Carine Lenders, Janey S. A. Pratt, R. Armour Forse, Adrienne O'Brien, and Michael Tarnoff, "Best Practice Guidelines in Pediatric/Adolescent Weight Loss Surgery," *Obesity Research* 13, no. 2 (2005): 275.

66 Ibid., 276; Kominiarek, "Pregnancy after Bariatric Surgery," 310.

67 Ziegler et al., "Medical Follow Up," 554.

68 "Bariatric Surgery: Side Effects," West Penn Allegheny Health System, accessed February 28, 2012, http://www.wpahs.org/specialties/bariatric-surgery/side-effects#Pregnancy.

69 The term is everywhere in the medical literature. For one example, see the National Institutes of Health publication *NIH Medline Plus* at http://www.nlm.nih.gov/med lineplus/magazine/issues/winter08/articles/winter08pg12.html.

70 Harriet Brown, "In 'Obesity Paradox,' Thinner May Mean Sicker," *New York Times,* September 17, 2012, http://www.nytimes.com/2012/09/18/health/research/more-data -suggests-fitness-matters-more-than-weight.html?_r=0.

71 Trivedi, "Bypass Cure."

72 Quoted in ibid.

73 Ibid.

74 Ibid.

75 Ann Harding, "Surgery Is No Quick Fix for Obese Teens," CNN.com, June 22, 2011, http://www.cnn.com/2011/HEALTH/06/22/surgery.obese.teens/index.html.

76 Anahad O'Connor, "Weight Loss Surgery May Not Combat Diabetes Long-Term," November 28, 2012, *New York Times Well Blogs,* http://well.blogs.nytimes.com/2012/11/28/weight-loss-surgery-may-not-combat-diabetes-long-term/.

77 Sarwer and Dilks, "Childhood and Adolescent Obesity," 101.

78 Valerie H. Taylor, Brian Stonehocker, Margot Steele, and Arya M. Sharmer, "An Overview of Treatments for Obesity in a Population with Mental Illness," *Canadian Journal of Psychiatry* 57, no. 1 (2012): 17.

79 Ibid.

80 Wendy C. King, Jia-Yuh Chin, James E. Mitchell, Melissa A. Kalarchian, Kristene J. Steffen, Scott G. Engel, Anita P. Courcoulas, Walter J. Pories, and Susan G. Yanovski, "Prevalence of Alcohol Abuse Disorders before and after Bariatric Surgery," *Journal of the American Medical Association* 307, no. 23 (2012): 2523.

81 Beverly Haynes, "Creation of a Bariatric Surgery Program for Adolescents at a Major Teaching Hospital," *Pediatric Nursing* 31, no. 1 (2005): 21.

82 S. Herpertz, R. Kielman, A. M. Wolf, M. Langafel, W. Senf, and J. Hebebrand, "Does Obesity Surgery Improve Psychosocial Functioning? A Systematic Review," *International Journal of Obesity* 27 (2003): 1310.

83 Latner and Schwartz, "Weight Bias," 61.

84 Meg H. Zeller, Helmut R. Roehrig, Avani C. Modi, Stephen R. Daniels, and Thomas H. Inge, "Health-Related Quality of Life and Depressive Symptoms in Adolescents with Extreme Obesity Presenting for Bariatric Surgery," *Pediatrics* 117, no. 4 (2006): 1159.

85 Rebecca M. Puhl, "Coping with Weight Stigma," in *Weight Bias: Nature, Consequences and Remedies,* ed. Kelly D. Brownell, Rebecca M. Puhl, Marlene B. Schwartz, and Leslie Rudd (New York: Guilford Press, 2005), 280.

86 Ibid.

87 Browne and Inge, "How Young for Bariatric Surgery," 177.

88 Ibid.

89 H. R. Clark, E. Goyder, P. Bissell, L. Blank, and J. Peters, "How Do Parents' Child Feeding Behaviours Influence Child Weight? Implications for Childhood Obesity Policy," *Journal of Public Health* 29, no. 2 (2007): 132.

90 Esther Jansen, Sandra Mulkens, and Anita Jansen, "Do Not Eat the Red Food!: Prohibition of Snacks Leads to Their Relatively Higher Consumption in Children," *Appetite* 49 (2007): 576.

91 Ibid.

92 Herpertz et al., "Does Obesity Surgery Improve," 1311.

93 Ibid.

94 Ibid.

95 Polivy's work on food restriction, eating disorders, and body image is too voluminous to cite exhaustively. She has authored or coauthored over forty journal articles on these issues since 1996.

96 Roker, *Never Goin' Back,* 67.

97 Ibid.

98 Jeremy R. Garrett and Leslie Ann McNolty, "Bariatric Surgery and the Social Character of the Obesity Epidemic," *American Journal of Bioethics* 10, no. 2 (2010): 24.

99 V. A. Shrewsbury, K. S. Steinbeck, S. Torvaldson, and L. A. Baur, "The Role of Parents in Adolescent and Pre-adolescent Overweight and Obesity Treatment: A Systematic Review of Clinical Recommendations," *Obesity Reviews* 12 (2011): 765.

100 I first saw foods referred to as "red light" foods in Kandi Stinson's 2001 *Women and Dieting Culture.* Recently, Dara-Lynn Weiss has also talked about red light foods in her memoir, *The Heavy: A Mother, a Daughter, a Diet* (New York: Ballantine Books, 2013). According to Weiss, the terminology of traffic lights was used by the nutritionist they visited as she was trying to get her daughter to lose weight (see p. 52).

101 Lisa, "Before Gastric Bypass Surgery." Wilson also eventually had surgery to remove her excess skin after weight loss. She writes about her excess skin and the surgeries in *I'm Still Hungry.*

102 Inge et al., "Challenges of Adolescent Bariatric Surgery," 160 (my emphases).

103 S. M. van Geelen, L. L. E. Bolt, and M. J. H. van Summeren, "Moral Aspects of Bariatric Surgery for Obese Children and Adolescents: The Urgent Need for Empirical-Ethical Research," *American Journal of Bioethics* 10, no. 12 (2010): 31.

104 "Childhood Obesity Deemed Child Abuse," Weight Loss Surgery Channel, February 21, 2013, http://www.weightlosssurgerychannel.com/breaking-wls-news/childhood-obesity-deemed-child-abuse-in-controversial-court-case.html/.

105 Asch, "Why I Haven't Changed My Mind," 248.

106 Ingelfinger, "Bariatric Surgery in Adolescents," 1365.

107 "Study Finds Bariatric Surgery Safe for Teens," TodayShow.com, January 3, 2013, http://video.today.msnbc.msn.com/today/47858507#47858507.

108 Zeller et al., 1159.

109 Sarwer and Dilks, "Childhood and Adolescent Obesity," 99.

110 Inge et al., "Challenges of Adolescent Bariatric Surgery," 159.

111 Michael G. Sarr, "The Problem of Obesity: How Are We Going to Address It?" *American Journal of Bioethics* 10, no. 12 (2010): 13.

112 Ibid., 12–13 (my emphasis).

113 Studies also show that even after losing weight, "residual stigma" remains. See Janet D. Latner, Daria W. Ebneter, and Kerry S. O'Brien, "Residual Obesity Stigma: An Experimental Investigation of Weight Bias against Obese and Lean Targets Differing in Weight-Loss History," *Obesity* 20, no. 10 (2012): 2035, and Puhl, Peterson, and Luedicke, "Weight-Based Victimization."

114 Latner, Ebneter, and O'Brien, "Residual Obesity Stigma."

115 Ibid.

116 Roker, *Never Goin' Back,* 72.

117 Peter Muennig, "The Body Politic: The Relationship between Stigma and Obesity–Associated Disease," *BioMed Central Public Health* 8, no. 128 (2008), accessed February 10, 2013, http://www.biomedcentral.com/1471–2458/8/128.

118 Ibid.; Daniel Engber, "Glutton Intolerance: What If a War on Obesity Only Makes the Problem Worse?" *Slate,* October 5, 2009, http://www.slate.com/articles/health_and_science/science/2009/10/glutton_intolerance.html.

119 Quoted in Harding, "Surgery Is No Quick Fix."

120 Hyman, Kooi, and Ficklen, "Bariatric Surgery in Adolescents," 452.

121 "Medical Missions and Program," *Operation Smile,* February 21, 2013, http://www.operationsmile.org/our_work/medical-missions/ (my emphasis).

122 "Donation Page," *Operation Smile,* January 5, 2013, https://secure.operationsmile.org/site/Donation2?df_id=15900&15900.donation=form1&utm_source=google&utm_medium=cpc&utm_term=operationsmile&utm_campaign=paid.

123 Alice Domurat Dreger, "What to Expect When You Have the Child You Weren't Expecting," in *Surgically Shaping Children: Technology, Ethics, and the Pursuit of Normality,* ed. Erik Parens (Baltimore, Md.: Johns Hopkins University Press, 2006), 254–255.

124 Ibid., 256–257.

125 Michalsky, "Adolescent Bariatric Surgery."

126 Roker, *Never Goin' Back,* 52.

127 Ibid.

128 I. A. Hughes, C. Houk, S. F. Ahmed, and P. A. Lee, "Consensus Statement on the Management of Intersex Disorders," *Archives of Disease in Childhood* 91, no. 7 (2006): 554–563.

129 Hartcollis," Young, Obese and in Surgery."

130 Kate Scannell, "Study on Weight Loss Surgery for Type 2 Diabetes Has Serious Problems," April 2012, accessed May 3, 2012, MevsDiabetes.com, http://mevsdiabetes-bloglapedia.blogspot.com/2012/04/dr-kate-scannell-study-on-weight-loss.html. Dr. Scannell's article originally appeared in the *Contra Times* but is no longer available from that site.

131 Tolulope A. Oyetunji, Ashanti L. Franklin, Gezza Ortega, Namita Akolkar, Faisal G. Qureshi, Fizan Abdullah, Edward E. Cornwell, Benedict C. Nwomeh, and Terrence M. Fullum, "Revisiting Childhood Obesity: Persistent Underutilization of Surgical Intervention?" *American Surgeon* 78, no. 7. (2012): 790–791.

132 Ibid., 792.

133 Love and Billett, "Obesity, Bariatric Surgery, and Iron Deficiency," 403.

CONCLUSION: A CRAMPED ROOM

1 This is, of course, a loose translation of the oath, but it's the one with which most people are familiar.

2 Harris and Conley, "Childhood Obesity."

3 These details are garnered from accounts of the case provided by scholars such as Sondra Solovay in *Tipping the Scales of Justice* and Paul Campos in *The Obesity Myth.*

4 Tommy Thompson, who was the secretary of health and human services at the time, declared the war on obesity at a press conference on December 13, 2001.

5 Jo Bridgeman, "Criminalising the One Who Really Cared," *Feminist Legal Studies* 6, no. 2 (1998): 246.

6 Alaina Anderson, "The Family Unit That Eats Together, Stays Together: Setting Table Standards for Childhood Obesity, Neglect and the Family Unit," *New England Law Review* 47, no. 189 (2012): 188–215.

7 Ibid.

8 Ibid.

9 Ibid.

10 Gard and Wright, *Obesity Epidemic,* 132–134.

11 Amy Bentley, "Martha's Food: Whiteness of a Certain Kind," *American Studies* 42, no. 2 (2009): 96.

12 Ibid.

13 Paula J. Caplan, "Mother-Blaming," in *"Bad" Mothers: The Politics of Blame in Twentieth-Century America,* ed. Molly Ladd-Taylor and Lauri Urmansky (New York: New York University Press, 1998), 131.

14 Bridgeman, "Criminalising the One," 246.

15 Brierly, "Family Law," 156–158.

16 Natasha Devon, "Dress Provocatively? Overweight? You're Not Asking for Trouble, Nor Are You the Root of the Problem; We Shouldn't Ask Women to Change the Way They Dress So as to Safeguard Themselves, Just as Children Shouldn't Have to Lose Weight So as Not to Attract Bullies," *Independent,* May 29, 2013, http://www.indepen dent.co.uk/voices/comment/dress-provocatively-overweight-youre-not-asking-for -trouble-nor-are-you-the-root-of-the-problem-8634750.html.

17 Ibid.

18 Victoria Haskins and Margaret D. Jacobs, "Stolen Generations and Vanishing Indians: The Removal of Indigenous Children as a Weapon of War in the United States and Australia, 1870–1940," in *Children and War: A Historical Anthology,* ed. James Marten (New York: New York University Press, 2002), 227–241.

19 John E. B. Myers, "A Short History of Child Protection in America," *Family Law Quarterly* 42, no. 3 (2008): 449–463.

20 Solovay, *Tipping the Scales of Justice,* 22.

21 Gard and Wright, *Obesity Epidemic,* 157.

Bibliography

"About Let's Move!" Let's Move! January 12, 2013. http://www.letsmove.gov/about.

"About Shape Up! America." Shape Up! America. Surgeon General of the United States. July 30, 2003. http://www.shapeupamerica.org/general/index/html.

Abrams, Lindsey. "A Case for Stigmatizing Obesity." *Atlantic.* January 23, 2013. http://www.theatlantic.com/health/archive/2013/01/a-case-for-shaming-obese-people-tastefully/267446/.

———. "Think of the (Fat) Children: Minnesota's 'Better Example' Anti-obesity Campaign." *Atlantic.* September 24, 2012. http://www.theatlantic.com/health/archive/2012/09/think-of-the-fat-children-minnesotas-better-example-anti-obesity-campaign/262674/.

Adler, Nancy E., and Judith Stewart. "Reducing Obesity: Motivating Action While Not Blaming the Victim." *Millbank Quarterly* 87, no. 1 (2009): 49–70.

Allan, Vicky. "The War on Fat People: Time for a Truce." *Sunday Herald,* September 11, 2011, 29.

American Heart Association and American Stroke Association. "Facts: Unhealthy and Unregulated Food Advertising and Marketing to Children." American Heart Association. December 20, 2012. www.heart.org/idc/groups/heart-public/@wcm/ . . . /ucm_301781.pdf.

American Psychological Association. "The Impact of Food Advertising on Childhood Obesity." February 13, 2013. http://www.apa.org/topics/kids-media/food.aspx?item=6.

"Americans with Disabilities Act of 1990, as Amended." March 25, 2009. http://www.ada.gov/pubs/ada.htm.

Amy, N. K., A. Aalborg, P. Lyons, and L. Keranen. "Barriers to Routine Gynecological Cancer Screening for White and African American Obese Women." *International Journal of Obesity* 30 (2006): 147–155.

Anderson, Alaina. "The Family Unit That Eats Together, Stays Together: Setting Table Standards for Childhood Obesity, Neglect and the Family Unit." *New England Law Review* 47, no. 189 (2012). http://newenglrev.com/archive/volume-47/volume-47-issue-1/anderson-the-family-that-eats-together-stays-together/.

Apovian, Caroline, Christina Baker, David Ludwig, Alison Hoppin, George Hsu, Carine Lenders, Janey S. A. Pratt, R. Armour Forse, Adrienne O'Brien, and Michael Tarnoff. "Best Practice Guidelines in Pediatric/Adolescent Weight Loss Surgery." *Obesity Research* 13, no. 2 (2005): 274–282.

Applebaum, Robin. E-mail message to author, November 2, 2012.

Arani, Shireen. "Case Comment: State Intervention in Cases of Obesity-Related Medical Neglect." *Boston University Law Review* 82, no. 875 (2002): 875–894.

Asch, Adrienne. "Critical Race Theory, Feminism and Disability: Reflections on Social Justice and Personal Identity." *Ohio State Law Journal* 62 (2001): 391–425. http://moritz law.osu.edu/students/groups/oslj/files/2012/03/62.1.asch_.pdf.

———. "Why I Haven't Changed My Mind about Prenatal Diagnosis: Reflections and Refinements." In *Prenatal Testing and Disability Rights,* edited by Adrienne Asch and Erik Parens, 234–258. Washington, D.C.: Georgetown University Press, 2000.

Asch, Adrienne, and Erik Parens. "The Disability Rights Critique of Prenatal Genetic Testing: Reflections and Recommendations." In *Prenatal Testing and Disability Rights,* edited by Adrienne Asch and Erik Parens, 3–43. Washington, D.C.: Georgetown University Press, 2000.

atchka. "Stormy Weather." Fierce, Freethinking Fatties. March 1, 2012. http://fiercefatties .com/2012/03/01/stormy-weather/.

Austin, Heather, Kevin C. Smith, and Wendy L. Ward. "Bariatric Surgery in Adolescents: What's the Rationale? What's the Rational?" *International Review of Psychiatry* 24, no. 3 (2012): 254–261.

Bacon, Linda. *Health at Every Size: The Surprising Truth about Your Weight.* Dallas, Tex.: Benbella Books, 2008.

Bacon, Linda, and Lucy Aphramor. "Weight Science: Evaluating the Evidence for a Paradigm Shift. *Nutrition Journal* 10, no. 19 (2011). http://www.nutritionj.com/content /10/1/9.

Bang, Kyung-Sook, Sun-Mi Chea, Myung-Sun Hyun, Hye Kyung Nam, Ji-Soo Kim, and Kwang-Hee Park. "The Mediating Effects of Perceived Parental Teasing on Relations of Body Mass Index to Depression and Self-Perception of Physical Appearance and Global Self-Perception in Children." *Journal of Advanced Nursing* 68, no. 12 (2012): 2646–2653.

"Bariatric Surgery: Side Effects." West Penn Allegheny Health System. February 28, 2012. http://www.wpahs.org/specialties/bariatric-surgery/side-effects#Pregnancy.

Barnes, Julie Anne, and Fiona Macrae. "Babies Treated in the Womb for Obesity: Overweight Mothers-to-Be Get Diabetes Pill to Cut the Risk of Having a Fat Child." *Mail Online.* April 1, 2012. http://www.dailymail.co.uk/health/article-2123700/Babies-treated-womb-obesity-Overweight-mothers-diabetes-pill-cut-risk-having-fat-child.html.

Barnett, Ron. "S. C. Case Looks on Child Obesity as Abuse. But Is It?" *USA Today,* July 17, 2009. http://usatoday30.usatoday.com/news/health/weightloss/2009-07-20-obesity boy_N.htm.

Belkin, Lisa. "Watching Her Weight." *New York Times,* July 8, 2001. http://www.nytimes .com/2001/07/08/magazine/watching-her-weight.html?pagewanted=all&src=pm.

Bennett-Smith, Meredith. "Geoffrey Miller, Visiting NYU Professor, Slammed for Fat-Shaming Obese PhD Applicants." HuffingtonPost.com. June 4, 2013. http://www .huffingtonpost.com/2013/06/04/geoffrey-miller-fat-shaming-nyu-phd_n_3385641 .html.

Bentley, Amy. "Martha's Food: Whiteness of a Certain Kind." *American Studies* 42, no. 2 (2009): 89–100.

Berkeley Media Studies Group. *Fighting Junk Food Marketing to Kids: A Toolkit for Advocates.* 2006. January 17, 2013. www.bmsg.org/pdfs/BMSG_Junk_Food_toolkit.pdf.

Bernstein, Gaia, and Zvi Triger. "Over-Parenting." *University of California Davis Law Review* 44, no. 4 (2011): 1221–1279.

Best, Mary. "The Growing Challenge of 'Diabesity.'" *NIH Medline Plus.* Winter 2008. http://www.nlm.nih.gov/medlineplus/magazine/issues/winter08/articles/winter 08pg12.html.

Biltekoff, Charlotte. "The Terror Within: Obesity in Post 9/11 U.S. Life." *American Studies* 48, no. 3 (2007): 29–48.

Boero, Natalie. "Fat Kids, Working Moms and the 'Epidemic of Obesity'; Race, Class and Mother Blame." In *The Fat Studies Reader,* edited by Esther Rothblum and Sondra Solovay, 113–119. New York: New York University Press, 2009.

———. *Killer Fat: Media, Medicine, and Morals in the American "Obesity Epidemic."* New Brunswick, N.J.: Rutgers University Press, 2012.

Bordo, Susan. *Unbearable Weight: Feminism, Western Culture, and the Body.* Berkeley: University of California Press, 1993.

Bradley, Quiet Storm. "Big Butt Theory." *Facebook.* https://www.facebook.com/Big ButtTheory/info.

Bridgeman, Jo. "Criminalising the One Who Really Cared." *Feminist Legal Studies* 6, no. 2 (1998): 245–256.

Brierly, Kristen E. "Family Law—Childhood Morbid Obesity: How Excess Pounds Can Tip the Scales of Justice in Favor of Removing a Child from the Home and/or Termination of Parental Rights." *Western New England Law Review* 35, no. 1 (2013): 129–160.

Brooks, Susan L. "A Family Systems Paradigm for Legal Decision Making Affecting Child Custody." *Cornell Journal of Law and Public Policy* 6, no. 1 (1996): 1–20.

Brown, Harriet. "Feeling Bullied by Parents about Weight." *New York Times,* January 9, 2013. http://well.blogs.nytimes.com/2013/01/09/feeling-bullied-by-parents-about -weight/.

———. "In 'Obesity Paradox,' Thinner May Mean Sicker." *New York Times,* September 17, 2012. http://www.nytimes.com/2012/09/18/health/research/more-data-suggests -fitness-matters-more-than-weight.html?_r=0.

Browne, Allen F., and Thomas Inge. "How Young for Bariatric Surgery in Children?" *Seminars in Pediatric Surgery* 18 (2009): 176–185.

Bruch, Hilde. *The Importance of Overweight.* New York: W. W. Norton, 1957.

Burrows, Lisette. "'This Is How "We" Do It': Pedagogising Families in Obesity Discourse." *Childrenz Issues* 13, no. 1 (2009): 9–11.

Burrows, Lisette, and Jan Wright. "The Discursive Production of Childhood, Identity and Health." In *Body Knowledge and Control: Sociology of Education and Physical Education and Health,* edited by John Evans, Brian Davies, and Jan Wright, 83–95. New York: Routledge, 2003.

Busis, Hillary. "Can Bariatric Surgery Be Reversed?" *Slate,* February 24, 2010. http://www. slate.com/articles/news_and_politics/explainer/2010/02/can_bariatric_surgery_be_ reversed.html.

Butterworth, Trevor. "Top Science Journal Rebukes Harvard's Top Nutritionist." Forbes

.com. May 27, 2013. http://www.forbes.com/sites/trevorbutterworth/2013/05/27/top
-science-journal-rebukes-harvards-top-nutritionist/.

Calhoun, Ada. "The Criminalization of Bad Mothers." *New York Times,* April 25, 2012.
http://www.nytimes.com/2012/04/29/magazine/the-criminalization-of-bad-mothers
.html?pagewanted=all.

Campbell, Kate, and Sue Levesque. "Mandatory Thinness and Mother Blame: The Newspaper Coverage of the Marlene Corrigan Trial." *Canadian Women's Studies* 18, no. 2–3
(1998): 69–73.

Campos, Paul. "Anti-obesity Ads Won't Work by Telling Fat Kids to Stop Being Fat." *Daily
Beast,* January 4, 2012. http://www.thedailybeast.com/articles/2012/01/04/anti-obesity
-ads-won-t-work-by-telling-fat-kids-to-stop-being-fat.html.

———. *The Obesity Myth: Why America's Obsession with Weight Is Hazardous to Your
Health.* New York: Gotham Books, 2004.

Caplan, Paula J. *Don't Blame Mother: Mending the Mother-Daughter Relationship.* New
York: Harper & Row, 1989.

———. "Mother-Blaming." In *"Bad" Mothers: The Politics of Blame in Twentieth-Century
America,* edited by Molly Ladd-Taylor and Lauri Urmansky, 127–144. New York: New
York University Press, 1998.

Centers for Disease Control. "Adult Obesity Facts." October 24, 2012. http://www.cdc.gov
/obesity/data/adult.html.

Charles, Nick. "Desperate Measure." *People Magazine,* September 11, 2000. http://www
.people.com/people/archive/article/0,,20132254,00.html.

"Childhood Obesity." American Heart Association. December 20, 2012. http://www.heart
.org/HEARTORG/GettingHealthy/WeightManagement/Obesity/Childhood-Obesity_
UCM_304347_Article.jsp.

"Childhood Obesity Deemed Child Abuse." Weight Loss Surgery Channel. February
2, 2013. http://www.weightlosssurgerychannel.com/breaking-wls-news/childhood
-obesity-deemed-child-abuse-in-controversial-court-case.html/.

"Childhood Obesity Facts." Centers for Disease Control. December 13, 2012. http://www
.cdc.gov/healthyyouth/obesity/facts.htm.

Childress, James F. "The War Metaphor in Public Policy: Some Moral Reflections." In *The
Leader's Imperative: Ethics, Integrity, and Responsibility,* edited by J. Carl Ficarrotta,
181–197. West Lafayette, Ind.: Purdue University Press, 2001.

Cincinnati Children's Hospital. "Teen-Longitudinal Assessment of Bariatric Surgery."
February 6, 2013. http://www.cincinnatichildrens.org/research/divisions/t/teen-labs/
default/?utm_source=Teen%E2%80%94Longitudinal%2BAssessment%2Bof%2B
Bariatric%2BSurgery%2B%28Teen-LABS%29&utm_medium=shortcut&utm
_campaign=teen-labs.

Clark, H. R., E. Goyder, P. Bissell, L. Blank, and J. Peters. "How Do Parents' Child Feeding
Behaviours Influence Child Weight? Implications for Childhood Obesity Policy." *Journal of Public Health* 29, no. 2 (2007): 132–141.

Cloud, John. "Why Your DNA Isn't Your Destiny." *Time Magazine,* January 6, 2010. http://
www.time.com/time/magazine/article/0,9171,1952313,00.html.

Cooper, Charlotte. "Headless Fatties." CharlotteCooper.com. 2007; December 11, 2012.
http://www.charlottecooper.net/docs/fat/headless_fatties.htm.

"Costs and Paying for Treatment." Fertility Associates. November, 30, 2012. http://www
.fertilityassociates.co.nz/paying-for-treatment.aspx.

Counihan, Carole M. *The Anthropology of Food and Body: Gender, Meaning and Power.*
New York: Routledge, 1999.

Creighton, S., J. Alderson, S. Brown, and C. L. Minto. "Medical Photography: Ethics, Consent, and the Intersex Patient." *British Journal of Urology International* 89 (2002): 67–72.

Critser, Greg. *Fatland: How Americans Became the Fattest People on Earth.* New York:
Houghton Mifflin, 2003.

———. "Let Them Eat Fat." *Harper's Magazine,* March 2000, 41–49.

Daniel, Lincia. "Body Mass Wars: Effective Use of Resources or Discrimination?" *British
Journal of Midwifery* 14, no. 10 (2006): 600.

Davison, Kirsten Krahnsoever, and Leanne Lipps Burch. "Weight Status, Parent Reaction,
and Self-Concept in Five-Year-Old Girls." *Pediatrics* 107, no. 1 (2001): 46–53.

Devon, Natasha. "Dress Provocatively? Overweight? You're Not Asking for Trouble, Nor
Are You the Root of the Problem; We Shouldn't Ask Women to Change the Way They
Dress So as to Safeguard Themselves, Just as Children Shouldn't Have to Lose Weight
So as Not to Attract Bullies." *Independent,* May 29, 2013. http://www.independent
.co.uk/voices/comment/dress-provocatively-overweight-youre-not-asking-for-trou-
ble-nor-are-you-the-root-of-the-problem-8634750.html.

Dixon, J. B., Dominic A. Fitzgerald, Lilian Kow, Deborah Bailey, and Louise A. Baur. "Adolescent Bariatric Surgery: ANZ Guidance and Recommendations." *Australian and New
Zealand Journal of Surgery* 81 (2011): 854–855.

Doherty, Brian. "Fatwa on Fat: The Surgeon General Snoops into Private Health, Again."
December 19, 2001. http://reason.com/archives/2001/12/19/fatwa-on-fat.

"Donation Page." *Operation Smile.* 2013; January 7, 2014. http://www.operationsmile.org/.

Dreger, Alice Domurat. "What to Expect When You Have the Child You Weren't Expecting." In *Surgically Shaping Children: Technology, Ethics, and the Pursuit of Normality,*
edited by Erik Parens, 253–266. Baltimore, Md.: Johns Hopkins University Press, 2006.

"Eligibility for Bariatric Surgery." Cincinnati Children's Hospital. January 20, 2013. http://
www.cincinnatichildrens.org/service/s/weight-loss/bariatric/eligibility/.

Elkins, James. *The Object Stares Back: On the Nature of Seeing.* New York: Harcourt, 1996.

Elwood, William N. *Rhetoric in the War on Drugs: The Triumphs and Tragedies of Public
Relations.* Santa Barbara, Calif.: Praeger Press, 1994.

Engber, Daniel. "Glutton Intolerance: What If a War on Obesity Only Makes the Problem
Worse?" *Slate,* October 5, 2009. http://www.slate.com/articles/health_and_science
/science/2009/10/glutton_intolerance.html.

Evans, John, and Brian Davies. *Body Knowledge and Control: Sociology of Education and
Physical Education and Health.* New York: Routledge, 2003.

Farquhar, C. M., and W. R. Gillett. "Prioritising for Fertility Treatments—Should a High
BMI Exclude Treatment?" *British Journal of Obstetrics and Gynaecology: An International Journal of Obstetrics and Gynaecology* 113, no. 10 (2006): 1107–1109.

Farrell, Amy Erdman. *Fat Shame: Stigma and the Fat Body in American Culture.* New York:
New York University Press, 2011.

Fat, Sick, and Nearly Dead. Joe Cross and Kurt Engfehr. 2010; July 20, 2012. http://www
.rebootwithjoe.com/watch-fat-sick-and-nearly-dead/.

Flashdance. Directed by Adriene Lyne. 1983. Los Angeles: Paramount Pictures, 2002. DVD.

Ford-Martin, Paula. *The Everything Parents Guide to the Overweight Child.* Avon, Mass.: Adams Media Corporation, 2005.

Fullmer, Michell A., Stephanie H. Abrams, Kathleen Hrovat, Lori Mooney, Ann O. Schemann, Jennifer B. Hillman, and David. L. Suskind. "Nutritional Strategy for Adolescents Undergoing Bariatric Surgery: Report of a Working Group of the Nutrition Committee of NASPGHAN/NACHRI." *Journal of Pediatric Gastroenterology and Nutrition* 54, no. 1 (2011): 125–135.

Galbincea, Pat. "Juvenile Court Judge Releases Obese 9-Year-Old Cleveland Heights Boy from Protective Supervision." Cleveland.com. May 10, 2012. http://www.cleveland .com/metro/index.ssf/2012/05/juvenile_court_judge_releases.html.

Gann, Carrie. "How Young Is Too Young for Bariatric Surgery?" ABC News. June 13, 2012. http://abcnews.go.com/Health/gastric-sleeve-helps-obese-12-year-shed-pounds /story?id=16552766#.UMziSIWvwm1.

Gard, Michael. *The End of the Obesity Epidemic.* New York: Routledge, 2011.

Gard, Michael, and Jan Wright. *The Obesity Epidemic: Science, Morality and Ideology.* New York: Routledge, 2005.

Gardner, Amanda. "Many Obese Americans Struggle with Stigma, Discrimination, Poll Finds." *U.S. News and World Report,* August 23, 2012. http://health.usnews.com/health -news/news/articles/2012/08/23/many-obese-americans-struggle-with-stigma -discrimination-poll-finds.

Garland-Thomson, Rosemarie. *Staring: How We Look.* New York: Oxford University Press, 2009.

Garrett, Jeremy R., and Leslie Ann McNolty. "Bariatric Surgery and the Social Character of the Obesity Epidemic." *American Journal of Bioethics* 10, no. 2 (2010): 20–22.

Geelen, S. M. van, L. L. E Bolt, and M. J. H. van Summeren. "Moral Aspects of Bariatric Surgery for Obese Children and Adolescents: The Urgent Need for Empirical–Ethical Research." *American Journal of Bioethics* 10, no. 2 (2010): 30–32.

George, Cheryl. "Parents Supersizing Their Children: Criminalizing and Prosecuting the Rising Incidence of Childhood Obesity as Child Abuse." *DePaul Journal of Healthcare* 13, no. 1 (2010): 33–74.

Gillett, W. R., T. Putt, and C. M. Farquhar. "Prioritising for Fertility Treatments—The Effect of Excluding Women with a High Body Mass Index." *British Journal of Obstetrics and Gynaecology: An International Journal of Obstetrics and Gynaecology* 113, no. 10 (2006): 1218–1221.

Gilman, Sander L. *Fat: A Cultural History of Obesity.* Malden, Mass.: Polity Press, 2008.

Goffman, Erving. *Stigma: Notes on the Management of Spoiled Identity.* New York: Simon and Schuster, 1963.

Goldberg, C. "Citing Intolerance, Obese People Take Small Steps to Press Cause." *New York Times,* national edition, November 5, 2000, 1, 30.

Goodman, W. Charisse. *The Invisible Woman: Confronting Weight Prejudice in America.* Carlsbad, Calif.: Gurze Books, 1995.

Gosman, Gabriella G., Wendy C. King, Beth Schrope, Kristene J. Steffen, Gladys W. Strain, Anita P. Courcoulas, David R. Flum, John R. Pender, and Hyagriv N. Simhan. "Reproductive Health of Women Electing Bariatric Surgery." *Fertility and Sterility* 94, no. 4 (2010): 1426–1430.

Gray, Emma. "Ragen Chastain Launches 'Support All Kids' Campaign to Counter Georgia Anti-obesity Ads." *Huffington Post.* February 23, 2012. http://www.huffingtonpost .com/2012/02/23/support-all-kids-ragen-chastain-georgia-anti-obesity-ads_n _1295047.html.

Gray, Wendyn, Nicole A. Kahhan, and David M. Janicke. "Peer Victimization and Pediatric Obesity: A Review of the Literature." *Psychology in the Schools* 46, no. 8 (2009): 720–727.

Grinberg, Emanuella. "Georgia's Child Obesity Ads Aim to Create Movement Out of Controversy." CNN.com. February 7, 2012. http://www.cnn.com/2012/02/07/health/ atlanta-child-obesity-ads/index.html.

Grundy, Melanie, Sean Woodcock, and Stephen E. Attwood. "The Surgical Management of Obesity in Young Women." *Surgical Endoscopy* 22 (2008): 2107–2116.

Guthman, Julie. *Weighing In: Obesity, Food Justice, and the Limits of Capitalism.* Berkeley: University of California Press, 2011.

Harding, Ann. "Surgery Is No Quick Fix for Obese Teens." CNN.com. June 22, 2011. http:// www.cnn.com/2011/HEALTH/06/22/surgery.obese.teens/index.html.

Harris, Dan, and Mikaela Conley. "Childhood Obesity: A Call for Parents to Lose Custody." ABC News. July 14, 2011. http://abcnews.go.com/Health/childhood-obesity -call-parents-lose-custody/story?id=14068280#.UKpFeYWvy2Q.

Hart, Dani. *I Want to Live: Gastric Bypass Reversal.* Fort Collins, Colo.: Mountain Stars, 2003.

Hartcollis, Anemona. "Young, Obese and in Surgery." *New York Times,* January 7, 2012. http://www.nytimes.com/2012/01/08/health/young-obese-and-getting-weight-loss -surgery.html?pagewanted=all&_r=0.

Hartley, Cecilia. "Letting Ourselves Go: Making Room for the Fat Body in Feminist Scholarship." In *Bodies Out of Bounds: Fatness and Transgression,* edited by Kathleen LeBesco and Jana Evans Braziel, 60–73. Berkeley: University of California Press, 2001.

Haskins, Victoria, and Margaret D. Jacobs. "Stolen Generations and Vanishing Indians: The Removal of Indigenous Children as a Weapon of War in the United States and Australia, 1870–1940." In *Children and War: A Historical Anthology*, edited by James Marten, 227–241. New York: New York University Press, 2002.

Haynes, Beverly. "Creation of a Bariatric Surgery Program for Adolescents at a Major Teaching Hospital." *Pediatric Nursing* 31, no. 1 (2005): 21–23, 59.

Hearnshaw, C., and K. Matyka. "Managing Childhood Obesity: When Lifestyle Change Is Not Enough." *Diabetes, Obesity, and Metabolism* 12 (2010): 947–957.

Herndon, April. "Collateral Damage from Friendly Fire?: Race, Class, Nation, and the 'War against Obesity.'" *Social Semiotics* 15, no. 2 (2005): 127–141.

———. "Disparate but Disabled: Fat Embodiment and Disability Studies." *National Women's Studies Association Journal* 14, no. 3 (2002): 120–137.

———. "Mommy Made Me Do It: Mothering Fat Children in the Age of the Obesity Epidemic." *Food, Culture and Society* 13, no. 3 (2010): 331–349.

———. "Thin Like Me." *Atrium: The Report of the Northwestern Medical Humanities and Bioethics Program* 9 (Spring 2011): 19–21.

Herpertz, S., R. Kielman, A. M. Wolf, M. Langafel, W. Senf, and J. Hebebrand. "Does Obesity Surgery Improve Psychosocial Functioning? A Systematic Review." *International Journal of Obesity* 27 (2003): 1300–1314.

Hughes, I. A., C. Houk, S. F. Ahmed, and P. A. Lee. "Consensus Statement on the Management of Intersex Disorders." *Archives of Disease in Childhood* 91, no. 7 (2006): 554–563.

Huh, S. Y., S. L. Rifas-Shiman, C. A. Zera, J. W. Edwards, E. Oken, S. T. Weiss, and M. W. Gillman. "Delivery by Caesarean Section and Risk of Obesity in Preschool Age Children: A Prospective Cohort Study." *Journal of Archives of Disease in Childhood* 97, no. 7 (2010): 610–616.

Human Fertilization and Embryology Authority. "NHS Fertility Treatment." May 9, 2012. http://www.hfea.gov.uk/fertility-treatment-cost-nhs.html.

Hyman, Bill, Kari Kooi, and David Ficklen. "Bariatric Surgery in Adolescents." *Journal of School Health* 78, no. 8 (2008): 452–454.

Inge, T. H., S. A. Xanthakos, and M. H. Zeller. "Bariatric Surgery for Pediatric Extreme Obesity: Now or Later?" *International Journal of Obesity* 31 (2007): 1–14.

Inge, Thomas, Michael Helmrath, Mark Vierra, and Sayeed Ikramuddin. "Challenges of Adolescent Bariatric Surgery: Tips for Managing the Extremely Obese Teen." *Journal of Laparoendoscopic and Advanced Surgical Techniques* 18, no. 1 (2008): 157–169.

Ingelfinger, Julie. "Bariatric Surgery in Adolescents." *New England Journal of Medicine* 365, no. 15 (2011): 1365–1367.

Inness, Sherrie A. *Secret Ingredients: Race, Gender, and Class at the Dinner Table.* New York: Palgrave Macmillan, 2006.

In re D. K. 202 WL 31968992 (Pa.com.PI.), 58 pa. (D. & C. 4th 353, 2002).

International Pediatric Endosurgery Group. "IPEG Guidelines for Surgical Treatment of Extremely Obese Adolescents." *Journal of Laparoendoscopic & Advanced Surgical Techniques* 19, no. 1 (2009): xiv–xvi.

In the Interest of L. T., a Minor Child. 494 N.W.2d 450 (Court of Appeals of Iowa, 1992).

In the Matter of Brittany T. N-0142–03/06 G (Family Court of New York, Chemung County, 2007).

Jansen, Anita, Tom Smeets, Brigette Boon, Chantelle Nederkoorn, Anne Roefs, and Sandra Mulkens. "Vulnerability to Interpretation Bias in Overweight Children." *Psychology and Health* 22, no. 5 (2007): 561–574.

Jansen, Esther, Sandra Mulkens, and Anita Jansen. "Do Not Eat the Red Food!: Prohibition of Snacks Leads to Their Relatively Higher Consumption in Children." *Appetite* 49 (2007): 572–577.

Janssen, Ian, Wendy M. Craig, William F. Boyce, and William Pickett. "Associations between Overweight and Obesity with Bullying in School-Aged Children." *Pediatrics* 113, no. 5 (2004): 1187–1194.

Jhally, Sut. *Tough Guise: Violence, Media, and the Crisis of Masculinity.* DVD. Media Education Foundation. 1999.

Jutel, Annemarie. "Weighing Health: The Moral Burden of Obesity." *Social Semiotics* 15, no. 2 (2005): 113–125.

Kaati, G., L. O. Bygren, and S. Edvinsson. "Cardiovascular and Diabetes Mortality Determined by Nutrition during Parents' and Grandparents' Slow Growth Period." *European Journal of Human Genetics* 10 (2002): 682–688.

Kassirer, David, and Marcia Angell. "Losing Weight: An Ill-Fated New Year's Resolution." *New England Journal of Medicine* 338, no. 1 (1998): 52–54.

Kent, Le'a. "Fighting Abjection: Representing Fat Women." In *Bodies Out of Bounds: Fatness and Transgression,* edited by Jana Evans Braziel and Kathleen LeBesco, 130–150. Berkeley: University of California Press, 2001.

Kersh, Rogan. "The Politics of Obesity: A Current Assessment and Look Ahead." *Millbank Quarterly* 87, no. 1 (2009): 295–316.

King, Wendy C., Jia-Yuh Chin, James E. Mitchell, Melissa A. Kalarchian, Kristene J. Steffen, Scott G. Engel, Anita P. Courcoulas, Walter J. Pories, and Susan G. Yanovski. "Prevalence of Alcohol Abuse Disorders before and after Bariatric Surgery." *Journal of the American Medical Association* 307, no. 23 (2012): 2516–2525.

Kirkland, Anna. *Fat Rights: Dilemmas of Difference and Personhood.* New York: New York University Press, 2008.

Knowles, David. "Al Roker: 'I Pooped My Pants' during 2002 White House Visit, Ditched Soiled Underwear in Bathroom and 'Went Commando.'" *New York Daily News,* January 2, 2013. http://www.nydailynews.com/entertainment/tv-movies/al-roker-pooped-pants-white-house-article-1.1235259.

Kolata, Gina. *Rethinking Thin: The New Science of Weight Loss—and the Myths and Realities of Dieting.* New York: Picador, 2007.

Kominiarek, Michelle. "Pregnancy after Bariatric Surgery." *Obstetrics and Gynecology Clinics of North America* 37, no. 2 (2010): 305–320.

Kral, John G. "Preventing and Treating Obesity in Girls and Young Women to Curb the Epidemic." *Obesity Research* 12, no. 10 (2004): 1539–1546.

Kral, John G., Ruth A. Kava, Patrick M. Catalano, and Barbara J. Moore. "Severe Obesity: The Neglected Epidemic." *European Journal of Obesity* 5, no. 2 (2012): 254–269.

Kubasek, Nancy. "The Case against Prosecutions for Prenatal Drug Use." *Texas Journal of Women and the Law* 8 (1999): 167–181.

Kukla, Rebecca. *Mass Hysteria: Medicine, Culture, and Mothers' Bodies.* New York: Rowman & Littlefield, 2005.

Ladd-Taylor, Molly, and Lauri Urmansky. "Introduction." In *"Bad" Mothers: The Politics of Blame in Twentieth-Century America,* edited by Molly Ladd-Taylor and Lauri Urmansky, 1–28. New York: New York University Press, 1998.

Laitinen, J., A. Jaaskalainen, A. L. Hartikainen, U. Sovio, M. Vaarasmaki, A. Pouto, M. Kaakanen, and M. R. Jarvelin. "Maternal Weight Gain during the First Half of Pregnancy and Offspring Obesity at 16 Years: A Prospective Cohort Study." *British Journal of Obstetrics and Gynaecology: An International Journal of Obstetrics and Gynecology* 119, no. 6 (2012): 716–723.

Landsman, Gail. "Real Motherhood: Class and Children with Disabilities." In *Ideologies and Technologies of Motherhood: Race, Class, Sexuality and Nationalism,* edited by Helene Ragone and France Winddance Twine, 169–190. New York: Routledge, 2000.

Latner, Janet D., and Marlene B. Schwartz. "Weight Bias in a Child's World." In *Weight Bias: Nature, Consequences and Remedies,* edited by Kelly D. Brownell, Rebecca M. Puhl, Marlene B. Schwartz, and Leslie Rudd, 54–67. New York: Guilford Press, 2005.

Latner, Janet D., Daria W. Ebneter, and Kerry S. O'Brien. "Residual Obesity Stigma: An

Experimental Investigation of Weight Bias against Obese and Lean Targets Differing in Weight-Loss History." *Obesity* 20, no. 10 (2012): 2035–2038.

Lawlor, Debbie A., George Davey Smith, Michael O'Callaghan, Rosa Alati, Abdullah Mahmun, Gail M. Williams, and Jake M. Najman. "Epidemiologic Evidence for the Fetal Overnutrition Hypothesis: Findings from the Mater-University Study of Pregnancy and Its Outcomes." *American Journal of Epidemiology* 165, no. 4 (2006): 418–424.

Leary, Christine. "Should Obese Women Be Denied Access to Fertility Treatment on the NHS?" *Biologist* 58, no. 2 (2011): 24–26.

LeBesco, Kathleen. "Quest for a Cause: The Fat Gene, the Gay Gene, and the New Eugenics." In *The Fat Studies Reader,* edited by Esther Rothblum and Sondra Solovay, 65–74. New York: New York University Press, 2009.

———. *Revolting Bodies: The Struggle to Redefine Fat Identity.* Boston: University of Massachusetts Press, 2004.

LeBesco, Kathleen, and Jana Evans Braziel. "Introduction." In *Bodies Out of Bounds: Fatness and Transgression,* edited by Kathleen LeBesco and Jana Braziel, 1–15. Berkeley: University of California Press, 2001.

Lee, C. Y. W., and G. Koren. "Maternal Obesity: Effects on Pregnancy and the Role of Pre-conception Counseling." *Journal of Obstetrics and Gynaecology* 30, no. 2 (2010): 101–106.

Levenstein, Harvey. *Paradox of Plenty: A Social History of Eating in Modern America.* New York: Oxford University Press, 1993.

Linton, Simi. *Claiming Disability: Knowledge and Identity.* New York: New York University Press, 1998.

Lipsitz, George. *American Studies in a Moment of Danger.* Minneapolis: University of Minnesota, 2001.

Lisa. "Before Gastric Bypass Surgery: What I Wish I Had Known." *Gastric Bypass Truth: The Skinny on Life after Weight Loss Surgery.* http://gastricbypasstruth.com/before-gastric-bypass-surgery/before-gastric-bypass-surgery-what-i-wish-i-had-known/.

"London, Ohio City Data." City-Data.com. November 3, 2012. http://www.city-data.com/city/London-Ohio.html.

Love, Aileen, and Henry Billett. "Obesity, Bariatric Surgery, and Iron Deficiency: True, True, True, and Related." *American Journal of Hematology* 83, no. 5 (2008): 403–409.

Lowe, Adrian. "Is This Child Abuse? Courts Think So." July 12, 2012. http://www.theage.com.au/victoria/is-this-child-abuse-the-courts-think-so-20120711-21wdb.html.

Macrae, Fiona, "Obesity Legacy of Mums-to-Be: Carrying Too Many Pounds during Pregnancy Can Give Your Baby a Life of Weight Problems." *Daily Mail,* May 14, 2012. http://www.dailymail.co.uk/health/article-2144243/Obesity-pregnancy-Carrying-pounds-baby-life-weight-problems.html.

Madowitz, J., S. Knatz, T. Maginot, J. Crow, and K. N. Boutelle. "Teasing, Depression, and Unhealthy Weight Control Behavior in Obese Children." *Pediatric Obesity* 7 (2012): 446–452.

Maher, JaneMaree, Suzanne Fraser, and Jan Wright. "Framing the Mother: Childhood Obesity, Maternal Responsibility and Care." *Journal of Gender Studies* 19, no. 3 (2010): 233–247.

Mann, Traci, A. Janet Tomiyama, Erika Westling, Ann-Marie Lew, Barbara Samuels, and Jason Chatman. "Medicare's Search for Effective Obesity Treatments: Diets Are Not the Answer." *American Psychologist* 62, no. 3 (2007): 220–233.

Martins, Nicole, and Kristen Harrison. "Racial and Gender Differences in the Relationship between Children's Television Use and Children's Self Esteem: A Longitudinal Panel Study." *Communication Research* 39, no. 3 (2012): 338–357.

Maya Joi's Journey to Being Strong4Life.com. January 2, 2013. http://mayajoi4life.blog spot.com/.

Mayo Clinic Staff. "Dumping Syndrome." MayoClinic.com. January 8, 2013. http://www .mayoclinic.com/health/dumping-syndrome/DS00715.

McDonnell, Jane Taylor. "On Being the 'Bad' Mother of an Autistic Child." In *"Bad" Mothers: The Politics of Blame in Twentieth-Century America,* edited by Molly Ladd-Taylor and Lauri Umansky, 220–229. New York: New York University Press, 1998.

McGraw, Seamus. "Teen Actress: Anti-obesity Ads Made Me More Confident." *Today Show.* May 6, 2011. http://www.today.com/id/42929825/site/todayshow/ns/today-today _health/t/teen-actress-anti-obesity-ads-made-me-more-confident/#.UTOM moWvxrd.

"Medical Missions and Program." *Operation Smile.* February 21, 2013. http://www.opera tionsmile.org/our_work/medical-missions/.

Meier, Conrad, and Diane C. Bast. "New Round Fired in Fat Wars." *Heartland Institutes Healthcare News,* May 1, 2012. http://news.heartland.org/newspaper-article/2002/05/ 01/new-round-fired-fat-wars.

Michalsky, Marc. "Adolescent Bariatric Surgery Best Practice Guidelines." American SocietyforMetabolicandBariatricSurgery.com. January 25, 2013. http://asmbs.org/2012 /01/adolescent-bariatric-surgery-best-practice-guidelines/.

Michalsky, Marc, Robert E. Kramer, Michelle A. Fullmer, Michele Polfus, Renee Porter, Wendy Ward-Begnoche, Elizabeth Getzoff, Meredith Dreyer, Stacy Stolzman, and Kirk W. Reichard. "Developing Criteria for Pediatric/Adolescent Bariatric Surgery Programs." *Pediatrics* 128, no. 2 (2011): 65–70.

Millman, Marcia. *Such a Pretty Face: Being Fat in America.* New York: W. W. Norton, 1980.

Mitgang, Melissa. "Childhood Obesity and State Intervention: An Examination of the Health Risks of Pediatric Obesity and When They Justify State Involvement." *Columbia Journal of Law and Social Problems* 44, no. 553 (2011): 553–587.

Mollow, Anna. "Sized Up: Why Fat Is a Queer and Feminist Issue." Bitch.com. 2013; March 1, 2013. http://bitchmagazine.org/article/sized-up-fat-feminist-queer-disability.

The Morning Show with Mike and Juliet. June 19, 2007. http://www.youtube.com/ watch?v=gBdLKNKqeAY.

Muennig, Peter. "The Body Politic: The Relationship between Stigma and Obesity–Associated Disease." *BioMed Central Public Health* 8, no. 128 (2008). http://www.bio medcentral.com/1471-2458/8/128.

Murray, Samantha. "Normative Imperatives vs. Pathological Bodies: Constructing the 'Fat' Woman." *Australian Feminist Studies* 23, no. 56 (2008): 231–224.

Murtagh, Lindsey, and David S. Ludwig. "State Intervention in Life-Threatening Childhood Obesity." *Journal of the American Medical Association* 306, no. 2 (2011): 206–207.

Mutcherson, Kimberly M. "No Way to Treat a Woman: Creating an Appropriate Standard for Resolving Medical Treatment Disputes Involving HIV-Positive Children." *Harvard Women's Law Journal* 25, no. 221 (2002): 221–279.

Myers, John E. B. "A Short History of Child Protection in America." *Family Law Quarterly* 42, no. 3 (2008): 449–463.

"Nathan Sorrell, Nike Olympic Commercial: Today Show Interviews Overweight Boy Running." NewsChannel5.com. August 13, 2012. http://www.wptv.com/dpp/news/local_news/water_cooler/nathan-sorrell-nike-olympic-commercial-youtube-video-today-show-interviews-overweight-boy-running.

Neergaard, Lauren. "Mom's Obesity Surgery May Help Break Cycle in Kids." YahooNews.com. May 27, 2013. http://news.yahoo.com/moms-obesity-surgery-may-help-break-cycle-kids-192322482.html.

Neumark-Sztainer, Dianne, and Marla Eisenberg. "Weight Bias in a Teen's World." In *Weight Bias: Nature, Consequences and Remedies,* edited by Kelly D. Brownell, Rebecca M. Puhl, Marlene B. Schwartz, and Leslie Rudd, 68–79. New York: Guilford Press, 2005.

Newcomb, Alyssa. "Obese Third Grader Taken from Mom, Placed in Foster Care." ABC News.com. November 27, 2011. http://abcnews.go.com/blogs/health/2011/11/27/obese-third-grader-taken-from-family-placed-in-foster-care/.

"Nike's 'Great' Fat Kid Commercial Is Not Great." Buzzfeed.com. August 7, 2012. http://www.buzzfeed.com/copyranter/nikes-great-fat-kid-commercial-is-notgreat?fb_comment_id=fbc_10152050583855145_34412435_10152051863405145#fbee8c1d5c4df4.

"Obesity and Extreme Slimness Cause Risks in Pregnancy." *Science Daily.* April 19, 2012. http://www.sciencedaily.com/releases/2012/04/120419090719.htm.

O'Connor, Anahad. "Weight Loss Surgery May Not Combat Diabetes Long-Term." November 28, 2012. *New York Times Well Blogs.* http://well.blogs.nytimes.com/2012/11/28/weight-loss-surgery-may-not-combat-diabetes-long-term/.

Okie, Susan. "The Epidemic That Wasn't." *New York Times,* January 26, 2009. http://www.nytimes.com/2009/01/27/health/27coca.html?_r=1&pagewanted=all&.

Oliver, Eric J. *Fat Politics: The Real Story behind America's Obesity Epidemic.* New York: Oxford University Press, 2006.

Olshanky, S. Jay, Douglas J. Passaro, Ronald C. Hershaw, Jennifer Layden, Bruce A. Carnes, Jacob Brody, Leonard Hayflick, Robert N. Butler, David B. Allison, and David S. Ludwig. "A Potential Decline in Life Expectancy in the United States in the 21st Century." *New England Journal of Medicine* 352, no. 11 (2005): 1138–1145.

Olson, Christine M., Myla St. Strawderman, and Barbara A. Dennison. "Maternal Weight Gain during Pregnancy and Child Weight at Age 3 Years." *Maternal and Child Health Journal* 13 (2009): 839–846.

Oyetunji, Tolulope A., Ashanti L. Franklin, Gezza Ortega, Namita Akolkar, Faisal G. Qureshi, Fizan Abdullah, Edward E. Cornwell, Benedict C. Nwomeh, and Terrence M. Fullum. "Revisiting Childhood Obesity: Persistent Underutilization of Surgical Intervention?" *American Surgeon* 78, no. 7 (2012): 788–793.

Pandey, S., A. Maheshwari, and S. Battacharya. "Should Access to Fertility Treatment Be Determined by Female Body Mass Index?" *Human Reproduction* 25, no. 4 (2010): 815–820.

Parker-Pope, Tara. "Better to Be Fat and Fit Than Skinny and Unfit." *New York Times*, August 18, 2008. http://www.nytimes.com/2008/08/19/health/19well.html?_r=0.

Patel, Deena. "Super-Sized Kids: Using the Law to Combat Morbid Obesity in Children." *Family Court Review: An Interdiscplinary Journal* 43, no. 1 (2005): 164–177.

"Paying the Price for Those Extra Pounds." *Harvard School of Public Health*. January 21, 2013. http://www.hsph.harvard.edu/obesity-prevention-source/obesity-consequences/economic/#costs-rising.

Peterson, M. M. "Assisted Reproductive Technologies and Equity of Access Issues." *Journal of Medical Ethics* 31 (2005): 280–285.

Pollan, Michael. "You Want Fries with That?" Nytimes.com. January 12, 2003. http://www.nytimes.com/2003/01/12/books/you-want-fries-with-that.html?pagewanted=all&src=pm.

Poulton, Terry. *No Fat Chicks: How Big Business Profits by Making Women Hate Their Bodies—and How to Fight Back*. Seacaucus, N.J.: Birch Lane Press, 1997.

Powell, G. F., J. A. Brasel, and R. M. Blizzard. "Emotional Deprivation and Growth Retardation Simulating Idiopathic Hypopituitarism—Clinical Evaluation of the Syndrome." *New England Journal of Medicine* 276, no. 23 (1967): 1271–1278.

"Public Health Grand Rounds." Centers for Disease Control. June 17, 2010. http://www.cdc.gov/about/grand-rounds/archives/2010/06-June.htm.

Puhl, Rebecca M. "Coping with Weight Stigma." In *Weight Bias: Nature, Consequences and Remedies*, edited by Kelly D. Brownell, Rebecca M. Puhl, Marlene B. Schwartz, and Leslie Rudd, 275–284. New York: Guilford Press, 2005.

Puhl, Rebecca M., and Chelsea A. Heuer. "The Stigma of Obesity: A Review and Update." *Obesity* 17, no. 5 (2009): 941–964.

Puhl, Rebecca, and Kelly D. Brownell. "Bias, Discrimination and Obesity." *Obesity Research* 9, no. 12 (2001): 788–805.

———. "Confronting and Coping with Weight Stigma: An Investigation of Overweight and Obese Adults." *Obesity* 14, no. 10 (2005): 1802–1815.

———. "Psychological Origins of Obesity Stigma: Toward Changing a Powerful and Pervasive Bias." *Obesity Reviews* 4 (2003): 213–227.

Puhl, Rebecca M., Marlene B. Schwartz, and Kelly D. Brownell. "Impact of Perceived Consensus on Stereotypes about Obese People: A New Approach for Reducing Bias." *Health Psychology* 24, no. 5 (2005): 517–525.

Puhl, R. M., T. Andreyeva, and K. D. Brownell. "Perceptions of Weight Discrimination: Prevalence and Comparison to Race and Gender Discrimination in America." *International Journal of Obesity* 32 (2008): 992–1000.

Puhl, Rebecca M., Jaimie Lee Peterson, and Joerg Luedicke. "Weight-Based Victimization: Bullying Experiences of Weight Loss Treatment–Seeking Youth." *Pediatrics* 31, no. 1 (2013): e1–e9. http://pediatrics.aappublications.org/content/early/2012/12/19/peds.2012–1106.

Rapp, Emily. "Notes from a Dragon Mom." *New York Times*, October 16, 2010. http://www.nytimes.com/2011/10/16/opinion/sunday/notes-from-a-dragon-mom.html?_r=0.

———. *Poster Child: A Memoir*. New York: Bloomsbury, 2007.

Reynolds, Gretchen. "Getting Fat but Staying Fit." *New York Times*, March 7, 2012. http://well.blogs.nytimes.com/2012/03/07/getting-fat-but-staying-fit/.

———. "Phys Ed: Can You Be Overweight and Still Be Healthy?" *New York Times,* January 6, 2010. http://well.blogs.nytimes.com/2010/01/06/phys-ed-can-you-be-overweight-and-still-be-healthy/.

Rimm, Sylvia. *Rescuing the Emotional Lives of Overweight Children: What Our Kids Go through and How We Can Help.* Emmaus, Pa.: Rodale Press, 2004.

Roberts, Dorothy E. "Punishing Drug Addicts Who Have Babies: Women of Color, Equality, and the Right of Privacy." *Harvard Law Review* 104, no. 7 (1991): 1419–1482.

Roehling, Mark V., Patricia V. Roehling, and L. Maureen Odland. "Investigating the V=Validity of Stereotypes about Overweight Employees." *Group and Organization Management* 23, no. 4 (2008): 392–424.

Roehrig, Helmut R., Stavra A. Xanthakos, Jenny Sweeney, Meg H. Zeller, and Thomas H. Inge. "Pregnancy after Bypass Surgery in Adolescents." *Obesity Surgery* 17 (2007): 873–877.

Roker, Al, with Laura Morton. *Never Goin' Back: Winning the Weight-Loss Battle for Good.* New York: New American Library, 2013.

"Roux-en-Y Bypass." Salt Lake Regional Medical Center. March 1, 2013. http://www.saltlakeregional.com/services/weight_loss_surgery/rouxeny/.

Rukavina, P. B., and W. Li. "School Physical Activity Interventions: Do Not Forget about Obesity Bias." *Obesity Reviews* 9 (2008): 67–75.

Ryan, Joan. "Monumental Task of Parenthood Far Outweighs Fat or Thin." *SFGate.* January 10, 1998. http://www.sfgate.com/politics/article/JOAN-RYAN-Monumental-Task-Of-Parenthood-Far-3016364.php.

Saguy, Abigail C. *What's Wrong with Fat?* New York: Oxford University Press, 2012.

Sargese, Lisa. "Gastric Bypass and the Pretzel Issue." LisaLovesLifeLessons.com. January 5, 2012. http://theskinnyonline.blogspot.com/2012/01/gastric-bypass-and-pretzel-issue.html.

Sarr, Michael G., "The Problem of Obesity: How Are We Going to Address It?" *American Journal of Bioethics* 10, no. 12 (2010): 12–32.

Sarwer, David B., and Rebecca J. Dilks. "Childhood and Adolescent Obesity: Psychological and Behavioral Issues in Weight Loss Treatment." *Journal of Youth Adolescence* 41 (2012): 98–104.

Saxe, Jessica Schorr. "Promoting Healthy Lifestyles and Decreasing Childhood Obesity: Increasing Physician Effectiveness through Advocacy." *Annals of Family Medicine* 9, no. 6 (2011): 546–548. October 8, 2013. http://www.annfammed.org/.

Scannell, Kate. "Study on WLS for Type 2 Diabetes Has Serious Problems." MeVsDiabetes.com. April 2012; May 3, 2012. http://mevsdiabetes-bloglapedia.blogspot.com/2012/04/dr-kate-scannell-study-on-weight-loss.html.

Scharmberg, Kristen. "Prosecutors Targeting Pregnant Drug Users: Some Fear Women Will Shun Treatment." *Chicago Tribune News,* November 23, 2003. http://articles.chicagotribune.com/2003-11-23/news/0311230450_1_prosecutions-pregnant-women-pregnant-drug-users.

Schoenberg, Nara. "Obese Children, Government Intervention: High-Profile Case Generates Fears among Families and Their Advocates." *Chicago Tribune,* December 20, 2011. http://articles.chicagotribune.com/2011-12-20/features/sc-fam-1220-obese-kids-2011 1220_1_obese-kids-obese-children-pediatrics.

Schvey, Natasha. "Weight Bias in Healthcare." *American Medical Association Journal of Ethics* 12, no. 4 (2010): 287–291.

Schwartz, Hillel. *Never Satisfied: A Cultural History of Diets, Fantasies, and Fat.* New York: Free Press, 1986.

Seavey, Todd. "Issuing a Fatwar." American Council on Science and Health. March 28, 2002. http://acsh.org/2002/03/issuing-a-fatwar/.

Sheeran, Thomas J. "Ohio Officials Take 200-Pound Boy from Mother." *Huffington Post.* November 29, 2011. http://www.huffingtonpost.com/2011/11/29/ohio-officials-take-200-p_n_1118186.html?.

Sherry, Michael. "The Language of War in AIDS Discourse." In *Writing AIDS: Gay Literature, Language and Analysis,* edited by T. Murphy and S. Poirer, 46–58. New York: Columbia University Press, 1993.

Shield, J. P. H., E. Crowne, and J. Morgan. "Is There a Place for Bariatric Surgery in Treating Childhood Obesity?" *Archives of Disease in Childhood* 93, no. 5 (2008): 369–372.

Shildrick, Margrit. *Leaky Bodies and Boundaries: Feminism, Postmodernism, and (Bio)Ethics.* New York: Routledge, 1997.

Shipley, Dean. "London Student Featured in Nike Ad." *Record Herald,* August 1, 2012. http://www.recordherald.com/main.asp?SectionID=1&SubSectionID=1&ArticleID=144055.

Shrewsbury, V. A., K. S. Steinbeck, S. Torvaldson, and L. A. Baur. "The Role of Parents in Adolescent and Pre-adolescent Overweight and Obesity Treatment: A Systematic Review of Clinical Recommendations." *Obesity Reviews* 12 (2011): 759–769.

Shulevitz, Judith. "Why Fathers Really Matter." *New York Times Sunday Review,* September 8, 2012. http://www.nytimes.com/2012/09/09/opinion/sunday/why-fathers-really-matter.html?pagewanted=all.

Simmons-Duffin, Selena. "New Anti-obesity Ads Blaming Overweight Parents Spark Controversy." NPR. September 27, 2012. http://www.npr.org/blogs/thesalt/2012/09/27/161831449/new-anti-obesity-ads-blaming-overweight-parents-spark-criticism.

Skuse, David, Assunta Albanese, Richard Stanhope, Jane Gilmore, and Linda Voss. "A New Stress-Related Syndrome of Growth Failure and Hyperphagia in Children, Associated with Reversibility of Growth Hormone Insufficiency." *Lancet* 348, no. 9024 (1996): 353–358.

Smith, J. Clinton. *Understanding Childhood Obesity.* Jackson: University Press of Mississippi, 1999.

Solovay, Sondra. "Remedies for Weight-Based Discrimination." In *Weight Bias: Nature, Consequences and Remedies,* edited by Kelly D. Brownell, Rebecca M. Puhl, Marlene B. Schwartz, and Leslie Rudd, 212–222. New York: Guilford Press, 2005.

———. *Tipping the Scales of Justice: Fighting Weight-Based Discrimination.* Amherst, N.Y.: Prometheus Books, 2000.

Sontag, Susan. *Illness as Metaphor and AIDS and Its Metaphors.* New York: Picador, 1989.

Stearns, Peter. *Fat History: Bodies and Beauty in the Modern West.* New York: New York University Press, 1997.

Steiner, Andy. "Fat Nation." *Utne Reader,* March-April 2002, 72–75.

Stone-Manista, Krista. "Protecting Pregnant Women: A Guide to Successfully Challenging Criminal Abuse Prosecutions of Pregnant Drug Addicts." *Journal of Criminal Law and Criminology* 99, no. 3 (2009): 823–856.

Story, Mary, and Simone French. "Food Advertising and Marketing Directed at Children and Adolescents in the US." *International Journal of Behavioral Nutrition and Physical Activity* 1, no. 3 (2004). 10.1186/1479–5868–1-3 http://www.ncbi.nlm.nih.gov/pmc /articles/PMC416565/.

Strong4Life. http://www.strong4life.com/.

"Study Finds Bariatric Surgery Safe for Teens." TodayShow.com. January 3, 2013. http:// video.today.msnbc.msn.com/today/47858507#47858507.

Stukator, Angela. "It's Not over until the Fat Lady Sings: Comedy, the Carnivalesque, and Body Politics." In *Bodies Out of Bounds: Fatness and Transgression,* edited by Jana Evans Braziel and Kathleen LeBesco, 197–213. Berkeley: University of California Press, 2001.

"Suing McDonald's over Happy Meals Won't Keep Kids from Getting Fat." *Crain's Chicago Business,* December 20, 2010. http://www.chicagobusiness.com/article/20101218 /ISSUE07/312189992/editorial-suing-mcdonald-s-over-happy-meals-won-t-keep-kids -from-getting-fat.

Tauber, Michelle, and Mark Dagostino. "100 and Counting." *People,* November 18, 2002, 104–110.

Taylor, Nicole L. "Guys, She's Humongous: Gender and Weight-Based Teasing in Adolescence." *Journal of Adolescent Research* 26, no. 2 (2011): 178–199.

Taylor, Valerie H., Brian Stonehocker, Margot Steele, and Arya M. Sharmer. "An Overview of Treatments for Obesity in a Population with Mental Illness." *Canadian Journal of Psychiatry* 57, no. 1 (2012): 13–20.

Thompson, Becky W. *A Hunger So Wide and So Deep: American Women Speak Out on Eating Problems.* Minneapolis: University of Minnesota Press, 1994.

Thorne, Barrie. *Gender Play: Girls and Boys in School.* New Brunswick, N.J.: Rutgers University Press, 1995.

Trivedi, Bijal P. "The Bypass Cure." *Discover Magazine,* December 2012. http://discover magazine.com/2012/dec/29-bypass#.UM44w4Wvwm1.

Tyre, Peg. "Fighting Anorexia: No One Is to Blame." National Association of Anorexia and Associated Disorders. December 5, 2005; September 3, 2012. http://www.anad.org /news/fighting-anorexia-no-one-is-to-blame-newsweek/.

US Department of Health and Human Services. "Childhood Obesity." October 12, 2012. http://aspe.hhs.gov/health/reports/child_obesity/.

Vahratian, Anjel, and Yolanda R. Smith. "Should Access to Fertility-Related Services Be Conditional on Body Mass Index?" *Human Reproduction* 24, no. 7 (2009): 1532–1537.

van Geelen, S. M., L. L. E. Bolt, and M. J. H. van Summeren. "Moral Aspects of Bariatric Surgery for Obese Children and Adolescents: The Urgent Need for Empirical-Ethical Research." *American Journal of Bioethics* 10, no. 12 (2010): 30–32.

Varness, Todd, David. B. Allen, Aaron L. Carrel, and Norman Fost. "Childhood Obesity and Medical Neglect." *Pediatrics* 123, no. 1 (2009): 399–406.

"Victory: Strong4Life Billboards Coming Down." Mamavation.com. February 26, 2012. http://www.mamavation.com/2012/02/victory-strong-4-life-billboards-coming -down.html.

Wang, Lucy. "Weight Discrimination: One Size Fits All Remedy?" *Yale Law Journal* 117, no. 8 (2008): 1900–1945.

Wann, Marilyn. "Foster Care for Fat Children? Gastric Bypass Surgery? Two Wrongs Call for a Fight." *San Francisco Weekly,* July 21, 2011. http://blogs.sfweekly.com/exhibitionist/2011/07/foster_care_fat_children_gastric_bypass.php.

Warin, Megan, Tanya Zivkovic, Vivienne Moore, and Michael Davies. "Mothers as Smoking Guns." *Feminism and Psychology* 22, no. 3 (2012): 376–387. Published online May 16, 2012.

Warschburger, P. "The Unhappy Obese Child." *International Journal of Obesity* 29 (2005): S127–S129.

"Weight-Loss Surgery and Children." US Library of Medicine and the National Institutes of Health. MedlinePlus.com. July 11, 2011. http://www.nlm.nih.gov/medlineplus/ency/patientinstructions/000356.htm.

The Weight of the Nation. Directed by Kevin Kindle. 2012. HBO Documentary Films and Institute of Medicine. http://theweightofthenation.hbo.com/.

Weiner, Jennifer. "The F Word." *Allure: The Beauty Expert.* October 2010. http://www.allure.com/allure-magazine/2012/10/fat-the-f-word.

Weiss, Dara-Lynn. *The Heavy: A Mother, a Daughter, a Diet.* New York: Ballantine Books, 2013.

Wendell, Susan. *The Rejected Body: Feminist Philosophical Reflections on Disability.* New York: Routledge, 1996.

West, Lindy. "It's Hard Enough to Be a Fat Kid without the Government Telling You You're an Epidemic." *Jezebel.* March 3, 2013. http://jezebel.com/5945955/its-hard-enough-to-be-a-fat-kid-without-the-government-telling-youre-an-epidemic.

———. "Nike Uses Fat Kids to Sell Shoes: Nation Rejoices." *Jezebel.* August 6, 2012. http://jezebel.com/5932248/nike-uses-fat-kid-to-sell-shoes-nation-rejoices.

"What Is Support All Kids?" Support All Kids. January 5, 2013. http://supportallkids.virb.com/.

"When Bone Breaks: Osteoporosis Health Center." WebMD.com. October 15, 2011. http://www.webmd.com/osteoporosis/osteoporosis-complications.

Widhalm, K., S. Dietrich, and G. Prager. "Adjustable Gastric Banding Surgery in Morbidly Obese Adolescents: Experiences with Eight Patients." *International Journal of Obesity* 28 (2004): S42–S45.

Wilson, Carnie, with Mick Kleber. *Gut Feelings: From Fear and Despair to Health and Hope.* Carlsbad, Calif.: Hay House, 2001.

Wilson, Carnie, with Cindy Pearlman. *I'm Still Hungry: Finding Myself through Thick and Thin.* Carlsbad, Calif.: Hay House, 2003.

Young, Iris Marion. *Throwing Like a Girl and Other Essays in Feminist Philosophy and Social Theory.* Bloomington: Indiana University Press, 1990.

Zeller, Meg H., Helmut R. Roehrig, Avani C. Modi, Stephen R. Daniels, and Thomas H. Inge. "Health-Related Quality of Life and Depressive Symptoms in Adolescents with Extreme Obesity Presenting for Bariatric Surgery." *Pediatrics* 117, no. 4 (2006): 1155–1161.

Ziegler, O., M. A. Sirveaux, L. Brunaud, N. Reibel, and D. Quilliot. "Medical Follow Up after Bariatric Surgery: Nutritional and Drug Issues; General Recommendations for the Prevention and Treatment of Nutritional Deficiencies." *Diabetes and Nutrition* 35 (2009): 544–557.

Zivi, Karen. "Contesting Motherhood in the Age of AIDS: Maternal Ideology in the Debate over Mandatory HIV Testing." *Feminist Studies* 31, no. 2 (2005): 347–374.

———. *Making Rights Claims: A Practice of Democratic Citizenship.* New York: Oxford University Press, 2012.

Index

Abrams, Lindsey, 20, 88–89
addiction transfer, 129
advertising, food, 36, 90–91. *See also* fast-food industry
advertising, weight-loss, 37, 145
African Americans, 10, 12, 20, 21, 43, 45, 94–95, 96, 147
AIDS epidemic. *See* HIV, war on
Allan, Vicky, 52
Allen, David B., 57
American Heart Association, 91
American Medical Association, 79–80
American Psychological Association, 90
American Society for Metabolic and Bariatric Surgery, 116, 136
Americans with Disabilities Act, 73
Anderson, Alaina, 143
Andreyeva, T., 54
anorexia, 66–68, 142
Asch, Adrienne, 131–132
Association for Action against Obesity, 59
Auld, Doug, 84–85, 87

Bariatric Longitudinal Outcomes Database, 117
bariatric surgery, 5, 6, 25–26, 29, 81, 114–139, 146, 148, 171n29, 171n45
Barnett, Ron, 59, 66
Barth, Fredric, 104
Battacharya, S., 52
Baur, L. A., 130
Beals, Jennifer, 36–37
beauty ideals, cultural, 95–96, 99–100, 108, 109, 132

Bentley, Amy, 144
Bernstein, Gaia, 58, 59, 60–61
Billett, Henry, 124
Biltekoff, Charlotte, 17
Binge Eating Disorder Association, 101–102
Birch, Leanne Lipps, 108
Blizzard, Robert, 74
Blue Cross and Blue Shield of Minnesota campaign, 87–89, 90, 91, 92, 108, 165n14
BMI (body mass index), 8, 27, 34, 50, 51, 53, 116–117, 118–119
BMI guidelines for, 116–117, 118–119
    on children and adolescents, 29, 30, 114–115, 116–119, 122–123, 124–125, 126–129, 130–139, 146, 148
    children born to mothers after, 25, 26
    complications and side effects of, 29, 114, 115, 116, 117–125, 128–129, 133
    and consent v. compliance, 29, 130–131, 137
    as cosmetic surgery, 134–137
    in diabetes treatment, 125–126, 138
    and "dumping syndrome," 114, 116, 120–122
    eating disorders attributed to, 128–129
    ethical questions surrounding, 137–139, 148
    FDA and, 116–117
    gastric banding in, 29, 115, 116, 118–119, 123, 124
    opposition to, 81, 115–116, 137
    parental consent to, 130–131, 133, 135–137
    and pregnancy, 124–125

court system, obese children and
in Corrigan case, 66–67, 141–142, 143,
148, 149, 176n3
and fast-food industry, 144
gender norms and expectations and,
27–28, 60–61, 72–73, 76–77
and *In re D. K.*, 61–62, 68–69, 71–77, 78,
79
and *In the Interest of L. T.*, 61, 62, 64, 67,
78, 162n58
and *In the Matter of Brittany T.*, 61, 62,
63, 68–71, 72, 76, 78, 80
and justifications for and against
removal from home, 57–62, 77–80,
81–82, 160n1
and obese mothers, 68–77
and the pathologizing of difference, 21
in Regino case, 1–3, 13, 19, 27, 78, 151n2
and single mothers, 61, 77
See also childhood obesity
crack cocaine, pregnancy and, 42, 43,
44–45
Crawford, Robert, 11
Critser, Greg, 7, 9, 10, 11–13, 20, 21, 23, 24
(figure), 47–48, 49, 96, 113

Davenport, Charles, 48–49
Davies, Brian, 2
Davies, Michael, 41
Davison, Kirsten Krahnstoever, 108
depression
among anorexics, 67–68
and bariatric surgery, 126–127, 128, 132
and childhood obesity, 18, 29, 78, 107,
131–132
in L. T. court case, 61, 62, 67
Deutsch, Donny, 98, 99
Devon, Natasha, 146–147
diabesity, 125, 151, 173n69
diabetes, 3, 18, 19, 22, 116, 125–126, 132, 135,
138
diets and dieting
and children, 103, 107–109, 128
and cultural differences, 21

and "fat talk," 154n62
norms of femininity and, 76
and "unhealthy others," 11–12
weight-loss industry and, 37, 76, 137, 145
"digestive bonsais," 115–116. *See also*
bariatric surgery
Dilks, Rebecca J., 119, 132
disability in American culture, 63, 74, 94,
100, 105. *See also* Rapp, Emily
discrimination, weight-based, 6, 11, 20–21,
45, 51, 54–55, 89–90, 127–128, 132–133,
138–139, 146–147, 163n73
Donna K. See *In re D. K.*
Dreger, Alice, 135–136
drugs, war on, 17–18, 42–45, 147–148
"dumping syndrome," 114, 116, 120–122

eating disorders
and anorexia, 66–68, 142
and bariatric surgery, 128–129
beauty ideals and, 95–96, 99–100, 108
among marginalized women, 94–96
as psychosocial issues, 74–75, 127,
129–130
public health campaigns and, 28
teasing and, 29, 103
Eberstadt, Mary, 23
Edison, Laurie Toby, 165n7
Elkins, James, 87, 93
Elwood, William N., 17
epigenetics, 25–26, 27, 39–40, 41
eugenics movement, 32, 47–49
Evans, John, 2

Farquhar, C. M., 53
Farrell, Amy, 12, 65–66
fast-food industry, 4, 9, 10, 11, 12, 17, 21–22,
23, 25, 88, 91, 143, 144
Fat, Sick, and Nearly Dead (documentary),
93–94
"fat hating," 12, 91–92
fatness. *See* childhood obesity; obesity
fatphobia, 12, 52–53, 66–67, 132–133
"fat talk," 19, 154n62

in gender ideology, 44
and HIV, 32–33, 37–38
and maternal weight gain, 38–39, 45–46
obesity treatment during, 47, 49
uterine environment during, 25, 31–32, 34, 38–39, 40, 41, 44–45, 145
and women's reproductive rights, 26–27, 30, 31–34, 39, 46–53, 146, 147–148
and women as "vessels," 26, 27, 37, 39
psychosocial dwarfism, 72, 74–75
public health campaigns, obesity and
and children's perception of self, 92–94, 100, 105
cultural organizing of fat and thin in, 104–105
fear and blame in, 8–10
and food advertising and food system, 90, 91–92
parents and, 92–93, 101, 107, 108
and results, 108
as "save the children" campaigns, 18–19
and shame, 28, 87–89, 89–90, 101, 109
socially sanctioned bullying via, 28–29, 101–105, 107, 109, 148–149
weight loss as focus in, 155n10
See also Blue Cross Blue Shield of Minnesota campaign; I STAND campaign; Let's Move! campaign; Shape Up America! (SUA); Strong4Life campaign
public health campaigns, smoking and, 90
Puhl, Rebecca, 54, 89, 107, 109

race and class
in drug-abuse prosecutions of pregnant women, 42–43, 44–45
in fat blame, 11–13
and maternal ideology, 43–44
in war on obesity, 2–3, 4, 21, 147–148
in weight-based discrimination, 45
and women's reproductive rights, 45–46, 48–49, 50

Rapp, Emily, 95–96, 99–100, 105, 109
Reagan, Nancy, 17
"red light" foods, 130, 174n100
Regino, Anamarie, 1–3, 13, 19, 27, 78, 151n2
reproductive rights, women's, 26–27, 30, 31–34, 39, 45–53, 146, 147–148
"residual stigma," weight loss and, 133–134, 174n113
Richter, Marla, 80
Roberts, Deborah, 121
Roberts, Dorothy E., 43, 45, 46
Roker, Al, 65–66, 120–121, 130, 134, 136–137, 139
Roth, Meme, 59
Roux-en-Y procedure, 29, 81, 115, 116–117, 118, 123, 124, 125. *See also* bariatric surgery
Rukavina, P. B., 103, 106

Saguy, Abigail, 20, 92, 114
Sargese, Lisa, 120, 122
Sarr, Michael G., 133
Sarwer, David B., 119, 132
Satcher, David, 6–7, 152n17
school lunch programs, 4, 8, 13–14, 160n1
Schvey, Natasha, 54
Schwartz, Hillel, 7–8
Schwartz, Marlene B., 108
"secondhand obesity," 145
sexuality, 10, 36–37, 65–66, 68, 77, 95, 156n27
shame and shaming, 28, 85, 87–90, 91–92, 96, 101, 109, 165n7
Shape Up America! (SUA), 33, 34, 41, 42, 44, 155n10
Sharmer, Arya M., 127
Sherry, Michael, 13
Shrewsbury, V. A., 130
Shulevitz, Judith, 40
Silverstein, Sara, 110 (figure)
single mothers, 60, 61, 77, 141
Smith, J. Clinton, 22–23, 31
Smith, Yolanda R., 53
socioeconomics. *See* race and class

soft drink companies, 3–4, 8

Solovay, Sondra, 64, 67, 68, 79, 176n3

Sontag, Susan, 8, 9, 10, 11, 14, 20

Sorrell, Nathan, 96–99, 97 (figure), 100, 101, 105–106, 109

staring, social aspects of, 84–85, 87, 93

starvation, forced, 66, 162n45

Stearns, Peter, 7

Steele, Margot, 127

Steinbeck, K. S., 130

stereotyping, obesity and, 41–42, 43, 53, 61, 91–92, 98, 99, 102–104, 163n73

Stinson, Kandi, 174n100

"stomach amputation," 115. *See also* bariatric surgery

Stonehocker, Brian, 127

Stone-Manista, Krista, 44

Story, Mary, 90, 91

Strong4Life campaign
  criticism of, 101–102, 166n34
  depictions of children in, 83–84, 85, 86 (figure), 87, 93, 109, 164n2
  gender norms in, 65, 77, 85
  Maya Joi and, 85, 86 (figure), 87, 92–94, 96, 97, 100, 101, 105–106, 166n37
  message of "choice" in, 76
  shame and, 28, 85, 87, 109
  and social aspects of staring, 85, 87, 93

Stukator, Angela, 65

supersize, defined, 168n87

Support All Kids campaign, 102, 109

Sweeney, Julia, 65

Taylor, Nicole, 103–105

Taylor, Valerie, 127

teasing. *See* bullying and teasing, weight-based

Teen-Longitudinal Assessment of Bariatric Surgery (Teen LABS), 117–118

Teixiera, Julio, 125–126

thinness
  in American culture, 42, 76, 104–105, 109, 136
  in beauty ideals, 95, 99–100, 108, 109
  and eating disorders, 66–68, 99–100, 142

parental responsibility for, 57, 58, 63, 77–78, 79, 94, 108, 114, 147
  as patriotic, 7–8

Thompson, Becky W., 95

Thompson, Tommy G., 6–7, 176n4

Thorne, Barrie, 104

Time (magazine), 9, 14, 16 (figure), 17, 26, 113, 114, 157n52

Today Show, 98, 99, 100, 120, 121, 132

Torvaldsen, S., 130

Triger, Zvi, 58, 59, 60–61

type 2 diabetes, 18, 19, 116, 125–126. *See also* diabetes

uterine environment, fetus in, 25, 31–32, 34, 38–39, 40, 41, 44–45, 145

Vahratian, Anjel, 53

Varner, Grant, 59

Varness, Todd, 57–58, 80

Wang, Lucy, 89

Wann, Marilyn, 109, 110 (figure), 115

war on drugs, 17–18, 42–45, 147–148

war on HIV, 8, 9, 13– 14, 32–33, 34, 36, 37–38, 146, 147–148

Warin, Megan, 35, 41

war on obesity
  culture of fear in, 2, 8–10, 17–18, 157n52
  gender, race, and class in, 2–3, 4, 14, 17–18, 21, 27–28, 147–148
  ice cream cone as symbol in, 14, 15 (figure), 16 (figure), 17–18, 41, 113–114, 157n52
  maternal ideology in, 27, 31, 33, 38, 53, 144–145
  mother blaming in, 18, 27–28, 33–34, 37–40, 61, 141–142, 144–145, 148–149
  official declaration of, 6–7, 8, 142, 151n2, 152n17, 176n4
  patriotism in, 6–8, 113
  shame in, 85, 87–90
  victim blaming in, 146–147
  as war against women and children, 2–3, 4

war on HIV equated to, 8, 9, 10, 13–14, 32–33, 34, 36, 37–38, 42, 46, 54, 146, 147–148
and war rhetoric, 7–8, 13–14, 20, 33, 113, 141
and women's reproductive rights, 26–27, 33–34, 146, 148–149
working mothers in, 18, 21–23, 144
See also court system, obese children and
war rhetoric, obesity and, 7–8, 13–14, 20, 33, 113, 141
Warschburger, P., 103
weight-loss industry, 37, 76, 137, 145
weight-loss surgery. *See* bariatric surgery
Weight of the Nation, The (documentary), 8–9, 19, 48
Weiner, Jennifer, 46

Weiss, Dara-Lynn, 174n100
West, Lindy, 88, 89, 91–92, 98, 106
Willett, Walter, 3–4
Wilson, Carnie, 121–122, 130, 171n42, 174n101
WLS (weight-loss surgery). *See* bariatric surgery
working mothers, 18, 21–23, 144
World War I, overconsumption of food and, 7–8
Wright, Jan, 1, 5, 23, 26, 40–41, 59, 60, 113, 144, 149

Young, Iris Marion, 65

Zivi, Karen, 6, 27, 31, 32–33, 36, 46, 47, 55
Zivkovic, Tanya, 41